FOOD LOVE

FOOD L
GUIDE TO

SAN FRANCISCO

The Best Restaurants, Markets & Local Culinary Offerings

1st Edition

Grace Keh

Guilford, Connecticut

Editor: Kevin Sirois
Project Editor: Heather Santiago
Layout Artist: Mary Ballachino
Text Design: Sheryl Kober
Illustrations © Jill Butler with additional art by Carleen Moira Powell
Maps: Daniel Lloyd © Morris Book Publishing, LLC

ISBN 978-0-7627-7316-9

Printed in the United States of America
10 9 8 7 6 5 4 3 2 1

All the information in this guidebook is subject to change. We recommend that you call ahead
to obtain current information before traveling.

To my two amazing girls, Sydney and Madison,
who have taught me more than I ever dreamed I'd learn . . .
this is just a small part of why all that had to happen.
I love you both immensely, and fiercely.

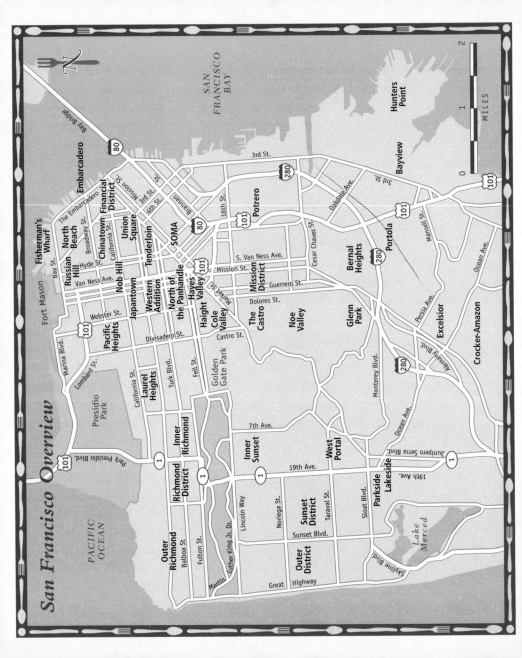

Contents

About the Author

Grace Keh is the food reviewer at San Francisco Food (http://sffood .net), her website dedicated to reviewing restaurants and amazing culinary experiences in San Francisco. For years, she has traveled the world eating at the world's greatest restaurants, but her main focus has always been on the food scene in San Francisco.

Born in New York, she grew up in Greenwich, CT before moving to California for college. Grace has lived in California for 20 years and spent 15 of those years in the San Francisco Bay Area. By day, she works in marketing communications and event management, and by night she visits as many San Francisco eateries as she can.

Grace spent much of her childhood living in Indonesia, Japan, and Korea where her love for foreign and delicious culinary presentations began. Eating out with her father, who introduced her to the world's most interesting foods, cooking alongside her mom and experimenting with cooking was a huge chunk of her younger years. While other kids went out and played, her fascination with cooking and food continued throughout the years.

As an avid cook, she has spent countless hours in the

kitchen preparing dishes for family and friends; very little in life brings her as much joy as when she is sharing great food and wine with loved ones.

Grace lives in San Francisco and has twin daughters, Sydney and Madison.

You can follow her on Twitter at @kgraciek or on Facebook at www.facebook.com/sffood.

Acknowledgments

I have to thank my mom, dad, sister, and aunt, who offered endless encouragement and support throughout the entire challenging experience of putting this book together while keeping the rest of my life afloat. I love you guys with all of my heart, and I could not have done this without your understanding and support.

I am being honest when I say that this book is brought to you by the generosity and love of my wonderful friends. "McMin," Dennis, Mikey, Will, Young, Woojae, Archie, and Ian—thank you for always being so willing to try out new places with me and letting me order entirely too much each time, without gasping in horror. Many thanks to Yuni and Lara for all of the administrative work you put into the book.

To all of my SF Food readers: Thank you for being the best readers in the world; it means so much to me that you follow my rants and ravings about food!

Rob . . . I want to thank you because it was only in going over all of the places I've eaten at that I could clearly see that so many of the San Francisco eateries I have tried, I tried with you.

To my editor, Kevin Sirois, and Globe Pequot Press—thank you for offering me this amazing opportunity; the trust you placed in me was the greatest compliment and I hope I lived up to your high expectations.

I also have to thank the chefs and restaurant staff members in San Francisco who made this entire experience so amazing. Your dedication to providing your customers the utmost in service, great food, and a memorable experience is what continues to make writing about the food scene in San Francisco so worthwhile and rewarding. You guys make San Francisco the hub of the greatest food in the world—and my job the envy of all.

And last but in no way the least, to KK—I always knew it was you out there, acting as my greatest fan. This is, unfortunately, the only way I can think of to thank you for believing in me.

Introduction

Very few cities in the world offer more diversity than San Francisco. This city has the great distinction of having the largest Chinese population outside of China; this city was also home to one of the greatest Japantowns in the United States at one point. This city welcomed the Russians and Irish, and even to this day, certain neighborhoods are known by the nationality of the original inhabitants. This city is home to some of the very businesses you use on the Internet daily, like Twitter and a slew of other dot-com companies, with satellite offices for bigwigs like Google and Cisco—and with these companies come the most talented folks from all over the globe whose skills are in high demand.

But this city also offers a bigger and greater variety of eating options than any other city in the country, rating No. 1 on the number of restaurants per capita for any city in the United States. Given that it's a city that is only 7 miles wide and long (i.e., 7x7), it's densely populated on each block—and virtually all neighborhoods have at least some eateries to accommodate the residents.

This, along with the incomparable assets that the city offers in terms of sightseeing (can you say "Golden Gate Bridge"?), might be one reason why the city was host to almost 16 million visitors in

2010. Pricewise, according to a 2010 Zagat survey, San Francisco is second only to New York City in cost per meal; New York City ranged in at an average of $41.76 per person per meal, and San Francisco followed close behind at a shocking $38.78. But people visit this city ready to dish out the funds; it's not news to anyone that living in, eating in, and existing in San Francisco is expensive.

San Francisco is, without a doubt, "foodie central"; this much is true. But one reason for the major influx of the finest chefs and their restaurants into this city is perhaps twofold. First, the resident foodies love to eat out in this city, not to mention the 16 million tourists who also visit this city with food at the top of their to-do list. If you offer good food, the people will come, so to speak. (Conversely, if your cooking is subpar, you'll close down before you know what hit you, too.) The second reason is perhaps the fact that this city offers chefs an incomparable proximity to fresh, local, and organic ingredients with which to cook, which anyone who cooks can tell you makes all of the difference in the end result.

The popular restaurants are booked months out, so plan ahead by making reservations before your trip, or call the restaurant to see if they can accommodate walk-ins. Many restaurants in San Francisco utilize OpenTable.com (www.opentable.com) but by no means the majority; when in doubt, call.

Our tastes may vary to some degree; you will love some, and perhaps you won't think of other restaurants as highly as I do—but rest assured these establishments offer some of the best that the talented chefs of San Francisco have to offer.

I truly hope you enjoy the San Francisco experience as much as I do on a daily basis.

How to Use This Book

With 89 "neighborhoods" in San Francisco (and soon to be more, if we leave it to the realtors), it was neither plausible nor sensible to list each chapter by every neighborhood. I've taken the best-known neighborhoods and grouped them into areas within the city (shown on the area map, p. iv) and created chapters out of them with restaurants listed in alphabetical order.

With the exception of the introductory chapter, which is devoted to the city and culture, the huge food cart movement, and the multitude of San Francisco's food-related events, the remaining chapters all focus on individual areas of the city. The Outside the City Limits chapter, however, covers a few must-try restaurants and feasting venues outside of the city, but all within driving distance; if possible, you might make the time to experience all that the Bay Area has to offer.

The Recipes chapter is devoted to giving you the chance to re-create the ultimate SF gastronomic experience for any of your special occasions or special needs. The Itineraries chapter helps you on your quest to fit in as much as possible within two days in San Francisco.

Foodie Faves

The restaurants that have made this section are the most noteworthy establishments that are worth a visit, from long-standing favorites to the latest on the scene. Bon appétit!

Landmarks

The listings in this section are the restaurants that have been San Francisco staples for a considerably long time and helped put San Francisco on the food map, or ones housed in historic buildings or locations.

Specialty Stores, Markets & Producers

Some truly notable butcher shops, specialized groceries, and bakeries exist within this fascinatingly diverse city. Here we give you a list of must-visit specialty stores.

Recipes

At the back of this book (p. 261), we give new meaning to the phrase "continuing education" and help you re-create some of our favorite local dishes from some of the city's best chefs.

Price Code

The price range is covered in this book, immediately following the address listing, using the following guide:

$:	Cheap—you can have a full meal for $10 or less here.
$$:	Economical—for $10–$25 per person, you can fill up and go.
$$$:	Moderate—a meal equivalent to an appetizer, entree selection, and one alcoholic beverage will run you $25–$50 per person.
$$$$:	Expect to spend $50–$75 at this establishment to order one appetizer, one entree, and a glass or two of wine.
$$$$$:	You will not walk out of this establishment having spent less than $75–$100 per person; the sky's the limit.

Getting Around San Francisco

Walking

Walking is, without a doubt, one of the best ways to get around the city. Within the grouped neighborhoods in these chapters, all but the last two chapters can be done relatively easily on foot, if need be. After all, it is a 7x7 city (approximately 7 miles across in all directions). When touring, you will inevitably get the best experience by walking around the neighborhoods. Do note, though, that San Francisco has many hills—some extreme—and walking up and down those hills is not easy or even feasible for everyone (e.g., elderly or children).

By Car

During rush hour, driving can be futile if you have to cross the city or get to one of the bridges. The remainder of the day, driving in San Francisco is not difficult, and getting from one place to another is rather easy. Be forewarned, however, that parking once you get to your location usually will take longer than the drive there; if you find a lot, expect to pay upward of $20 for a couple of hours. If you find valet parking options at these businesses—which, ironically, are not that common in this impossible-to-park city—it can cost you anywhere from $10 (a bargain) to $60 per day if the hotel valet parks your car!

By Taxi

There are many taxi options in San Francisco, though they are nowhere near as commonly available on the streets as in New York City, for example. The busier areas of the city will obviously have more taxis cruising; if the light is on it means the taxi is available to passengers. You can also call the taxi companies, like Arrow Cabs (415-648-3181) or Luxor Cabs (415-282-4141) to request taxi service. Alternatively, iPhone applications like Cabulous have worked quite nicely within city limits.

Bus, Light-Rail & Trolleys

San Francisco has a very well-established Muni (myoo-nee) system that can get you anywhere within the city limits. That said, not all routes are created equal. Some routes are easy as can be, getting you from the west end of the city to the east end, and other routes require massive planning to figure out how you will get from here to there. The public transportation mode in Google Maps, the mobile application http://nextbus.com, or the website http://511.org should assist you with this planning. Well-planned as it may be, taking the Muni (http://sfmta.com) will require allotting a considerable amount of extra time to your travel time. But at $2 per ride, which includes the next 90 minutes of transport, however many buses or light-rails you need, is about as economical as you will get in this city. Trolleys and streetcars also operate under MUNI and will provide transport, depending on the final destination.

Cable Cars

When someone thinks of San Francisco, images of cable cars inevitably pop up. Contrary to what you might imagine, this mode of transportation only covers a small portion of the city, but it does go through some of the prime neighborhoods of San Francisco. Taking one (or taking many) will cost you $5 each time you hop on. There's nothing quite like getting on one of these cable cars with no windows and open-air seating; children and adults enjoy this experience equally. As the cable car operator tracks you through the city, you'll inevitably think to yourself, "So this is what being in San Francisco is all about!" When needing to go places between Fisherman's Wharf and the Financial District, or through prime areas like Nob Hill and Russian Hill, consider this mode of transportation. This is also operated by Muni.

Passport

Alternatively, you can purchase a Passport that will allow unlimited travel on all Muni transportation for a predetermined amount of time. Visit www.sfmta.com/cms/mhome/home50.htm for additional information on all Muni options.

BART (Bay Area Rapid Transit)

Starting from San Francisco (SFO) or even Oakland (OAK) airports, you can take BART into the city of San Francisco. Intracity travel has limited stops within city limits, but it can be convenient to get you from Embarcadero to Mission or Civic Center, for example. Cost will differ based on the distance traveled to your final destination. BART is also useful for travel from San Francisco to the Peninsula or East Bay. Visit www.bart.gov for more information.

Keeping Up with Food News

In an ever-changing restaurant industry like San Francisco's, it takes a lot of work, eating, and reading to keep up with what's hot—and what's not. The city has many critics, legitimate or otherwise, but, each having different tastes, I find that I agree with some and vehemently disagree with others. Furthermore, when those "best of" lists come out, sometimes I am nodding with each listing, whereas at other times I'm stunned at almost every place listed.

But to each his/her own, and below is a list of some well-known sites by the best of the best of San Francisco foodies. Some are acclaimed critics, others are bloggers and/or food reviewers, and still others are phenomenal sites about food and cooking in this city. Take some time to visit the sites and read all about their dining experiences!

SF Weekly Blogs (http://blogs.sfweekly.com/foodie): This is the food blog linked to the publication *SF Weekly*. They often generate lists of top five or ten of the city's "best" and the daily coverage of recent food news is comprehensive. With Jonathan Kauffman as the new food critic, *SF Weekly* provides current reviews for many San Francisco eateries.

Cooking with Amy (http://cookingwithamy.com): This is a blog by author, food writer, cook, and recipe creator Amy Sherman. She covers a wide array of food-related topics, including everything from restaurants to new recipes she's trying out, and the site is chock-full of nice photos and write-ups that will have you wiping drool off your chin.

Grub Girl (www.grubgirl.com): Fun and lighthearted but equally informative, food blogger Liz Kao (also known as "Grub Girl") takes her crew and scours the city to find delicious and cheap eats. Her reviews list what's good, what's not, and other pertinent details in an easy-to-read format. Who doesn't want to save some money?

Inside Scoop SF (http://insidescoopsf.sfgate.com/blog): Michael Bauer, the *San Francisco Chronicle*'s food critic, posts his thoughts in this blog on the publication's website. The blog visits some of the city's and area's best eateries, and whether you agree with him or not, it makes for an interesting read.

San Francisco Grub Street (http://sanfrancisco.grubstreet.com): This is the food segment of *New York* magazine's website, and it's often the first site I visit every morning to keep up-to-date on what's happening in San Francisco. Information is accurate and updated constantly for major food scenes across the country, and while they do review restaurants and food, I use it more as a news source.

Eater SF (http://sf.eater.com): One of the better sites to keep up with what's new on the restaurant and food scene in San Francisco. It's not really useful as a restaurant guide, nor do they provide any in-depth "reviews," but they do cover what other critics think.

Tablehopper (http://tablehopper.com): Marcia Gagliardi, food writer extraordinaire, covers everything from restaurants to bars, San Francisco food news to star sightings in the city. Subscribe to the newsletter for up-to-date information.

UrbanDaddy San Francisco (www.urbandaddy.com/home/sfo): A classy and elegant site that covers hot stories in the food and wine industry. Based in New York, the SF edition is sleek, and when a story is interesting, it's quite fantastic.

Yelp San Francisco (www.yelp.com): Take it all with a grain of salt. You can read up on restaurants here and find out what's popular these days, but count on reading at least 50 reviews to get a decently accurate picture of a restaurant—and don't even bother with the forums. Some Yelpers may be prolific foodies, but with just anyone posting a review, there's little consistency or accuracy in what they report.

Food Events

Nearly every weekend has some kind of a event—be it a show, festival, fair, or production—going on somewhere in San Francisco. The city is full of free events to attend (though food and drinks are your own responsibility), and when there is an associated cost for an event, it will almost always involve food of some sort. The residents of the city value every moment of nice weather and/or sunshine, so if the weather is nice, you can rest assured that the city will be crazy with all the people getting their dose of sunshine.

Here are the most popular food-oriented events that happen annually in San Francisco.

January

Chinese New Year, www.chineseparade.com. This is one of the most colorful and festive events in San Francisco, given the large Chinese population in this city. This event includes a fancy parade and a lot of street vendors. Takes place on the lunar calendar's New Year's Day; dates change annually.

Dine About Town, www.opentable.com. This two-week "event" is a great opportunity for anyone to try new restaurants. Hosted by OpenTable (www.opentable.com), the list of restaurants offering Dine About Town pricing on their prix-fixe menu grows each time this event takes place. Lunches are offered in the $17 range, and dinner is in the $35 range. This takes place a second time in June of each year for another two weeks. There is usually a grand launch party that showcases foods from various restaurants offering the Dine About Town menu, enticing customers to visit them during these two weeks.

February

Union Street Has a Crush on You Valentine Wine Walk, www.sresproductions.com/union_street_valentine_wine_walk.html. This fun walk extends from Pacific Heights to Union Street, dropping in on merchants and restaurants for food and wine tastings. A tasting wrist band needs to be purchased separately, but people are welcomed to join in on the walk.

March

St. Patrick's Day Parade, www.sresproductions.com/sfstpatricks day.html. Every Irish bar in San Francisco becomes packed by mid-afternoon (if not earlier) as the St. Patty's Day parade takes place. Vendors providing typical Irish cuisine are present throughout the city, and in general, it's a lot of debauchery and fun.

Rhone Rangers San Francisco Grand Wine Tasting, www .rhonerangers.org. In spring, this massive group of winemakers offers an incredible tasting of many different wines, and tickets include a sit-down dinner with the winemakers, followed by an auction of their wines. It's an experience worth trying at least once.

San Francisco International Beerfest, www.sfbeerfest.com. In spring (Mar or Apr), this extraordinary event takes place with tons of beer stands and unlimited kegs offering generous tastings, as food trucks adorn the outside lot to pair eats with whatever beer strikes your fancy. More information is available at their website, including next year's event information.

April

Northern California Cherry Blossom Festival, www.nccbf .org. Japantown is transformed into a mecca of food stands as the parade passes through slowly. From stands serving sake tastings to stands selling Japanese food and beer, this all-afternoon event is always popular and fun.

May

Asian Heritage Street Celebration, www.sanfranciscochinatown
.com/events/asianheritagestreet.html. There's food galore during
this festival, as Asian food trucks, carts, and vendors line up
throughout Little Saigon in San Francisco, offering cuisine from
China, Vietnam, Korea, Thailand, Philippines, and more! With per-
formances scheduled throughout the entire event, this one is sure
to please the masses.

Bay to Breakers, www.zazzlebaytobreakers.com. On the third
Sunday in May, over 100,000 San Franciscans and tourists head
out to the streets to walk or run the entire distance of the city,
equivalent to 7 miles across town. Some are there to run; some
are in costumes just because it's a tradition; some are downright
naked—and most are drinking, though the city has attempted to
cut out all drinking in recent years, due to the mass destruction
to people's properties near where the race happens to run. It's
chaotic and a traffic mess, but it's also a long-standing tradition
that the residents truly enjoy. Food stands and carts will be all
over the running route, providing eats to the runners and specta-
tors alike.

Noodle Fest, www.chinatowncdc.org or www.northbeachmerchants
.com. Since 2010, The Chinatown Community Development Center
and the North Beach Merchants Association have come together to
host a popular event in North Beach. Right in between Chinatown

and Little Italy, the streets are closed and the vendors set up to offer a great variety of noodle dishes. The purchase of a ticket includes a tasting of a set number of Asian noodle dishes and an equal number of pasta dishes.

San Francisco Carnaval's Grand Parade and Festival, www .sfcarnaval.com. With a parade going through one part of town, this Memorial Day festival celebrates Brazil's Carnaval. While it's on a much smaller scale, the festive mood reigns supreme, and Latin American and other ethnic foods are sold throughout the event.

June

Union Street Festival, www.unionstreetfestival.com. This one is always crowded and always full of gourmet vendors and other eateries offering food on the streets. It happens on the first weekend of June and is one of the largest festivals in the country. Come one, come all—it's free, and it's a madhouse!

Fiesta Filipina, www.fiestafilipinausa.net. This is the largest Filipino festival in the country—and the many Filipino food carts and stands give the city an opportunity to taste a lot of ethnic foods, and appreciate the art, dance, and culture of the Philippines.

Bayview District Sunday Streets and Music Festival, www .sundaystreetssf.com The streets are closed down, and people are encouraged to roam about as freely as they want for this all-out party on the streets. With food contests, bike rentals, and entertainment, the City of San Francisco, in conjunction with various local sponsors, hosts several of these events throughout the city via Sunday Streets. More information can be found on the website if you want to find different dates and locations.

North Beach Festival, www.northbeachchamber.com. Mayhem ensues in North Beach in June when this festival takes place. All kinds of eateries set up food stands on the streets to serve customers, while drinks are served freely to anyone willing to pay a few bucks. With arts and crafts, street painting activities, and cooking demonstrations, North Beach Festival is a happy occasion for all.

SF Gay Pride Parade, www.sfpride.org. The last Sunday in June, people from the gay and lesbian community—and a massive number of people from the heterosexual community—get dressed up in their most flamboyant costumes and join this parade. Colorful, exciting, and always fascinating, there are plenty of vendors ready to feed your hunger and quench your thirst.

Dine About Town, www.opentable.com. This is the second time Dine About Town takes place annually. See the January listing for more details.

July

Fillmore Street Jazz Festival, www.fillmorejazzfestival.com. It's focused on jazz music, but what's jazz without some drinks—and what are drinks without some food? The food lineup for this festival is always impressive, with culinary delights from all over the world being represented.

August

La Cocina Street Food Festival, www.sfstreet foodfest.com. Music, drinks, fun, and food! La Cocina promotes food entrepreneurs who have income barriers to opening their own food establishments; a ticket bought to this event includes food and drinks (how much depending on which ticket), and the event is a gastronomic delight! This group also hosts a conference in August at Fort Mason Center, meant for foodies and investors alike.

San Francisco Aloha Festival, www.pica-org.org. It's a full-blown celebration of all things Hawaiian and Polynesian as San Francisco hopes for warm weather in an often-chilly August. The hula dancers are beautiful, the music is mesmerizing, but the real focus is on the food: loco moco, Spam musubi, and other Hawaiian fare are served here. Aloha! (A separate Polynesian Pride Festival takes place in the same month. Call 415-586-7474 for more information about this particular event.)

SF Chefs, www.sfchefs2011.com. It's a world-class event at Union Square with an impressive of array of San Francisco's best-known chefs gathering to put on food productions like you've never seen, hosted by the Golden Gate Restaurant Association (http://ggra.org). It covers the entire range, from cooking classes by these chefs to private tastings and wine tastings, and there's an impressive array of winemakers and food industry folks, all present to create a one-of-a-kind experience. Going on for a full week, this is the foodie event to experience.

October

Oktoberfest by the Bay, www.oktoberfestbythebay.com. German beers, food, and entertainment take over Fort Mason as thousands come out to experience a mini Oktoberfest in San Francisco.

Street Food Culture

The food truck industry has exploded in San Francisco in the last few years. It's no surprise, really; given the high cost of eating out in San Francisco—the cheaper option of tasty and creative food trucks serving "good eats" is a welcome addition to the food scene.

Many times a month, an organization called **"Off the Grid"** **(OTG)** puts together a food truck and mobile vendor gathering at various locations throughout the city; check www.offthegridsf .com/weekly-markets for the various locations at which OTG takes place. This organization was started by Matthew Cohen in hopes of promoting food trucks and the food vendor movement—and very rapidly it became hugely popular in the city.

On Fridays during the temperate months, OTG takes place at Fort Mason with some 30 trucks and tents serving up the city's best examples of "truck food." Residents from all over the city come to try the food, drink some beer, and spend an evening outdoors. As many of these don't have permanent locations at which you can find them within city limits, and most utilize Twitter to announce their location, they are posted below, separately from the chapter listings, for those of you who want to give these awesome entre-preneurs' cooking a whirl. These aren't your typical food stands serving hot dogs—they are trucks cooking with fresh ingredients and serving up all sorts of great fare from the confines of a small space. The list is by no means comprehensive, but just some of my favorites at these events; the trucks/stands with permanent loca-tions are included in the neighborhood chapters.

An The Go, OTG; Twitter: @anthegosf. The An family, famous for their restaurant **Thanh Long** (p. 202), took their famous garlic noodles and decided to make them mobile. This truck is worth fol-lowing, and the food is worth trying—and it's often present at Off the Grid and Bay Area events. It's a simple wheat noodle, stir-fried in garlic sauce and served plain, or with meat or vegetables for an additional cost. Buttery and on the greasier side, they taste great and feel lighter than eating a burger, but less so than a salad. Try one of the beef skewers to accompany this dish.

Chairman Bao, OTG; Twitter: @chairmantruck. Take a fluffy steamed bun, add a braised slice of pork belly that has also been seared, put a couple drops of hoisin sauce on it, and top it with pickled daikon (which helps cut through the heaviness and richness of the meat)—and you have one addictive and savory treat that will make you change facial expressions several times with each bite. Get two to start, or else you'll have to stand in line again. Of the baked buns, the duck with mango salsa is a nice balance of sweet and savory, but it doesn't hold a candle to the pork belly bun.

Eat Curbside, OTG; Twitter: @eatcurbside. What image do you see when I write "deep-fried mac/cheese/bacon balls"? That's what Eat Curbside serves; cheesy mac and cheese with bacon bits, made into balls and deep-fried to a light crisp so that each bite oozes hot cheese, creamy pasta, and smoky bacon. (I know; I feel like saying "Amen!" too.) Get this, the thick steak fries, and the ahi tuna sliders served with wasabi sauce, or the grilled brie on toasted buns with capocollo and sun-dried tomatoes; it's a really ferocious blend of sweet and savory that tingles your taste buds long after the sandwich is gone.

4505 Meats, Ferry Building; Twitter: @4505_ Meats. Despite how many excellent burger choices there are in this city, some will argue to the death that the burgers from 4505 are the best in San Francisco. They'd be making a valid point. The hefty patty is placed on what appears to be a small brioche bun, and it's piled high with the condiments; request an egg to be put atop your cheeseburger. You can barely get your mouth around this thing to take a bite; when the bun crunches, the egg yolk pops, the cheese oozes out, and the juices from the steak-like meat run down your chin.

Yeah, it's up there with the best burger in San Francisco.

They make homemade *chicharrónes,* too; and while you realize what these are and how unhealthy they are—each light and crispy bite really leads you to believe they're little cloud chips until, much to your horror, you see the entire bag is gone. It's unfair that these are fried pork rinds; why can't toasted artichokes taste this good?

Gorilla Pete's Hot Dogs, Twitter: @gorillapetesf. After a night of drinking, who doesn't want a big bratwurst in a bun, piled high with onions and sauerkraut, and topped with—cream cheese? Grilled onions? Jalapeños? Sriracha is available—a must for many Asian folks! Pete has beef hot dogs, chicken hot dogs, and even veggie hot dogs. Follow him on Twitter to find out where he will be on any given day; the food cart's location seems to be less than regular at the time of this writing, but it's primarily in the North Beach area.

FERRY BUILDING FARMERS' MARKET

The **Ferry Building Farmers' Market** (http://ferrybuilding
marketplace.com/farmers_market.php) is also a great place to
find food vendors. Many restaurants in San Francisco set up food
stands at these markets, or sometimes even host guest chefs who
will prepare ingenious dishes to sell to the public.
It's a real treat to devour these dishes while
shopping for some of the freshest organic
produce available in the area. A visit to
this farmers' market is not just about
buying fresh ingredients—it's about
coming hungry and leaving stuffed!
Given that many chefs themselves
shop at this farmers' market, it's
appropriate that many of them will use
the ingredients on the spot to prepare
their take on fresh cooking. Some food
trucks will also make an appearance at this
market to provide sustenance to the shoppers. Some of the best
stands at the Thursday and Sunday farmers' market are also listed
in this section for your enjoyment.

Hapa Ramen, Ferry Building; Twitter: @haparamen. This food
stand offers freshly made ramen to the masses during the farmers'
market. On a brisk San Francisco day, very little is as comforting as
the piping-hot bowl of soup and noodles served here. They offer the

typical add-ons to the ramen, like a slice of slow-cooked pork or a *sous vide* farm egg for $1. Depending on what you order, you will spend somewhere between $10 and $15 for a small bowl of ramen; hearty as it is, it doesn't look like a big serving, though it is surprisingly filling. They also started offering smoked meats—it's good, though I don't really know what the connection between smoked meat and ramen is.

JapaCurry, OTG; Twitter: @japacurry. Sticky Asian rice is laid on the serving plate with whatever meat source you ordered on top; the curry—as spicy as you request it—is served in a separate bowl. The chicken *katsu* curry means you will get one crispy-fried chicken cutlet that retains its juices inside, sliced into rows and perfectly crunchy with each bite until you pour the curry sauce all over the creation. Personally, I like my white rice and I like dipping my cutlets into the curry sauce—but it's up to you. The curry is flavorful and both the chicken *katsu* and Kurobuta sausages are excellent additions to the plate/bowl of curry. At $8 per plate, not a bad deal for spicy and flavorful curry!

Namu, every Thursday at the Ferry Building; Twitter: @namusf. $3 for one taco, or $5 for two—opt for these unusual seaweed-wrapped tacos with rice, kimchee, well-marinated slices of juicy *galbi* (ribs) topped with green onions. Call it a Korean twist on the Mexican staple, these small but tasty treats are perfect bites to stave your hunger. Eat them quickly, though, as the nori will soften if you wait. Their Gamja fries are french fries topped with steak, hot chile paste, kimchee, a dollop of mayonnaise, and green onions—unusual, yes, but sinfully good.

Roli Roti, Ferry Building; Twitter: @roliroti. This is a rotisserie truck that makes one mean *porchetta* sandwich. Found at the farmers' market but also at Blue Bottle Coffee or other locations in the city, it's worth following this crew to get a bite of this mouthwatering creation. Atop a meat-juice-soaked Acme bun goes thick slices of *porchetta,* topped with onion marmalade that offers sweetness and a dose of bitterness, enhanced only by the pile of arugula on top. Order it with the roasted potatoes that are soaked in meat drippings. Need I really say more?

Sam's Chowdermobile, OTG; Twitter: @chowdermobile. Perhaps my favorite truck to hit up on colder San Francisco days, this one serves clam chowder that's soupy rather than thick, with large chunks of clam and potatoes in it. The fish-and-chips are huge pieces of battered fish served with french fries; the shrimp po'boy is also lightly battered and served with lettuce, tomato, a secret aioli-type sauce, and piled on top of a toasted brioche bun. But the real superstar at this truck is the lobster roll: large chunks of Maine lobster meat are tossed in hot butter and piled on a toasted (and buttered) bun. It's the epitome of simplicity, but with each bite—you realize this sandwich doesn't need a single thing added to it.

North Beach, Chinatown, Fisherman's Wharf & Embarcadero

Almost every district/neighborhood in San Francisco is populated by at least some tourists or tourist attractions. The most popular must-see districts are included in this chapter. Unlike some cities, where "tourist spot" is synonymous with bad, overpriced food, San Francisco offers some exquisite foodie spots scattered evenly throughout this region. Plenty of tour companies offer bus trips around these neighborhoods and you can easily go back and forth between these areas with a cab ride below $10, or a bus ride.

North Beach

This is the Little Italy of San Francisco, or San Francisco's sweetheart, if you will. It's almost always busy here with a great number of restaurants and cafes; when the restaurant scene dies down late at night, you'll find it bustling with nightclubs and bars. This is also the region that could be called the red-light district of San Francisco, and if you're going to find shady "clubs" anywhere, this is the spot.

Historically, North Beach was heavily populated by Italians. Today, the residents are completely mixed with perhaps fewer Italians than Chinese, but you will find more Italian restaurants per block in this district than anywhere else in the city.

North Beach is also the home to the annual North Beach street fair (p. 16), as well as the Noodle Fest that highlights noodles from both Little Italy and Chinatown, one neighborhood over.

Chinatown

Outside of Asia, the Chinatown in San Francisco is purported to be the largest in existence at the time of this writing (and the oldest in the United States). It has also the largest community of Chinese people outside of Asia. It's no surprise, considering the Chinese have inhabited San Francisco since 1848. Chinatown takes up about a square mile within city limits, but given that San Francisco is only about 49 square miles in size, this is a considerable area. Naturally, this is perhaps the most popular tourist destination in the city, even beating out the Golden Gate Bridge in number of vacationers per year. With over 300 restaurants and over 100,000 residents packed into the area, this is a section of San Francisco not to be missed. You might as well take half a day and stroll through the area on foot; traffic in this area can become unmanageable.

Fisherman's Wharf

Since the days during the gold rush when Italian fishermen popu-lated this area to fish for Dungeness crab, Fisherman's Wharf has been a hot spot in San Francisco. While those fishing fleets still dock in at the wharf, this northwestern point of San Francisco is one of the city's busiest tourist locations. With beautiful views of the San Francisco Bay, this area has plentiful seafood restaurants and is home to landmarks like Pier 39, Ghirardelli Square, and the Wax Museum. Plenty of streetcars and cable cars give you the feeling that you are, indeed, in the beautiful city of San Francisco.

Embarcadero

You have clear water views on three sides of San Francisco; the beach is on the far west side in the Sunset district (p. 176), the Presidio offers the Golden Gate, and the gorgeous bay with a clear view of the Bay Bridge is on the west side of the city in the Embarcadero district. While the area was originally busy as a sea-port, it went through a depressed state prior to the rebuilding of the area. Today, it is a gorgeous palm tree–lined area adorned with many piers, and modern buildings and eateries galore that offer some of San Francisco's best (and priciest) cuisines. The price is no surprise when you look out the window and see the views. The Ferry Building is one of the most popular locations even for the locals, and the **Ferry Building Farmers' Market** (p. 22) always attracts a good crowd. As its name implies, it's also where the ferry picks up and drops off the passengers heading to Marin County. On the rare warm day in San Francisco, it often feels like all of San Francisco decided to gather in the Embarcadero.

Foodie Faves

Albona Ristorante Istriano, 545 Francisco St., North Beach, San Francisco, CA 94133; (415) 441-1040; www.albonarestaurant .com; Italian/Istrian; $$$. Tucked away in the middle of a quiet street in North Beach, Albona is one of the best-kept secrets in San Francisco. The cuisine is from Istria, which is the largest peninsula in the Adriatic Sea, bordered by Italy on one side; the flavors are familiarly Italian yet not quite that. The ambience in this restaurant feels like a classic Italian restaurant. In the kitchen, Chef Samuel Hernandez is the executive chef, with his wife and pastry chef, Beatriz Hernandez. They create masterpieces on a nightly basis from Tuesday to Sunday. Not to be missed on this menu are the gnocchi starter—perfectly crispy on the outside and so soft on the inside, covered in a rich cumin-based sauce—and the strudel, Albona's outstanding twist on Italian lasagna, which consists of thin layers of pasta mixed with a tangy, bright, and flavorful tomato sauce and a generous amount of cheese laid between the sheets of pasta. Be sure to leave room for the *bonet*—the rich chocolate flan-like creation; check out Albona's recipe for **Bonet (Chocolate Flan)** on p. 276.

Ana Mandara Restaurant, 891 Beach St., Fisherman's Wharf, San Francisco, CA 94109; (415) 771-6800; www.anamandara.com; Vietnamese; $$$$. Vietnamese fusion cooking has been the latest rage in San Francisco. Ana Mandara offers that, along with perhaps one of the most beautiful and romantic venues of the city's restaurant scene. There's a spiraling staircase that leads from the grand first-floor dining hall to the beautiful second floor, where you find that they even have an outdoor patio that is simply perfect. The food is clearly geared toward a more Americanized palate, with sauces tending to be on the sweeter side of things. However, the menu is creative. The fresh lobster is always a good choice here, as well as the juicy chunks of beef tenderloin served with sweet onions and peppery cress. They have changing fish specials, and all are worth trying. Be aware that parking in this neighborhood can be impossible, especially on the weekends.

Boudin Sourdough Bakery & Cafe, 160 Jefferson St., Fisherman's Wharf, San Francisco, CA 94133; (415) 928-1849; www .boudinbakery.com; Bakery; $. When in often blustery San Francisco, nothing sounds as appealing as a hot bowl of clam chowder in a sourdough bread bowl. This might be one of Fisherman Wharf's most popular destinations for tourists. Boudin bakes bread fresh daily, which is then hollowed out to hold a piping-hot serving of New England clam chowder. The bread is good, and the creamy soup contains chunks of clams and potatoes, albeit with a more liquid consistency than the norm. The combination is almost a mandatory must-try item when visiting Fisherman's Wharf. They also sell other edibles like sandwiches and baked goods. The location is large and designed for tourists to shop around and buy Boudin/San Francisco items. While it's usually quite busy, don't be deterred as the line moves pretty fast. Although this one is the most popular, there are five other locations spread out in the city; check the company website for addresses.

City View Restaurant, 662 Commercial St., Chinatown, San Francisco, CA 94111; (415) 398-2838; Chinese/Dim Sum; $$. Smack dab in the middle of Chinatown, City View is a large dim sum restaurant with a loyal following. Frequented by an equal number of Chinese natives as tourists, it's definitely one of the nicer dim sum restaurants in the city. While the *siu mai* (steamed pork dumplings with shrimp on top) is not quite as impressive compared to other SF restaurants, the *har gow* (shrimp dumplings) has fresh shrimp meat inside the dumpling; the seafood pan-fried noodles are crispy with a pile of shrimp, squid, scallops and vegetables on top, with a clear gravy poured over. Mix it all up and enjoy. Expect service typical of Chinese restaurants; while a smile is hard to come by, they are efficient and get the job done. It's an ideal location at which to begin your day if you intend to tour Chinatown and North Beach after a late breakfast or early lunch. Parking is also considerably easier for lunch than dinner.

Coi Restaurant, 373 Broadway, North Beach, San Francisco, CA 94133; (415) 393-9000; www.coirestaurant.com; California; $$$$$. Eating at Coi (pronounced "kwa") is quite a pricey and lengthy experience, but one that will seduce all of your senses. It's ranked as the 75th of the world's best restaurants on the 2011 San Pellegrino World's Best Restaurants List and has even earned two Michelin stars. Chef Daniel Patterson puts together a creative menu that truly gives you a new admiration for ingredients you previously found underwhelming. For instance, if you thought porridge was rather boring before, you'll leave Coi thinking differently after trying the chanterelle porridge with root vegetables—the scent of mushrooms pervades this dish and elevates a basic porridge into a world-class offering. In fact, by the end of the meal, you realize you've really not had a lot of meat or fish, as you would at other 11-course restaurants, but that somehow Coi took something as simple as beets and hay, of all things, and made them a culinary explosion of flavors. For two people, expect to pay close to $350, or near $500 for the meal if you will be opting for the wine pairing.

√ **Crab House at Pier 39,** 203 C Pier 39, Fisherman's Wharf, San Francisco, CA 94133; (415) 434-2722; www.crabhouse39.com; Seafood; $$. It's a crab feast! This isn't high-end dining, though the meal will cost a considerable amount since it is seafood. But if there's a single seafood most often associated with San Francisco, it's the crab (move over, Maryland!), and Crab House is one of the best places to go. If you like clam chowder, don't miss their creamy crab chowder with generous chunks of crabmeat. Try their shrimp-and-crab combo plate, and definitely order the garlic fries. Their killer crab is similar to that of **Thanh Long** (p. 202) or **PPQ Dungeness Island** (p. 194) but Crab House offers a much greater variety of fresh seafood choices. Order the mussels and clams; both are spectacular and cooked in a light butter broth that lets all the flavors explode as you chew; don't forget to dip the bread into the buttery sauce. The aura is casual and feels more like a diner than a fancy seafood restaurant, but the view is absolutely breathtaking.

√ **E' Tutto Qua,** 270 Columbus Ave., North Beach, San Francisco, CA 94133; (415) 989-1002; www.etuttoqua.com; Italian; $$$. It'll feel like you've come home to family, even if you've never seen these people before. It might even feel like a bit much, but you'll find yourself smiling as they're so jovial. This restaurant is classically Italian in aura, service, music, and—most especially—the food. Homemade pastas and dough, and the use of completely fresh ingredients make all of their dishes as authentic as eating at someone's home in the Tuscan hills. While E' Tutto Qua is known for its pastas, do try the pizza, as it is about as simple and delicious as you will find in San Francisco. Their seafood pasta dishes start with the spaghetti *neri* at the top—a pasta made with squid ink in a white wine sauce with fresh clams and shrimp—it's like a seafood party in your mouth. Definitely save room for the tiramisu, as it could be the best $5 you spend in San Francisco. Be prepared for lots of hugs and kisses; the staff here love what they do and love you for choosing their restaurants for dinner.

Gary Danko, 800 N. Point St., Fisherman's Wharf, San Francisco, CA 94109; (415) 749-2060; www.garydanko.com; American; $$$$$. Chef Gary Danko's name has become synonymous with "amazing food." This is consistently San Francisco's most popular restaurant, and reservations must be made a couple months prior, but they do have walk-in seating for canceled reservations or bar seating, so it might be worth pursuing at the last minute. Gary Danko offers 3- to 5-course meal choices with an optional caviar course. The caviar course is stellar, with perhaps the best buckwheat blinis known to mankind; the buttery goodness of these little "toasts" paired with

DIM SUM CULTURE

San Francisco 's official Chinatown, starts at the colorful and grand Dragon's Gate at Grant Avenue and Bush Street. Most locals, especially the Chinese, refer to this as the "tourist Chinatown," lined with shops, offering trinkets and other items equivalent to souvenirs or bargains available only in Chinatown, and little restaurants scattered in with some huge banquet-style Chinese restaurants.

Dim sum is a fabulous dining option in this Chinatown, or clear across town in the Richmond District on Clement Street— the other Chinatown, or "the new Chinatown," where for blocks on end, Chinese markets, stores, and restaurants have placed their roots—and nearly every person on the street is Chinese. Various dim sum–style restaurants have emerged on Irving Street in the Sunset District, as well.

This style of eating is most similar to small plates or tapas, except ordinarily carts filled with freshly prepared food are rolled around the restaurant and make a stop at tables that request it in lieu of ordering via server.

Many dim sum restaurants will have servers who don't speak much English, but luckily, words really are not necessary, as the server will open up the lids to the baskets in the cart to show you what's inside. With dim sum, it's worth giving whatever looks good a try, as you'll find some new favorites by doing so.

Most popular at dim sum are dumplings. Pork, shrimp, scallop, vegetable, or beef fillings are wrapped in a wheat flour–based wrapper or sometimes rice-based wrappers, and steamed in bamboo baskets. Once cooked, the items are put into the cart and brought directly out to you, usually retaining all that heat. Fried or boiled dumplings are also available, though the majority are steamed.

Normally, prices are very cheap with one "serving" of dumpling being anywhere between $1.50 and $4, depending on filling, size of order, and restaurant. You can have as many or as few orders as you want.

Other popular items are fresh Chinese broccoli, steamed and drizzled with oyster sauce; lotus-leaf-wrapped sticky rice *(lo mai gai)*; braised spare ribs; chicken feet; barbecue pork buns *(char siu bao)*; or *cheung fun,* which are sticky rice sheets with a shrimp, pork, or beef filling, offered steamed or fried. Those with a sweet tooth will love the mango pudding or deep-fried sesame-seed balls with red beans offered on the dessert carts.

Dim sum for the Chinese is almost a way of life; it represents a break mid-morning to take some time alone with a newspaper and hot tea while slowly ordering a basket or two on which to snack. For others, it's a chance to get friends or family together over a drawn-out meal, catching up over good food and good tea.

Some notable dim sum spots have been included in this book, but in the nooks and crannies of the tourist's Chinatown, you can find little stores serving up fresh dim sum. Feel free to walk in and share a couple baskets with a friend, and move on after a cup of tea to try another place.

the saltiness of the roe and the creaminess of the crème fraîche is in a league of its own; order with a crisp glass of Champagne. The oysters with osetra caviar were lightly cooked and presented in a flavorful cream broth, sprinkled throughout with caviar. The salmon fillet is offered rolled and crusted in bread crumbs, and then stuffed with cucumber, horseradish, and a cream sauce that titillates every note on the palate. For your meal, choosing the wine pairing option will be rewarding as Gary Danko offers some creative and delectable accompaniments. For dessert, opt for the chocolate soufflé, as it's an experience in and of itself. Valet parking is offered, and you might as well use it; you are, after all, dining at the world-famous Gary Danko.

Golden Flower Vietnamese, 667 Jackson St., Chinatown, San Francisco, CA 94108; (415) 433-6469; Vietnamese; $. This is one of the only Vietnamese restaurants located in the middle of Chinatown. Perhaps that's why it's also really popular in the area and during lunch, it will almost always be a full house. My first choices for pho are in the Richmond district in "the other Chinatown," but Golden Flower is a good choice when you're on this side of town. The pho broth is very meaty and herb infused, and the noodles have always been consistently well cooked. What they really prepare well is the rare beef salad, and if you haven't tried this, Golden Flower is a good place for an introduction. Consider it a Vietnamese version of carpaccio with thin slices of raw beef, topped with peanuts, basil, and a load of onions, dressed in a delicious fish-sauce preparation and sprinkled with fresh lemons. One order is good enough to share between two and four people—depending on how much your party loves raw meat.

The House Restaurant, 1230 Grant Ave., North Beach, San Francisco, CA 94133; (415) 986-8612; www.thehse.com; Vietnamese/Asian Fusion; $$$. You have quite a selection of choices for Vietnamese fusion restaurants in the city, and at the top of that list is The House. It's a tiny place, and while not shabby in decor, it's not fancy either. Tables are rather jammed in together, and although it can't hold a candle to some of its competitors in ambience, it blows its competitors out of the water in the taste of food. Nowhere else will you find a large sea bass, broiled until the oils start flowing, served up with garlic noodles that are sweet and garlicky and will melt in your mouth—this restaurant is famous for this dish. The cod and butterfish entrees are also excellent choices, and the vegetables and sauces carry a distinctly Asian influence. But most surprising is how good their rib eye steak is, as you don't quite expect that out of a tiny Asian fusion location. It's a family-owned place and the service is friendly. Locals love it, and tourists in-the-know will stand in line to get a taste of food at The House.

Hog Island Oyster Company, 1 Ferry Building, #11A, Embarcadero, San Francisco, CA 94111; (415) 391-7117; www.hog islandoysters.com; Seafood; $$$. All you can think of when you visit Hog Island at the Ferry Building is "This is living!" Whether you sit outside on the patio or inside at the oyster bar, you have a clear view of San Francisco Bay and the Bay Bridge, along with the boardwalk between piers. The oysters here are from their own oyster farm north of San Francisco, and they are all plump and fresh, and depending on what's offered, some are sweeter than others. They serve complimentary Acme bread here, and you'll find that nothing accompanies oysters and a drink as well as this bread with the butter. Every Monday and Thursday they have happy hour, offering $1 oysters (selected varieties only) from 4 to 7 p.m. Order some Champagne or a nice white wine to go with your oysters, and if you have the appetite for it, definitely order the grilled cheese. Filled with cheese from the famous **Cowgirl Creamery** (p. 232), it balances out the crispness of the oysters with something wonderfully creamy and heavy. At the end of the meal, order a clam chowder; it's soupier than it is chunky, but you can see the pieces of fresh clams inside.

Hot Spud, 2640 Mason St., Fisherman's Wharf, San Francisco, CA 94133; (415) 399-1065; www.hotspudsf.com; American; $–$$. Who doesn't love a baked potato? This fun restaurant is one place in Fisherman's Wharf you have to visit. The concept is genius, and it's the first of its kind to pop up in the city. The execution is also great: You can have your baked potato with basically anything your heart desires. The potato is scooped out, mashed, and nicely mixed with everything you order, then piled back into the skin, making for one of the best baked potatoes you will ever eat. Never again will you have a bite of just sour cream or just potatoes. Topping choices include peas, steak, chicken, shrimp, crab, onions, sour cream, sausage, cheese, corn—and the list goes on. All potatoes start at under $10, and there's also a good selection of healthy salads to balance out your creamy, starchy potato entree. The restaurant also states that 90 percent of their ingredients are gluten-free.

Kennedy's Irish Pub and Curry House, 1040 Columbus St., North Beach, San Francisco, CA 94133; (415) 441-8855; www.kennedys curry.com; Indian; $$. It's a game hall. It's a pub. No, wait—it's . . . an Indian restaurant? Kennedy's is perhaps one of San Francisco's strangest combinations as it really is all of the above. You have a dive-like Irish pub with an incredible amount of beers on tap; I've even found Murphy's Stout here on occasion, which is a rarity outside of Ireland! But then you have a dining area that looks like a diner in the Midwest, serving Indian food—and good Indian food, at that. But then the entire dining area is surrounded by games: video games, air hockey, pool tables, and so forth. It's a large space that can accommodate large parties. It even has an obscure outdoor patio in the very back. As for the food, it's one of the few places in San Francisco that takes your request for "extremely spicy" very seriously. I've been totally impressed with their lamb vindaloo with generous amounts of tender lamb engulfed in spicy vindaloo sauce, the chicken roll, and the moist and juicy chicken tikka masala with basmati rice. Service is friendly enough, and they are open until 2 a.m., with delivery in the local area until 1 a.m.

La Mar Cebicheria Peruana, Pier 1.5, Embarcadero, San Francisco, CA 94111; (415) 397-8880; www.lamarcebicheria.com; Peruvian; $$$$. Prepare for an explosion of flavors at La Mar—at a hefty price, too. There's a lot of beautiful people and beautiful food here. It's refreshing to have this upscale yet unpretentious restaurant on the San Francisco food scene, with gorgeous views of the San Francisco Bay, but a rather casual interior. The patio is a great option on all but the chilliest of days. Most notable is the food, though, with every refreshing order packed with freshness and flavor. Peruvian staples like ceviche and *crudo* items are excellent here; try the nikei ceviche consisting of ahi tuna, avocado, red onions, and seaweed, mixed in with tiger's milk with a hint of tamarind, bringing out the sweetness of the fish and the nuttiness of the avocado. Also try the *limeña causa,* a potato cake stuffed with crabmeat, avocado, and a quail egg—it's served cold and makes for a great starter dish. Be sure to try the skewer options and the lamb shank that falls apart on the plate. Their short ribs *(asado de tira)* and risotto options are always a huge hit, too.

La Trappe Cafe, 800 Greenwich St., North Beach, San Francisco, CA 94133; (415) 440-8727; www.latrappecafe.com; Belgian; $$. Peering in the window, you'd never know how lively La Trappe Cafe really is. The first floor is intended for the diners, but not many go to this local secret joint for dinner. Downstairs is where San Francisco beer lovers and connoisseurs unite after work to select from an immense choice of beers while slurping mussels that are brought to you in a huge cauldron, with bread to dip into the buttery and herbal sauce. The order of mussels come with fries and an option of dipping sauces; try the wasabi mayo, which offers a nice balance between creamy, tart, and spicy. After a few beers, you may end up dipping the bread into the wasabi mayo—or worse, the beer—but you won't care much as the action is lively and the beer keeps flowing. Try the boudin blanc, La Trappe's take on the pork sausage infused with milk and served over a potato-leek gratin; it's rich and creamy and begs for the perfect pint of cold beer.

Mama's on Washington Square, 1701 Stockton St., North Beach, San Francisco, CA 94133; (415) 362-6421; www.mamas-sf .com; American; $$. Brunch doesn't get much better than Mama's. It also doesn't get busier than Mama's does, as even on weekdays there is often a line down the block to get into the restaurant. It's really no wonder, given that the food is so fresh and tasty, and they serve up San Francisco's finest omelets! The Northern Italian Omelet is a prime example of what Mama's offers: a fluffy egg exterior stuffed with pancetta, tomatoes, mushrooms, basil, and a good dose of garlic Jack cheese. Served with crunchy home fries and sourdough toast, this omelet offers a world of flavors and textures. The Dungeness crab eggs Benedict is expensive and worth every penny, as  large portions of crabmeat are laid on English muffins, topped with perfectly poached eggs, and slathered in hollandaise sauce. Each bite yields a nice balance of moist crabmeat and the richness of the eggs and cream sauce. While a french toast sampler is offered, stick to the Swedish Cinnamon Toast; it's piled high with fresh fruits, topped with powdered sugar, and with just a slight drizzle of maple syrup—it can easily replace dessert in my world on any given day.

Mo's Grill, 1322 Grant Ave., North Beach, San Francisco, CA 94133; (415) 788-3779; www.mosgrill.com; American; $$. If you ask a local what their favorite burger in San Francisco is, a good percentage of them will tell you "Mo's!" This classic diner has mastered the art of making a good burger. This is not your fancy burger with cheese from distant lands; this is the good ol' American burger that has the best-quality beef packed generously and loosely to enhance flavor and texture, sandwiched between 2 toasted buns, topped off with some fabulous choices. Order a "belly buster," which is a large burger with perfectly caramelized onions and mushrooms, topped with a load of melted cheddar cheese. Opt for the soup instead of the fries if, after the sound of that burger, you decide to be concerned about calories or fat. (I'm not sure what the point would be, but the tomato soup is excellent.) They have many specials as well as a full lunch and dinner menu, including comfort foods like meat loaf for those of you who don't want what might be San Francisco's finest hamburger.

Osha Thai Restaurant, 4 Embarcadero Center, Embarcadero, San Francisco, CA 94111; (415) 788-6742; www.oshathai.com; Thai; $$. When you have a large group of friends, or if you are looking for a restaurant that will suit all palates and wallets, Osha Thai is one of the first that comes to mind. All 7 locations throughout San Francisco are very popular, and each has its own vibe, but all offer the same level of food. The one on Embarcadero is the nicest as far as ambience and serves as the flagship restaurant for Osha Thai, but there is, quite literally, an Osha Thai in almost every San Francisco neighborhood. Appetizers to try are the duck rolls, which are egg rolls stuffed with juicy duck meat; the tuna tower of raw tuna with a soy marinade, served with chips; and the calamari, which comes accompanied with a spicy yet creamy aioli sauce. The entrees to consider are the Volcanic Beef (sweet), spicy string bean (rather punchy), lemongrass sea bass (fresh and flavorful), or any of the curries, which all make up for in taste what they may lack in authenticity. The pad thai or the pineapple fried rice are both popular items with the San Francisco crowd. Visit the website to find the best location for you if you're staying in a particular neighborhood of San Francisco; some of the locations also offer delivery.

Pier 23 Cafe, Pier 23, Embarcadero, San Francisco, CA 94102; (415) 362-5125; www.pier23cafe.com; Seafood; $$. There's nothing about the exterior of this place that would grab your attention as you drive up the Embarcadero, but you'd be missing out if you didn't go in through the restaurant to the patio on the back end of the restaurant. With a full bar and good drinks, Pier 23 is a casual restaurant that serves up great seafood fare. You have the standard fish-and-chips along with other goodies like bacon-fried oysters. You also have fresh seafood like shrimp cocktail, but one item that must be ordered is the shrimp and crab sandwich. It's fresh shrimp and crabmeat with a creamy mayo-based sauce, piled high on sourdough—absolutely perfect with a beer. With a full brunch and lunch menu that is served well into dinner, Pier 23 is always fun and inviting, with friendly service. Sitting at the water, the restaurant is open nightly and often has live bands performing.

R & G Lounge, 631 Kearny St., Chinatown, San Francisco, CA 94108; (415) 982-7877; www.rglounge.com; Chinese/Seafood; $$$$. This Chinatown staple is at the top of most folks' lists for one reason only: The food is excellent. The stewed oxtails served in a clay pot are delicious—they're served in a thick, gravy-like sauce and the seasoning is completely infused into the oxtail meat. Order the Three Treasures: peppers stuffed with a shrimp, tofu, and eggplant concoction and doused in a delectable black bean sauce; after the dish is gone, make sure to mix some rice into the sauce. R&G is well-known for the crab presentation—whole crab is served to the table, flash-cooked in a variety of ways, keeping the meat tender and juicy throughout. Try the salt-and-pepper method, and if ordering more than one, do try the ginger scallion method as well; it elevates the sweetness of the crab a couple of notches higher.

The Slanted Door, 1 Ferry Building, #3, Embarcadero, San Francisco, CA 94111; (415) 861-8032; www.slanteddoor.com; Vietnamese; $$$. For visitors coming from areas where Vietnamese fusion is not rampant, this could be "foodie heaven": It takes the great flavors of Vietnam and melds them with other cuisines to create something totally unique and delightful. Even if you don't like Vietnamese food, you will most likely enjoy a meal at Slanted Door, as much of it is geared toward the Western palate. Located on the back-end corner of the Ferry Building, it offers terrific views in a contemporary and hip venue with a massive dining room and an equally impressive lounge and bar area. The rib eye with garlic-soy sauce, the green papaya  salad, or the moist and buttery Alaskan halibut are all chock-full of flavors ranging between sweet and savory; the cellophane noodles with green onions and Dungeness crab are consistently sautéed so that the noodles are just right and the crabmeat takes center stage with each bite. One visit and you'll see why Chef Charles Phan has made a huge name for himself in San Francisco and is here to stay.

Sotto Mare Seafood Restaurant, 552 Green St., North Beach, San Francisco, CA 94133; (415) 398-3181; www.sottomaresf.com; Seafood; $$$. What's not good at Sotto Mare? This is classic North Beach Italian, but the true highlight of this restaurant, as the name implies, is the seafood. Their claim to fame is the cioppino for two, packed with shrimp, crab, clams, chunks of fish, mussels, and even pasta in a savory tomato broth that begs for bread dipping. But the sand dabs take a close second place; lightly breaded and pan-fried, this fish exudes freshness and flavor, and the texture is buttery, soft, and flaky. In fact, all of their seafood is excellent; the linguine with clams is a huge hit, and best of all is the clam chowder. The seafood ravioli is truly delicious, and it's always a toss-up between that or the linguine with clams. It's a small spot and gets packed early. Run as a family establishment, the service is pointedly better to the regulars, but everyone tends to have a fun time at Sotto Mare. The ambience is extremely casual; this is not your "get dressed up to go have seafood" type of joint; it's a casual meal with fantastic food. Make reservations, as it's not a quick dining experience, and your wait will inevitably be long.

Vicoletto, 550 Green St., North Beach, San Francisco, CA 94133; (415) 433-5800; www.vicolettosfcom; Italian; $$$. Here's another classic Italian restaurant in Little Italy. Vicoletto has a warm and friendly staff that truly welcomes you into their establishment. On some evenings, I've seen the owner outside the restaurant, greeting passersbys who then are just enticed enough to give Vicoletto a try. In the sea of Italian restaurants available in North Beach, one has to do something to stand out, and Vicoletto's claim is the warmth that they exude. But the food is also terrific. The *burrata* cheese offered here is one of the best I've tried in San Francisco, and the veal cutlets drizzled in a lemon-caper sauce have been outstanding on each visit. The salmon with asparagus is always cooked to retain the moisture and flavor in the fish, and the fresh asparagus keeps much of its crunchiness and contributes some sweetness to this dish. The wine list is wholly Italian, and the choices they have made for us over the years have always been fairly priced and completely perfect with the meal. Do order the tiramisu at the end of the meal.

Yuet Lee, 1300 Stockton St., North Beach, San Francisco, CA 94133; (415) 982-6020; Chinese; $. Despite how many Chinese restaurants exist in Chinatown, the cream of the crop is undoubtedly Yuet Lee, and not necessarily because it's the best. It's cheap, it's fast (incredibly fast), it's fresh, and it's open late. In San Francisco, that is the recipe for success, especially given the lack of late-night dining options. It's a bit astonishing how fast this restaurant can bring your order out; it's as if they have psychics working in the kitchen. From Thursday to Saturday night, Yuet Lee begins to fill up at midnight and it doesn't stop until 4 a.m.; it often seems like every person who was out at the bars ends up craving Yuet Lee, and they all gather here to eat what is most likely their second dinner. Everything at Yuet Lee is packed with flavor, from the soups to the salt-and-pepper squid, which is served lightly breaded and flash-fried, to the porridge with abalone or the thousand-year egg. The menu is quite vast, and there's something for basically anyone. After a night of barhopping, you'd be well-served to cab it to North Beach to try some food at the city's most popular late-night restaurant.

Landmarks

Scoma's Restaurant, Pier 47, Fisherman's Wharf, San Francisco, CA 94133; (415) 771-4383; www.scomas.com; Seafood; $$$$. Walking into this landmark restaurant that is nearing 50 years of age, you can feel the history of San Francisco in its walls. Almost half a million visitors come through Scoma on a yearly basis, and surprisingly, they have never become "just a tourist location." Instead, the food seems to get better each year, and the seafood is about as fresh as you're going to find. Everything from oysters on the half shell to crab cocktails is good here. The crab cakes full of crabmeat and the steamed clams bordelaise are most notable on the hot appetizer list. Definitely have someone at the table order the shellfish sauté, which is big enough to share—2 lobster tails, chunks of crabmeat, shrimp, and scallops are sautéed and piled high on top of a bed of pasta and rice. The cioppino is also very good; the portions are generous and the seasoning is just enough to bring

San Francisco Ferry Building

As the name implies, this is the ferry terminal for all ferries supporting the Bay Area. The building itself has undergone massive renovations over the years; the current structure was completed in 2003. The **Ferry Building** (1 Ferry Building, San Francisco, CA 94111; 415-983-8030; www.ferrybuildingmarketplace .com) is home to many upscale markets and restaurants, including many listed in this chapter. A stroll through the building will yield many tastings from the high-end markets like stores selling only olive oil varieties or special cheese or meats. It's also the location for the popular famers' market, described on p. 22. Expensive valet parking is offered in front for those who drive here, but public transportation is highly recommended. Parking is very limited on the Embarcadero, and when available in private lots, it tends to be equal to the cost of using the valet service. The boardwalk behind the Ferry Building should be enjoyed by anyone who visits San Francisco.

the subtle seafood flavors to life. Some of the servers have been here almost as long as the beautiful restaurant, and they have mastered the art of providing service to you. From beginning to end, a dinner at Scoma's is a classic San Franciscan dining experience, and one you should not miss. With complimentary parking available, there's no reason not to go.

Teatro Zinzanni, http://love.zinzanni.org. Cast away whatever your previous notions about dinner theaters are, as you'd be remiss to not give this landmark theater a whirl. It is, without a doubt, one of the most fun, entertaining, and spectacular venues in San Francisco, and with a new show every 3 months or so, Teatro Zinzanni is worth visiting time and again. Your experience, of course, will depend mostly on the quality of the show, but their lineup is usually amazing. The dinner is spaced ingeniously between acts, and many of the actors themselves are also the servers and will dance your plate to you. The food is provided by Taste Catering, and given the sheer number of people they have to serve at once, each of the 5 courses was surprisingly delicious. The first course was just a starter plate with nuts, **Cowgirl Creamery** (p. 232) cheeses, brioche, and olives; the second course was a creamy and uniquely filling tortilla soup; the third course was a spinach and marinated fennel salad with almonds and a sweet but light dressing; the fourth course was a beef filet, paired wonderfully with asparagus and carrots; and the dessert was one of the best panna cottas I have had. The talents displayed within this unassuming and deceivingly small tent on Embarcadero is astonishing—with great acting, singing, acrobatics and more laughs than you can handle.

Tommaso's Ristorante Italiano, 1042 Kearny St., Downtown, San Francisco, CA 94133; (415) 398-9696; www.tommasos.com;

Italian; $$. This has been a staple in North Beach for over 75 years, and generation after generation has visited the Tommaso family establishment to enjoy the pizza. The dimly lit, small restaurant exudes a deeply embedded sense of family, and the owner himself will welcome you warmly, in a truly Italian fashion. The pizzas are large and extremely generous in toppings; order anything with their prosciutto, and with your first bite, you'll note that the quality of the cheese, dough, and every single topping you've ordered is top-notch. The pastas have always been cooked al dente, and from the regular spaghetti and meatballs to a fettuccine with salmon in a tomato cream sauce, Tommaso's impresses meal after meal. Definitely squeeze in an order of the linguine with clams as this might be the only place where you can't see the pasta for the seafood!

Specialty Stores, Markets & Producers

Eastern Bakery, 720 Grant Ave., Chinatown, San Francisco, CA 94108; (415) 982-5157; www.easternbakery.com. It's an unassuming little hole-in-the-wall bakery that offers some of Chinatown's finest baked goods. The best of all is the coffee crunch cake, which is about the last thing you'd expect from a Chinese bakery, but this is their claim to fame. Also notable are their pork buns, which are freshly made throughout the day and offered for only $1, and their combination steamed chicken buns. They offer standard bakery items like chocolate chip and almond cookies, and if you ask nicely, they will also heat them to soften them up for you.

Ferry Plaza Farmers' Market, 1 Ferry Building, Embarcadero, San Francisco, CA 94111; (415) 291-3276; www.ferrybuilding marketplace.com/farmers_market.php. On any given Saturday, a significant portion of San Francisco's population will head to the Embarcadero to visit the Ferry Plaza Farmers' Market. It's reported that nearly 25,000 shoppers visit this San Francisco farmers' market on a weekly basis! It's a great place to spot many restaurateurs who come to stock up on locally grown, organic produce, and others who come to put on cooking demonstrations as guest chefs; some well-known restaurants will sell their creations to visitors. From fresh produce to specialty honeys, cheeses, breads, and prepared foods, this market aims to educate and promote sustainable foods while providing a priceless service to San Francisco residents every weekend. On Tuesday and Thursday, farmers will display their goods at the front of the Ferry Building; on Saturday, it's a full-blown show with both the front and back end of the Ferry Building chock-full of stands. The produce is not cheap, but all are extremely high quality. Some of the trucks and stands available at this market are listed in the introduction of this book (p. 1); at the end of your eating and shopping expedition, finish up with a nice cup of Blue Bottle Coffee, when available.

Downtown: Financial District, Union Square, Tenderloin, Nob Hill & Russian Hill

San Francisco really doesn't have a designated downtown area except the Financial District; most people refer to any of the western neighborhoods surrounding the Financial District as "downtown." For the purpose of this book, "downtown" will include the Financial District, Nob Hill and Russian Hill, and the area surrounding the posh Union Square along with the shabby but wonderful Tenderloin district. Those are the main areas where the bustling activities take place, though not necessarily all business activities.

Financial District

The majority of high-rise buildings are located in the Financial District, with some more recently scattered throughout Embarcadero (in the previous chapter). The well-known TransAmerica Pyramid is also located here, home to many recognized businesses. This area during business hours is reminiscent of a smaller and cleaner Manhattan, with a large number of people on the streets bustling about with their cup of Starbucks coffee, walking rapidly to their destinations. Due to the number of businesses here, there are also many restaurants and bars, all suitable for after-work entertaining, business events, and expense-account expenditures.

Union Square

This 1-block plaza, named after the rallies that took place for the Union Army during the Civil War, is home to some of the finest shopping in the world. Many large hotel chains, as well as many boutique hotels, are located here, tempting tourists to spend money at the high-end stores throughout the area, including two Macys, Neiman Marcus, and Saks Fifth Avenue. Union Square refers to this entire area, not just the square itself, and there are such a vast number of restaurants, theaters, bars, and nightlife in the area that it could be considered active for nearly 24 hours a day.

The Hills: Nob Hill & Russian Hill

Sometimes jokingly referred to as "Snob Hill," Nob Hill is one of the more affluent neighborhoods of San Francisco. It follows suit that some of the city's most popular eateries are spread out through

Stanford Ct
great teatime

this neighborhood, along with the most expensive hotels within city limits: the Fairmont Hotel and Intercontinental Mark Hopkins Hotel.

Russian Hill is named after a small Russian cemetery discovered at the top of this area during the gold rush era. The demographic is similar to Nob Hill, albeit a bit on the lesser side, but the proximity to downtown and other neighborhoods keeps demand for housing in this area high. This is also home to Lombard Street, commonly known as "the crookedest street in the world," with eight hairpin turns to make the steepness of this hill manageable, which is also one of the city's most popular tourist attractions.

Tenderloin

Though there is crime in every major city, each city has certain neighborhoods that are considered worse than others, and in San Francisco it is the Tenderloin district. While it's true that crime is higher here, I've found it to be more dangerous for cars than people. Avoiding the Tenderloin means missing out on some of the best ethnic food in San Francisco, particularly Vietnamese food; living in San Francisco means that one has to visit the Tenderloin. At the time of this writing, much effort is being put into revamping the neighborhood, and with large companies like Twitter planning a move into the area, it should only be a matter of time before the area becomes safer.

Acquerello, 1722 Sacramento St., Nob Hill, San Francisco, CA 94109; (415) 567-5432; www.acquerello.com; Italian; $$$$$. If I had to pick my top five restaurants in the city, Acquerello would be in the top three, and not because of the Michelin star they earned. Executive Chef Suzette Gresham's cooking rivals that of any high-end dining location in the world, offering combinations of unique flavors that explode on the tongue. The wine list is full of every varietal you would ever want to try, with the best suggestions coming from truly impressive sommeliers, led by co-owner Giancarlo Paterlini, who pair wine with the food masterfully. The poached egg with farro and asparagus tips, the grilled lamb's tongue with celery and salsa verde, and the Kobe beef tartare served with salmon roe, basil and arugula flowers all make excellent starters. Not to be missed while at Acquerello is the ridged pasta with *foie gras* for the second course; the pasta is cooked al dente, and then smothered in a *foie gras* and Marsala sauce with truffles, which all combine to highlight sweet, savory, and intense flavors in this dish. The faux cannelloni with meat offers the whole spectrum of flavors but doesn't have a lick of pasta in it; I was honored to secure the recipe in this book. The cheese cart is also world-class. Order the coffee service with the bourbon caramel semifreddo for dessert—it's topped with amaretto crumbs and drizzled in rich chocolate sauce. See Acquerello's recipe for **Potato-Wrapped Cannelloni of Beef Brasato with Truffled Verdure** on p. 270.

Anh Hong Restaurant, 808 Geary St., Tenderloin, San Francisco, CA 94109; (415) 885-5180; www.anhhong.com; Vietnamese; $$. With a menu that touts 7 courses of beef, it's easy to sell people on Anh Hong. It's a simple and completely casual restaurant located in the middle of the Tenderloin that serves up some delicious Vietnamese food. For $18.95 per person, you can order the famous "7 courses of beef," which focus on wrapping your own fresh spring rolls. The first course is a beef salad; the second is a raw beef course that comes with a hot pot of herb-infused water in which to boil your beef, and wrap it up with many other vegetables like sprouts and carrots and herbs like basil and mint. The third, fourth, and fifth courses of beef are various sausages, also used to wrap into the rice sheets; the sixth course is a beef pâté or patty-type mound that is actually quite tasty. The final course is a delicious bowl of porridge meant to share, with a noticeable scent of ginger, boiled in a beef broth. Always order the vermicelli patties, which are noodle patties that are sprinkled with peanuts; including these into your spring rolls makes them taste even better.

Big 4 Restaurant, 1075 California St., Nob Hill, San Francisco, CA 94108; (415) 771-1140; www.big4restaurant.com; American; $$$$. With wooden walls and a fashionable old-school lounge area, Big

4 is a hidden gem adjacent and attached to the Huntington Hotel in Nob Hill. If under the age of 40, you can easily be the youngest person in the restaurant—and it's obvious the clientele frequenting Big 4 are old-time regulars. The atmosphere and food are ideal for dates, as it's dark, woody, and plush. Start the meal with the shrimp-avocado salad, served with wild arugula and shaved fennel; this dish was fresh and invigorating, and provided a nice balance between the seafood and nuttiness of the avocado in relation to the herbal flavors of the arugula and fennel. The osso buco was fascinatingly tasty, the tender pork falling apart and served with pancetta-roasted tomatoes, heirloom white beans, and potatoes. Also supreme was the rack of lamb with a rosemary rub; it was served with a slightly sweet quinoa, asparagus, and a Zinfandel pan jus sauce. Interestingly, the only steak worth eating is the filet mignon with Gorgonzola, so long as you request the cheese on the side, as it masks the great flavors in the meat itself.

BIX Restaurant, 56 Gold St., Financial District, San Francisco, CA 94133; (415) 433-6300; www.bixrestaurant.com; American; $$$$. The ambience of this place makes you want to wear a red flapper dress here. Something about the decor and mood takes you back to the early 20th century, and you can almost envision the patrons in the cozy booths smoking pipes and cigarettes during their meals while sipping on fine spirits. The large staircase heading to the second floor really sets the mood, which makes it suitable for fancy dinner dates, even with the masses of business suits downstairs by the bar. A live jazz band plays on and off through the night and really elevates the restaurant to high-end dining. The tuna tartare with toast was a blissful mix of fresh and comforting, and their crab cakes are actually little sandwiches with large chunks of crabmeat in between. The pork chop is large and extremely juicy, but the menu changes often, so ask one of the great servers for his/her recommendation. The entire menu is available at the bar area; you could just as easily enjoy a couple cocktails while ordering to eat and enjoying the music and ambience.

Brenda's French Soul Food, 652 Polk St., Tenderloin, San Francisco, CA 94102; (415) 345-8100; www.frenchsoulfood.com; Soul Food; $$. When you combine anything deep-fried with grits and 2 eggs any style, there's really not much more you can ask for in a true comfort meal. The grillades and grits at Brenda's consist of 2 beef cutlets covered in their house gravy, served with a whopping lump of grits with butter, eggs (get them poached if you like!), and a hot biscuit. It might require an ER visit post-dinner, but it's still worth it. The shrimp po'boy is a must, with battered shrimp and sauce, tucked plentifully with lettuce and tomatoes into a perfectly toasted French baguette, as is the shrimp and grits. One of the most beautiful sights at this restaurant is the braised ribs with cheddar grits and a sunny-side-up egg on top. The meat hardly requires a knife, and combined with the creaminess of the grits and the egg, it's a mandatory order at Brenda's. The restaurant is almost always busy, lunch or dinner, but the line moves relatively fast. Be patient and you will be in for the feast of a lifetime at minimal cost!

Cafe Claude, 7 Claude Ln., Union Square, San Francisco, CA 94108; (415) 392-3505; www.cafeclaude.com; French; $$. The interior of this restaurant is very nice, but the outdoor patio is what makes it special. If you let your imagination wander, you might as well be sitting at some cafe on Champs Elysees, sipping on espresso and pondering food. With the mostly French staff and their accents, you can forget for an instant that you are, in fact, down a small alleyway in downtown San Francisco, just seconds away from high-rise buildings. Their sandwiches are excellent (try the pork loin sandwich), as are the pommes frites; definitely request the house aioli as it was stellar when spread on the sandwich, extending a definite kick to the meal. The arugula salad was fresh, crisp, and lightly dressed and made for a perfect accompaniment to the meal.

Cotogna, 470 Pacific Ave., Downtown, San Francisco, CA 94133; (415) 775-8508; www.cotognasf.com; Italian; $$$. New on the San Francisco food scene, Cotogna is as popular as it gets these days, located next door to the beautiful sister restaurant **Quince** (p. 75), which has already made a name for itself. Cotogna focuses primarily on pastas and other casual Italian fare. All of their pastas are good to excellent; items like the ravioli with farm egg in butter was almost too rich for my taste, but their gnocchi was a mass of pillowy potato puffs and nothing short of outstanding. The pizzas are freshly prepared and are as authentic as any you might grab in Italy, with fresh slices of mozzarella and large chunks of whatever you ordered on it—perfect to share between two people. The most impressive of all was the pork loin; I daresay this was the best pork loin I've ever had. It was as juicy as can be, packed full of flavor, and the fennel that was paired with this dish made it soar to heights never before touched by pork loin. Cotogna has a massive wine list of Italian wines and an ingenious concept of pricing all wines at $40 per bottle or $10 per glass, regardless of which bottle you choose.

Crepes A Go Go, 1220 Polk St., Downtown, San Francisco, CA 94109; Creperie; $. The storefront window faces the streets, enticing late-night Polk Street dwellers to come in and grab a crepe with Nutella. This location makes good crepes, whether it is sweet with your standard strawberries, bananas, and Nutella, or a savory one, like their famous chicken and cheese crepe that is served hot with cheese oozing out. With late-night hours, it gets quite busy after midnight, especially as patrons leave Lush Lounge across the street. Service is friendly, and they can customize as much as you request. They have a really popular crepe food cart that serves up much of the same, located at 350 11th St., SOMA, San Francisco, CA 94103; (415) 503-1294. There is a third location in San Francisco, located at 2165 Union St., Marina, San Francisco, CA 94123; (415) 928-1919.

Curry Up Now, 225 Bush St., Financial District, San Francisco, CA 94104; (650) 477-3000; www.curryupnow.com; Twitter: @Curry UpNow; Indian; $. At any given weekday lunchtime, there's a line down the block of people wanting a chicken tikka masala burrito. In line with all the fusion cuisine this city has witnessed, it was only a matter of time before someone took flavorful Indian food and wrapped it up in a burrito. Try any of the tikka masala burritos, or the paneer burrito if you don't want meat, which is a homemade Indian cheese that is great in texture and creamy in taste. The burrito is filled with rice, juicy cuts of meat, and onions, with distinct notes of cumin and tamarind and a general curry sauce drizzled throughout. Keep in mind that their "mild" is considered spicy by some—but I've requested "extra extra spicy," which the staff confirmed twice before agreeing to it, and suffice to say they challenged even my idea of spicy (and nobody can eat spicier than me).

farm:table, 754 Post St., Tenderloin, San Francisco, CA 94108; (415) 292-7089; www.farm tablesf.com; Twitter: @farmtable; American; $$$. You just don't know what you're going to get when you go to farm:table. Well, okay, if you follow them on Twitter, you can find out the menu as it changes every single day. Therefore, it's impossible to make suggestions on what to order, but one thing about farm:table is that whatever they are serving up is always good! The restaurant has a communal table inside and 2 outdoor tables; they also have

some counter space where you can stand and eat, but if there's no room, you might as well take it to-go and enjoy the great food elsewhere. It's a great concept, following the style of food trucks tweeting locations and changing the daily menu, and it works because the friendly folks at farm:table know how to cook great food. For example, a *pain de mie* sandwich with perfectly crunchy bacon, arugula, and thin slices of apples, or braised pork atop a brioche with a soft egg and green onions are the types of items that farm:table offers. Due to the frequent menu changes, your mileage may vary, but more often than not, farm:table will deliver good food for good prices. Definitely try the coffee, iced or hot.

Farmerbrown Restaurant, 25 Mason St., Tenderloin, San Francisco, CA 94102; www.farmerbrownsf.com; Soul Food; $$. Food is sustenance, but sometimes, food makes you glad to be alive. Eating at Farmerbrown is a bit of the latter, even if eating there often might shorten your overall lifespan due to clogged arteries. But one look at the menu and you realize why they call it "soul food," or even better, "comfort food," as this food grounds you, even if it is by weighing you down. Just reading the menu elevates your mood. Farmerbrown offers some good ol' Southern fried chicken that is crispy on the outside and juicy on the inside, with mac and cheese (with Tillamook cheese!), but also the collard greens, po'boy sandwiches, pork chops (definitely try these), and grits are reminiscent of a lunch or dinner in the South. Some other recommendations would be the jambalaya and fried okra, which will make you take a second look at okra. They have a brunch for $16 per person every Saturday and Sunday with the breakfast usuals like eggs and potatoes—but with unlimited Southern fried chicken and desserts. I can't really think of a better brunch for a Saturday morning, can you?

This restaurant also runs **Farmerbrown: Little Skillet,** a pick-up window located at 360 Ritch St., SOMA, San Francisco, CA 94107; (415) 777-2777; www.littleskilletsf.com. Little Skillet put chicken and waffles on the map (in San Francisco), but I'm still not convinced that the two should ever be put together.

5A5 Steak Lounge, 244 Jackson St., Financial District, San Francisco, CA 94111; (415) 989-2539; www.5a5stk.com; Steakhouse; $$$$$. Half lounge and half steakhouse, 5A5 is a beautiful restaurant that is home to more parties every weekend than any other establishment. The steakhouse itself is modern in design with roomy booth seating and a menu that propels the restaurant to what some might call the best steakhouse in San Francisco. 5A5 has a huge selection of fusion-style appetizers, from oyster or *hamachi* shooters to strangely addictive truffle fries. Chef Alex Chen, originally from **Alexander's Steakhouse** (p. 89), heads up this restaurant with its fantastic food lineup. 5A5 is home to the best buffalo steak I've ever had; cooked medium rare, this juicy but lean cut of meat can make most sake-infused cows shrink away in shame due to its tenderness. The T-bone steak is served with a bone marrow sauce and fried bone marrow—seriously! The A5 Wagyu, reportedly the finest cut of meat known to the world, has almost uniform marbling throughout the meat. One bite into it, you realize there is something in the world that is actually better than real butter.

Frascati Restaurant, 1901 Hyde St., Downtown, CA 94109; (415) 928-1406; www.frascatisf.com; Italian/Mediterranean; $$$. Like Old Faithful, this is a great go-to restaurant choice in San Francisco. Starting with the bread and olive oil, both are of excellent quality and taste, you can overeat before your appetizers are delivered. One memorable creation is the watermelon salad, with a balsamic reduction lightly drizzled over mint leaves, nuts, and smoked ricotta sprinkled throughout. The combination comes to life as the mint and fruit mesh into one mouthful. If you're in the mood for something a little heavier, consider a bread salad with Mediterranean notes from olives and feta cheese, or the smoked trout salad with arugula, oranges, and pomegranate. For your entree, consider the sweet corn risotto—while technically vegetarian, you will never miss meat while eating this—or the roasted half chicken with artichokes— with crispy skin and juicy meat, the flavors of artichoke, lemon, and onions resound in this dish. If you have room for dessert, the flourless chocolate meltdown cake is decadent and rich; pairing each bite with a creamy vanilla gelato, drizzled in a raspberry sauce, you'll leave knowing Frascati is San Francisco's sweetheart for good reason.

Gitane Restaurant & Bar, 6 Claude Ln., Union Square, San Francisco, CA 94108; (415) 788-6686; www.gitanerestaurant.com; French; $$$. This might be one of the best-decorated restaurants in the city; every nook and cranny in this place had someone's talented eye and care put into it, and it shows. If you're a bit cramped in the dining area of the restaurant, they make up for it with putting romance in the air. But it's such a mishmash of cuisines from—well, basically, all over the world. There are some flavors from each continent, including Africa, Italy, then a culinary stroll to Spain, with a short stopover in France, then to Morocco, and finally to a cuisine you don't think you are even aware of yet. However, the food is tasty, and the dishes are very creative. They have Bacon Bonbons, which are worth a try if you love bacon. Overall, the experience is pleasant when you're on a date. It's a small, sexy, and intimate restaurant ideal for a date, but make sure your date is willing to eat food from any and all regions, as while the restaurant lists itself as "French," they really do offer a small taste of food from various regions around the world!

Globe Restaurant, 290 Pacific Ave., Financial District, San Francisco, CA 94111; (415) 391-4132; www.globerestaurant.com; American; $$$. It's commonly said that all the chefs in San Francisco head to Globe for their late-night dinner once they're off duty from their restaurants. It is true that once you get past the main dinner hours, Globe gets busier, as they offer good food and do so into the late-night hours. The New York steak for two is much like the "porterhouse for two" concept at Wolfgang's or Peter Luger's in New York; it's not normally a cut I'm impressed by, but Globe prepares it to a medium-rare and slices it up prior to serving to ensure it stays that way. It tends to be seasoned on the heavy-handed side of things, but, paired with the scalloped potatoes, the combination hits every culinary note. No other restaurant in San Francisco, at least to date, has utilized this concept of serving a particular cut of steak for the number of people in your party. The macaroni and cheese at Globe is phenomenal; using large pasta tubes with Tillamook cheese, it's so simple and plain yet so rich and cheesy. The live oysters, served all night, have always been fresh. With a full bar and good wine list that are available past midnight in a city where kitchens tend to go dark past 10 p.m., Globe is where almost all San Franciscans will end up at one time or another.

Ha Nam Ninh, 337 Jones St., Tenderloin, San Francisco, CA 94102; (415) 346-3100; Vietnamese; $. "Number 25, dry, please." Those are really the only words you need to use when visiting Ha Nam Ninh. It's a bowl of noodles with freshly cooked shrimp, squid, fish balls, marinated chicken, and pork with vegetables, served up with a brown fish sauce concoction and a small bowl of beef soup used for pho on the side. Pour in as much as you want of each liquid, some hot sauce if you can handle it, and mix up everything together, and you have their signature dish that people stand in line for during mealtimes. It's perfect for lunch in that it's light and not as filling as a regular bowl of pho, and on cold days it can't be beat. The sweet and savory flavors play together pleasantly, and it's impressive what removing the soup from what is essentially the same dish (pho) can do to enhance the flavor of the noodles and ingredients. The service can be excruciatingly slow sometimes, but otherwise, it's well-kept and clean despite its location in the Tenderloin.

Harris' the San Francisco Steakhouse, 2100 Van Ness Ave., Downtown, San Francisco, CA 94109; (415) 673-1888; www.harris restaurant.com; Steakhouse; $$$$$. This is the quintessential steakhouse in ambience, service, and price. The location is large with a gorgeous lounge area that offers full dining service, and a dining room that is graced with dark wood panels and murals on the walls, with large, roomy booths that make you feel like royalty. In the front room, you can see all the meat being aged with visible marbling throughout. Knowing your meat has gone through this process makes you salivate before you even sit down. Every meal starts off with their warm bread and butter; I'm not sure if anyone dislikes bread and butter, but this is irresistible. For appetizers, order the fresh oysters, sweetbreads that will make you fall in love with organs in general, and the crab cakes, full of crabmeat and fried to a nice crisp outside. Their rib eye choices are excellent in preparation and presentation, and the filet mignon Rossini is spectacular: a nice filet with a generous chunk of *foie gras* on top of it, seared perfectly. For sides, the creamed spinach and scalloped potatoes make this one of San Francisco's perfect meals from start to finish. I have yet to know anyone who has room for dessert after this layout.

Katana-Ya Restaurant, 430 Geary St., Union Square, San Francisco, CA 94102; (415) 771-1280; Japanese; $$. As a tiny place on Geary Street, Katana-Ya does really well by offering good ramen combinations. You can order just ramen, but they have nice add-ons for a small additional fee that include a roll, tuna over rice, or tempura, as not every appetite will be satiated on ramen alone. While they have a full sushi bar, the selling point of this little restaurant is not the sushi; rather, they have a comforting bowl of ramen with tasty soup, albeit a bit on the greasier side of things. Then again, you don't eat ramen for the health benefits, so the generous slices of pork and bamboo are a nice touch, particularly since your options for a warm bowl of ramen are limited in this area. Their donburi (pork cutlet on top of rice with gravy) and other rice plate items are well-priced and filling. Service is friendly and fast; most of the time, the ramen will be on your table within 10 to 15 minutes.

Kokkari Estiatorio, 200 Jackson St., Financial District, San Francisco, CA 94111; (415) 981-0983; www.kokkari.com; Mediterranean; $$$. Nowhere else in San Francisco will you find lamb chops as delicious as Kokkari's. Order them medium-rare, and if you didn't love lamb before, you'll realize it was only because nobody made them quite like this. The location is beautiful, and the menu is vast. I highly recommend you choose the zucchini cakes with homemade Greek yogurt for your appetizer, grilled octopus that is so soft and juicy, and the meatballs. If you have room, perhaps include the hummus with pita bread as this is not your usual store-bought hummus; it's a mash of beans and herbs that seem to have increasing levels of taste with each bite. The goat soup is definitely worth a try, filled with artichoke hearts, goat meat, and feta cheese that works magic into the soup. For your entree, despite the fact that this not a steakhouse, Kokkari offers a 20-ounce rib eye steak that is worthy competition to any steak in the city. Valet parking is offered in front.

La Folie, 2316 Polk St., Russian Hill, San Francisco, CA 94109; (415) 776-5577; www.lafolie.com; French; $$$$$. This staple restaurant has always been associated with fine and romantic dining, and from the moment you step in, you'll see why. With warm and attentive service, La Folie and Chef Roland Passot offer top-notch French cooking with no pretense. From *amuse-bouche* like a poached egg served in an egg shell with truffle shavings and brioche, to lobster with a curry-and-cauliflower puree, the cooking is creative and enables every ingredient to sing. While some restaurants pair *foie gras* with Sauternes, La Folie pairs it with cherries and maple syrup, and, surprisingly, it works. The rack of lamb served here is cooked to a beautiful medium-rare and paired with butter beans for texture, chorizo for a hint of smokiness, and the olive jus for a slight but sharp saltiness. Most impressive was a beef tenderloin entree that was so lean and tender on its own, but topped with a bone marrow–custard concoction, the flavors just jumped off the plate. For dessert, opt for the apple-tart bread pudding; it's served with Maker's Mark ice cream and an apple fritter.

Leopold's, 2400 Polk St., Russian Hill, San Francisco, CA 94109; (415) 474-2000; www.leopoldssf.com; German; $$. Leopold's gives you a peek into the very best representation of German food; not even in Germany have I tasted food this delightful. From the starters, be sure to try the crispy pig trotters with poached egg and potatoes. The slight fattiness of the pig's feet, chopped into indiscernible size, made into a patty and fried, just begs for a small sip of Franziskaner to balance it out. Try the potato pancakes with cured salmon; the fish is cured just enough so as not to be salty, and placed atop a piece of the lightly fried, soft potato pancake. The goulash is slightly different from stew in that the meat has more chewiness and texture, but the gravy that it's stewed in is so full of depth and spices. Each bite is accompanied with the buttery and flavorful spaetzle, and the combination is a huge success. Leopold's trout is wrapped in pancetta, stuffed full of leeks, garlic, fennel, and peas, and then roasted with potatoes until it becomes as delicious as any other fish in the world. Trout is not a particularly flavorful fish, and this was most impressive. Be prepared for good times each time someone orders Das Boot, a super-sized boot-shaped beer glass for truly dedicated and able beer-drinkers, and the entire restaurant goes into a momentary uproar.

Masa's Restaurant, 648 Bush St., Downtown, San Francisco, CA (415) 989-7154; www.masarestaurant.com; French; $$$$$. Chef Gregory Short, originally from the French Laundry, heads up what used to be the love child of Chef Masataka Kobayashi, also known as "Masa." The location has exchanged hands between quite a few chefs since 1983, and today, it still holds onto its Michelin star. Masa's is French cooking California-style. The ingredients are wonderful, and the presentation is beautiful. The concept at Masa's— allowing 2 choices for all 7 courses—is wonderful, enabling two people to try everything on their menu for the evening. With items like sea urchin custard with osetra caviar, or chilled Dungeness crab with edamame and cilantro, the flavors are distinct and meld together beautifully to create a surprise on your tongue. The poached lobster served at Masa's still reigns supreme; it was lightly poached in butter, just enough to enhance the sweetness of the lobster but not mask the subtle flavors of the sea. While assuredly French, the food at Masa's is noticeably light on cream and butter, and each dish aims to highlight the main ingredient.

Michael Mina, 252 California St., Downtown, San Francisco, CA 94111; (415) 397-9222; www.michaelmina.net; Contemporary American, French/Asian/Fusion; $$$$$. Michael Mina, the restaurant, recently moved to a new location on California Street, and the old location inside the St. Francis has been changed to Bourbon Steak, also from Michael Mina. His signature "trio presentation" of offering one item cooked three ways is now gone, but in its place are some imaginative and creative menu items. First and foremost, any chef who serves sourdough bread with a blended mix of ricotta and mascarpone cheese drizzled with honey and sprinkled with salt is a deity in my book. Amen, Michael Mina. The chilled shellfish platter is worth paying the extra money for, as the seafood is of a quality only Chef Mina can access. With crab, lobster, oysters, blue shrimp, crawfish, and ceviche on one platter, $35 per person is a bargain. For your entree, always order the Deconstructed Maine Lobster Pot Pie; need I really say more about this?

Nick's Crispy Tacos, 2101 Polk St., Nob Hill, San Francisco, CA 94109; (415) 409-8226; Mexican; $$. This might be the world's messiest and most sinful taco—"Nick's way." Every Tuesday is $2 Taco Night, and it's a madhouse—and for good reason, as Nick's Crispy Tacos are addictive. Every taco can be ordered "Nick's way." On the outside, you have a flour tortilla; on the inside, you have a deep-fried crispy tortilla. Then the magic begins inside the taco, depending on what you order. Best on the menu are the fish tacos, and a close runner-up is the *carne asada*. Whichever you order, it's piled thick with cabbage, then cheese is dumped on it with a huge dollop of fresh guacamole. If this is "Nick's way," I like Nick. Though their claim to fame is the taco, the burritos are equally delicious. They also supply you with 2 kinds of salsa; the habañero sauce is delightfully spicy and adds a real punch to everything. Note that Nick's Crispy Tacos shares the same space as Rouge Nightclub.

✓ **Pearl's Deluxe Burgers,** 708 Post St., Downtown, San Francisco, CA 94109; (415) 409-6120; www.pearlsdeluxe.com; American; $$. This is a classic American burger in more ways than one. First, it's huge; the regular burgers are half-pound patties and the mini burgers are quarter-pounders. Then, you can add any of the deep-fried burger accompaniments to your meal: thick-cut fries, garlic fries, sweet potato fries that everyone loves, onions rings—or mix them all up. This place is some San Franciscans' favorite burger joint, and they love the fat and oil dripping from the burger. There's a custom burger here for anyone, including those with enormous appetites. The King Burger is a beef patty with a whopping amount of Thousand Island sauce, American cheese, and a split hot dog on top—perfect for those of you who can't decide if you want a hot dog or a burger. There are a lot of ordering options, and you can customize to your heart's content, but definitely opt for the $4 Kobe burger upgrade; it will make all the difference in taste.

Perbacco: San Francisco Restaurant + Bar, 230 California St., Downtown, San Francisco, CA 94111; (415) 955-0663; www.perbacco sf.com; Italian; $$$. Taking up two floors and offering Italian fare,

Perbacco is a go-to restaurant downtown for client lunches, business dinners, and even dates. Almost always busy, the restaurant can require a wait if you don't have reservations, but the offerings reward you for your patience. Start off with the *burrata* cheese appetizer. While this dish is commonly offered in San Francisco restaurants, Perbacco's is especially good; the *burrata* is silky smooth on the outside and the outer layer of the cheese "pops" to release the soft and creamy cheese inside, with texture reminiscent of ricotta cheese. Served with arugula and roasted friarelli peppers and anchovies, the combination hits every flavor imaginable. Also exemplary is the *hamachi* with blood orange, drizzled with olive oil; it's not the combination you'd expect, but it is an explosion of distinct flavors, and the fish is extremely fresh. Don't miss out on the hand-cut tagliatelle that is served al dente with a pork *sugo* that's been stewed for five hours. Also notably good was the chanterelle risotto, which highlighted the mushrooms exquisitely.

Quince Restaurant, 470 Pacific Ave., Downtown, San Francisco, CA 94133; (415) 775-8500; www.quincerestaurant.com; Italian; $$$$$. If there's a list of must-try tasting menus in San Francisco, Quince would be in the top five. While the more economical sister restaurant, **Cotogna** (p. 60), has recently opened up next door and offers up simple and great pizzas and pastas, Quince retains

DRESSING FOR SAN FRANCISCO

When packing for San Francisco during spring and summer months, you really need to pack for summer and winter. A nice leather jacket or something to block the wind from passing through you is crucial. You will need a scarf or two, and at least a couple of sweaters. But if the weather is nice, you will also need your tank tops and shorts with flip-flops (it is California!), too.

In the warmer areas of San Francisco, like Potrero Hill and the Marina, a nice day may enable you to wear a light dress or tank top and feel comfortable. One short cab ride later as you go to eat in the Richmond, you will suddenly freeze as the sun sets and the wind blows, if the mist and fog haven't already rolled in!

Wherever we go, we always wear about two layers, a sweater in our bags, and a jacket or coat in the car that we can get if it becomes necessary.

Pack a pair of reasonable heels and a little black dress or two for the nice restaurants (and there are a lot in this city), but pack a couple pairs of comfortable shoes for walking—because walk you will. Jeans, flats, turtlenecks, sweaters, leggings, and boots—you get the drift: casual and comfortable.

Gentlemen, jackets will be required in some restaurants, so don't pack for just the beach; a pair or two of nice slacks, button-down shirts, and a nice dinner jacket should suffice for most occasions.

Unlike New York City where fashion outranks comfort despite the pain, San Francisco is all about looking and feeling comfortable but stylish!

the classy and luxurious dining with prices to match. Diners have the choice between 5- ($95) and 7-course ($125) menu options, and the highly recommended wine pairings will be an additional cost. Chef Michael Tusk forces sweetbreads and butter to make music on your plate, and very few restaurants can offer sweetbreads that compare to this. The pasta dishes, especially the ravioli and tortellini options, are exemplary, with fresh pastas enveloping generous portions of meat fillings that are seasoned to bring out intense flavors with each bite. If offered, don't hesitate to order the pasta with *uni* (sea urchin) options. One sip of the paired wine with each course raises the culinary bar for most pasta items. The menu changes nightly, but you can go to Quince expecting to be ecstatically surprised.

Saigon Sandwich, 560 Larkin St., Downtown, San Francisco, CA 94102; (415) 474-5698; Vietnamese; $. Something about a Vietnamese sandwich, also called banh mi, makes for the perfect lunch item. These sandwiches are filled with delicious Vietnamese ingredients and always served on a Vietnamese version of the French baguette. The bread is on the lighter end with a crispy crust on the outside and soft on the inside (they usually warm up the bread), and the flavor of the bread pairs perfectly with the sweet and savory tastes of the ingredients. The common fillings offered at Saigon Sandwiches are rated as some of the best in the city; the most popular are the barbecued pork and the roasted chicken, or if you're the more adventurous type, try the pâté sandwich, or any combination with pâté. The meats are roasted to retain the juices, and the seasoning is just enough that the ingredients remain the highlight of the sandwich. Pickled carrots and fresh cucumbers are added to the sandwich along with a slab of mayonnaise and a dab of soy sauce; fresh cilantro and jalapeños finish off the toppings.

Seasons, 757 Market St., Union Square, San Francisco, CA 94103; (415) 633-3000; www.fourseasons.com; Steakhouse; $$$$. This large and upscale restaurant inside the Four Seasons Hotel has rebranded itself recently as a steakhouse, which is just as well considering the steak they serve here has always been of the utmost quality, prepared exactly as requested. Start with the fresh oysters and a glass of Prosecco; the best Miyagi oysters I've ever had were at Seasons. Order the salmon; you'll find it grilled to the ultimate juiciness and flavor. For those with a hankering for meat, Seasons offers one of the best aged rib eye steaks, a 28-day dry-aged rib eye; it's the juiciest cut of well-seasoned meat, and every bite confirms in your mind that meat is best when aged properly. Order a la carte the family-style side dish of sautéed mushrooms or creamed spinach that make for the heartiest dinner, especially when paired with one of Seasons' great wines from its impressive wine list. Seasons is also open for lunch, and the crab sandwich, with huge chunks of fresh crabmeat piled high, is always a treat; split that and share the salmon salad with your dining companion for the best of both worlds.

Sons and Daughters Restaurant, 708 Bush St., Downtown, San Francisco, CA 94108; (415) 391-8311; www.sonsanddaughterssf.com; American; $$$$. As a newcomer to the city's restaurant scene, Sons and Daughters has quickly made itself known for fascinatingly imaginative cooking, utilizing trendier cooking methods like "spherification," a process by which you make spherical caviar-like balls out of the gelatinizing of liquid, and "sous-vide," a French method of cooking food by enclosing the food in a vacuum-sealed bag and immersing it in hot water for as many hours as needed to cook to the right texture. It's also become known for a really economical 4-course tasting menu ($58) that offers fascinatingly creative foods, but offers such small portions that all but the smallest of appetites may leave hungry. A seared *foie gras* with ginger-apple oats is worth trying; the richness of the *foie gras* plays wonderfully in your mouth with the sweetness and texture of the oats. If you're lucky enough to find that the chef is offering the raw lobster with pomegranates, do order this as you'll find that the lobster sashimi, paired with a lime-basil sauce, is the ideal partner to crunchy pomegranate seeds. Because the portions are small, this is one place you can gorge on the really tasty bread and salted butter; even with your main entree of honey-roasted squab (really good!), you will hardly be stuffed, but you will be satisfied.

Swan Oyster Depot, 1517 Polk St., Downtown, San Francisco, CA 94109; (415) 673-1101; Seafood; $$. A small, unassuming storefront on Polk Street is home to a restaurant that serves up some of San Francisco's freshest seafood. With only a handful of stools on which to sit and enjoy your meal, the line can be dauntingly long, but I daresay it's worth the wait as at Swan Oyster Depot. You will taste seafood the way it was meant to be devoured, without the dressing and heavy additions that often take away from the taste of fresh seafood. The bluepoint oysters at Swan are among the city's freshest, and you can't miss out on the shrimp cocktail while here. Keeping up the healthy theme, do try a combination salad, which is a favorite; topped with huge chunks of crabmeat and a generous amount of shrimp, the salad is made of iceberg lettuce and topped off with large pieces of prawns. The dressing is similar to Thousand Island, but so much better, but more often than not, I just sprinkle salt and pepper on it, and leave the dressing on the side to dip in at will. While quite pricey, it will be one of your most memorable seafood expeditions in San Francisco, despite the fact that it's not located anywhere near the water.

Taco's Sandwiches, 6 6th St., Tenderloin, San Francisco, CA 94103; (415) 863-8226; Sandwiches; $$. Contrary to the name, Taco's doesn't sell tacos; the owner's name is Taco, and his business is selling sandwiches. It's worth taking a drive to this shadier area of San Francisco to spend $6–$7 for one of his creations. For instance, the adobo pork sandwich is on a toasted bun with juicy chunks of heavily braised pork, topped with an aioli that has some kick to it, their homemade slaw, and grilled onions; one whiff of this and you start contemplating ordering one more to-go, despite how generous the portion size is, because you know you will be craving it again in a few hours. Also a must-try on the menu is the blackened-fish po'boy, which consists of two nicely sized fillets, lightly breaded, then subtly blackened, and slid into a toasted roll with lettuce, slaw, and a chipotle aioli. It's everything you would expect of a po'boy sandwich and is real "comfort food."

Turtle Tower Restaurant, 631 Larkin St., Tenderloin, San Francisco, CA 94109; (415) 409-3333; www.turtletowersf.com; Vietnamese; $. There are now 3 locations for this ever-popular pho restaurant: The original, smaller, and perhaps most popular location is this one in the Tenderloin district. The Richmond restaurant is bigger, newer, and cleaner, serving up the same great northern-style pho, and the 6th Street location is the newest. The beef soup commonly served with pho, while available, is not the highlight here—you must try the No. 9 or No. 10 varieties of pho ga, which consist of thick rice noodles served in what might be the most comforting chicken soup, sprinkled with scallions and cilantro—without a basil leaf or sprout in sight. The pho is served with some slices of jalapeño peppers and a wedge of lemon, both to be used in the soup at will. The No. 10 option comes with chicken gizzards; the No. 9 is served with only chicken meat, and you can request white or

dark meat. Expect a long line over the weekends while San Francisco residents come to cure their hangovers; it's not surprising as this may be the city's best pho. The second location is at 5716 Geary Blvd., Richmond, San Francisco, CA 94121; (415) 221-9890; the third location is at 501 6th St., SOMA, San Francisco, CA 94103; (415) 904-9888.

Vietnam House, 642 Eddy St., Tenderloin, San Francisco, CA 94109; (415) 885-3361; Vietnamese; $$. There's one thing you must try here, and it's the *banh khot*. I describe them as little puffs of heavenly clouds: cup-shaped rice cakes with mung beans and shrimp that you wrap in lettuce and dip in fish sauce. Let your eyes roll to the back of your head as you enjoy the crisp exterior of the rice cake and the lettuce, the deeper flavors of the beans, and the high notes of the shrimp with fish sauce. They have a full menu, including noodle soups, but because it's staffed by a husband-and-wife team, service can be extremely slow, though very friendly.

Wayfare Tavern, 558 Sacramento St., Downtown, San Francisco, CA 94111; (415) 772-9060; www.wayfaretarvern.com; American; $$$. This is San Francisco's new sweetheart. Chef Tyler Florence and team have created what is truly the epitome of San Francisco dining—taking fresh, local ingredients and cooking simple items but giving a significant high-end spin to each masterfully executed dish. Starting with the complimentary hot popovers that start each meal, your choices are expansive on this menu. Don't forgo the

Wayfare Burger, served on brioche bread with a huge, juicy patty, topped with a Petaluma Farms sunny-side-up egg and bacon. The steak tartare is a great shared appetizer, entirely too large (and heavy) for one person; rarely will you try raw meat that is this flavorful, and it's also topped with a (raw) egg. The Hangtown Fry, which they describe as "a dying man's last meal," is rich and decadent: a generous portion of eggs topped with fried oysters, cheese, crispy bacon, potatoes, and an exorbitant amount of crème fraîche. They're become well-known for their organic fried chicken, too. Another classic that Wayfare Tavern perfects is the crispiest chicken with a scent of rosemary, served in enormous portions. Squeeze lemon over it and the dish reaches a whole new level.

Landmark

House of Prime Rib, 1906 Van Ness Ave., Downtown, San Francisco, CA 94109; (415) 885-4605; www.houseofprimerib.net; American; $$$$. For over 60 years, San Francisco has had a love affair with House of Prime Rib (more commonly referred to by locals as HOPR). It's one of the city's favorite restaurants, but it's also a landmark now; almost every visitor wants to try it. Compared to other steakhouses, HOPR costs less for more food, excellent service, and old-school decor and an all-around enjoyable experience. With a name like HOPR, it's no surprise that they make one stunningly delicious and juicy prime rib. First, your sourdough bread is served on a cutting board with a knife and butter. Just as you gorge on this addictive bread, the salad presentation comes out. How or why this salad with beets tastes so delicious is anyone's guess, but even with the bread, everyone finishes the generous salad portion. Finally, the gorgeous silver meat cart comes around with a gigantic slab of prime rib sitting, and the carver asks you how you'd like your meat. Everything from totally cooked to "as rare as can be" is available, though I recommend the medium-rare for the greatest tenderness. For the heartier appetites, HOPR even offers a complimentary additional slice of meat (a thin cut, but still!) without question or judgment. Save room to order the tiramisu or apple pie a la mode, and the dinner rises into the "unbelievable" category. This is one restaurant you do not want to miss when in San Francisco.

Specialty Stores, Markets & Producers

California Golden Cookies, 255 Kearny St., Union Square, San Francisco, CA 94108; (415) 956-3070. It's an odd find in the middle of Union Square, as the reason I noticed this place was not because of their baked goods but their sign reading FALAFELS AND SHAWARMAS. Walking by one late night, I was compelled to enter and discovered a fascinatingly good lamb shawarma here. It's a pita-type wrap rolled big and filled to the brim with juicy slices of lamb, cucumbers, lettuce, tomatoes, and yogurt along with some hummus and other interesting herbal flavors that simply hits the spot when you want a classic gyro. It's hearty but healthy, and for under $10, you can feast like a king here; this includes baklava, which is just sweet and flaky enough. Their German chocolate bar is also heart-stoppingly good; it's a thick brownie-like bar with caramel and walnuts that can satisfy any sweet tooth.

Salama Halal Meat, 604 Geary St., Tenderloin, San Francisco, CA 94102; (415) 474-0359. With a friendly owner and a clean shop, this is one of the few butcher shops in San Francisco offering the best of halal meat. Many kinds of hummus and all types of Middle Eastern delicacies are available here, including specialty jams and breads. Salama carries goat, lamb, and beef, along with a slew of other animal parts, including organ meat. If you're in need of particular organ meats for your home cooking, this is the first place to call. *Merguez*, a lamb-beef sausage in lamb intestinal casing, though not readily available elsewhere in the city, is also for sale here.

SOMA, Mission, Noe Valley & Potrero Hill

These neighborhoods are located toward the eastern part of San Francisco. SOMA and the Mission are adjacent to the Downtown district previously covered, and Noe Valley and Potrero Hill lie just beyond SOMA and the Mission. Sometimes called the "better weather district," all four of these neighborhoods are blessed with fairer skies and slightly warmer weather compared to the eastern areas that are prone to mist and fog, and all four have different characteristics. If downtown caters to the workers in San Francisco, this area caters to the young yuppies, young couples, new families, and the trendy crowd with more up-and-coming eateries and newer housing and urban developments.

South of Market (SOMA)

Considered by many to be San Francisco's hippest neighborhood, SOMA is a vast area of the city that is filled with urban warehouses housing new lofts, sprawling apartment and condominium buildings, and bars and restaurants, along with many dot-com companies that survived the bust. For those not into the old San Francisco architecture, this area is considered most desirable, though not much of it resembles what people have come to equate with San Francisco. After all, the only Costco in San Francisco took up residence in this neighborhood. With the nightlife and the AT&T Ball Park located in this district, it's always busy and home to many of the city's finest dining spots.

Potrero Hill

One of the only "mostly sunny" areas of the city, Potrero Hill has developed into quite the residential area with patches of good eateries and shopping along its main streets. With close proximity to the Caltrain station and the 101 Freeway (US 101), it's an appealing location for commuters who travel into the city or down to Silicon Valley. With new condominiums popping up throughout the area and old warehouses being transformed into new living spaces, the area continues its massive growth.

The Mission

Without a doubt, the Mission district of San Francisco is one of the most diverse, colorful, bustling, and interesting areas of the city. Down a few blocks, you will encounter nothing but great butcher shops with organ meats, dollar stores, cheap clothing shops, street vendors, and check-cashing stores. Down another few blocks, you will have some of the best taquerias outside of Mexico, intermingled with cafes and bars. And in yet another area of the Mission, you will run into some of the finest dining available in the city with hopping nightlife and lounges. Some areas of this large district can get dangerous at night, but most are relatively safe during the day. Almost all parts of the Mission are busy, and many of the stereotypical "San Franciscan hippies" reside in this area, along with most anyone who appreciates the wealth of eateries and bars that keep the Mission popular at all times of the day and night.

Noe Valley

Everyone who gets married, buys a dog, and has a baby seems to move to this area, if the number of strollers and leashes are any indication, or so it feels when you stroll through this mostly residential area of San Francisco. There are plenty of specialty stores,  particularly eclectic stores selling trinkets for the home or feng shui items, and a few good restaurants and cafes exist in this area to serve the relatively well-off residents of this neighborhood. Unlike most city neighborhoods, this is one area of San Francisco where your neighbors from a few buildings down actually may know your name, and having an address here makes a statement about you and your lifestyle.

Alexander's Steakhouse, 448 Brannan St., SOMA, San Francisco, CA 94107; (415) 495-1111; www.alexanderssteakhouse.com; Steakhouse; $$$$$. First there was the famous Alexander's Steakhouse in Cupertino, California; then the owners took over the old Bacar Restaurant space and opened their San Francisco location on all three floors. The ambience is not quite like a steakhouse, but it is a gorgeous building fit for a restaurant of this caliber. Start with a couple of the fresh *hamachi* ponzu shooters—it's the only fish that should be ordered here. Order the Wagyu carpaccio with sous vide egg, which uses the highest-grade slices of raw beef. You can't help but get a little excited as you pop the poached egg and let the yolk expand all over the raw beef. The rib eye cuts here are aged and marbled like artwork and cooked exactly as requested; nearly every bite offers a flavorful "sliver" of fat. Try the prime dry-aged rib eye, served with watercress and a mushroom-and-porcini butter. The so-called "Perfect Porterhouse" is an enormous chunk of meat served up with bone marrow on the side; it's rich, it's full of flavor, and it's grilled to the exact color and temperature you want. With steaks going as high as $200 per cut, dinner here can be very expensive.

Ame Restaurant, 689 Mission St., SOMA, San Francisco, CA 94105; (415) 284-4040; www.amerestaurant.com; Asian Fusion; $$$$$. On the ground floor of the St. Regis Hotel is a minimalist yet sexy and sleek restaurant that combines the tastes and cuisines of Japan with that of other countries, and they do it well. Pricey as it may be, the freshest ingredients are used to delight your palate, like the *uni* in Sea Urchin Bruschetta with Lardo and Salt. They have a tasting menu that is offered on a nightly basis, but the main selection here that you must try is the broiled sake-marinated Alaskan black cod and shrimp dumplings in shiso broth that is always on the menu. Ame creates a masterpiece out of this dish with flavors galore, and the buttery broiled cod sits in the shiso broth, which brings out the sweetness of the fish itself, along with the shrimp filling inside the dumplings. The texture of this fish makes sea bass hang its head low. The grilled steak with *foie gras* is also delicious for those who prefer meat, and it's the epitome of tenderness. Save some room for dessert and try the strawberry parfait with strawberry ice milk (not quite ice cream) and sesame honeycomb.

Andalu, 3198 16th St., Mission, San Francisco, CA 94103; (415) 621-2211; www.andalusf.com; Spanish; $$. It's hard to tell you what to avoid here because, as many things as I have tried on the menu, they are all good to fabulous. It's a tapas (small plates) place where each individual will order 2 to 4 plates each, depending on appetite, and all the dishes are shared between the group. This enables you to try a little of everything, and with a few visits, you will have tried the whole menu. Start with the salmon tartare piled atop chips, along with the ahi tartare tacos, also a delightful mix of light and heavy with citrus notes. Then you move onto the heavier items on the menu, like their signature Coca-Cola-braised short ribs, which are heavily braised and hardly need a knife, and the lettuce cups with miso-glazed sea bass, a playful balance of sweet and savory. Definitely try the polenta fries! Pair it all with their red sangria, which is deceivingly strong.

Aperto Restaurant, 1434 18th St., Potrero Hill, San Francisco, CA 94107; (415) 252-1625; www.apertosf.com; Italian; $$. Order anything off the pasta menu and you'll be delighted with Aperto. Unlike other good Italian restaurants, the place is not exactly reminiscent of Italy, but the food shines, each pasta dish is perfectly prepared to al dente, and the sauces are rich. Share the crab cakes for the appetizer, and the octopus salad with arugula. So rarely in this city do you taste octopus served this tender! Mixed with the bitter and unique flavors of the arugula, the sweetness of the octopus meat emerges. Ask the kitchen to split an order of the Caesar salad, which is light with the distinct flavor of anchovies. The sweet-corn ravioli and the pea ravioli, when offered, are phenomenal; you will wonder why other restaurants don't combine these fillings with ravioli. Don't hesitate to try their fish or meat offerings; the sea bass with farro and the lemon cucumber salad still make my mouth water.

Arinell Pizza Inc., 509 Valencia St., Mission, San Francisco, CA 94110; (415) 255-1303; Pizza; $. This is as close to a New York pizza as you will get in San Francisco, or the Bay Area, for that matter. It's a hole-in-the-wall place that is dinky, at best, but they have a loyal following of patrons who swear by Arinell Pizza. The crust is thin, and you tell them what you want on your pizza, and they will take one of their large cheese pies, pile on everything you ordered, throw it back in the oven for you—then a few minutes later, you have a hot pizza piled high with toppings. Order extra cheese or your toppings will just be heated on top of the cheese pizza. I find that the thin crust and heaviness of the toppings doesn't lend itself well to being taken home; this is definitely one of those places where you order a couple slices and eat while there—standing against the wall with your pizza on a napkin.

Bar Agricole, 355 11th St., SOMA, San Francisco, CA 94103; (415) 355-9400; www.baragricole.com; American; $$$. The space is extraordinary: modern, sleek, sexy and hip. With great service and a loyal following, Bar Agricole has quickly made a name for itself in San Francisco. Equally well-known for its cocktail menu as it is for good food, the drinks are very creative and tasty and even the classics, like The Old Fashioned, were exemplary. Each dish at Bar Agricole is passionately prepared and exquisite in flavors. The cucumber salad with quinoa and spinach was lightly mixed with a citrus dressing that made each ingredient take center stage in this simple dish; the duck breast, prepared to a perfect medium-rare, was enhanced by the cabbage and soft-boiled egg that accompanied this dish. The spaghetti, which was totally vegetarian including only rapini, pimiento, green olives and pecorino cheese, also offered clean and distinct flavors. Bar Agricole is the only place where I've tried battered and deep-fried mussels; the mussels remained juicy and the crisp batter plus aioli provided a nice contrast in texture and a jubilee of flavors.

Benu Restaurant, 22 Hawthorne St., SOMA, San Francisco, CA 94105; (415) 685-4860; www.benusf.com; American/Asian Fusion; $$$$$. You can dine a la carte, or opt for the $160 per person, 15-course menu that Chef Corey Lee has designed to wow the senses. But with 15 courses, there are bound to be some hits and misses, and Benu is no exception. With ingenious creations like a creamy risotto topped with slivers of *uni* (sea urchin) to take it to another realm of creaminess, or an eggplant soup with Parmesan croutons and tomatoes that offers rich and bold flavors, Benu combines the best of many ingredients to create a small serving of often wondrous tastes. The star of the evening was the monkfish *torchon;* aptly called the *"foie gras* of the ocean," it was blended to a custard-like texture and served with toasted brioche and apple relish. Also notable were the breaded sweetbreads, served fresh and only with pickled celery that took nothing away from the subtle taste of sweetbreads and added only a refreshing crunch to each bite. Many dishes, like the oyster, pork belly and kimchee course, were decidedly Korean-influenced. Benu presents creativity and imagination and takes risks to reach new realms in flavor, which I appreciate. While stated as American cuisine, there's a distinct Asian flair to Chef Lee's cooking that extends a welcomed accent to every dish.

Beretta, 1199 Valencia St., Mission, San Francisco, CA 94110; (415) 695-1199; www.berettasf.com; Italian; $$. A beautiful and modern space on an unusually quiet segment of the Mission, Beretta offers late-night hours with some truly outstanding food. They have a good wine list that is priced reasonably and is meant to go with the great food that is offered more in small-plates fashion, followed by an individual entree. Share the bruschetta with fava beans and the meatballs in spicy tomato sauce; the meatballs are tender, the flavors of the sauce are deeply embedded in each bite and will leave you contemplating one more order. For the pizza, request extra *burrata* on any of them, and consider ordering the spicy Italian sausage pizza, or the *funghi misti* (mushroom). The lamb chops are prepared medium-rare, and served with fresh arugula that is completely devoid of any dressing (my favorite!) and a dipping sauce of goat milk yogurt; this makes for a fabulous entree, especially paired with a Zinfandel.

Chez Papa Bistrot, 1401 18th St., Potrero Hill, San Francisco, CA 94107; (415) 824-8205; www.chezpapasf.com; French; $$$.

This is Potrero Hill's sweetheart, and dare you say this place is not good, there are some residents who will go into an uproar. Chez Papa does have a niche market, providing decadent French cooking at moderate prices in a small yet cozy space. The food is rich, and you will most likely leave here in a food coma. Their claim to fame is the burger, served with Gorgonzola cheese and a fried egg. Their seared Sonoma *foie gras* is served with blackberry-ginger compote and a crisp salad, and the meat, jam and vegetables work together to create a great combination of richness, sweetness, and texture. While I am ordinarily not a fan of mussels, I always order them when I visit Chez Papa. Served in a bucket, the mussels are tender and flavorful, and the soup they are boiled in makes the ultimate dipping sauce for the bread.

Chez Spencer, 82 14th St., Potrero Hill, San Francisco, CA 94103; (415) 864-2191; www.chezspencer.net; French; $$$. I'm not sure if I go here for the bread or the food. The rolls served here are ridiculously addictive, and if I didn't know that my palate was about to be delighted, I'd lose control. The aura of this place is so romantic, and with a good bottle of French wine, a perfect evening begins. Normally, I order everything offered on the appetizer section of the menu, and I barely make it into the entrees. Order the bouillabaisse, which is a French fish stew, served hot with a piece of toast and cream. Then, share the *foie gras au torchon*, which consists of thick pâté-like slices of delicious, mashed-up *foie gras*. Unlike seared *foie gras*, this is served a bit on the colder side and makes for an amazing spread on the *campagne* bread with a dash of the compote that comes with this dish. If you like duck, the smoked duck with poached egg is not to be missed; cooked with lardons (small bits of pork fat), the flavors will make you salivate for days to come. If available, request patio seating; it's reminiscent of European outdoor dining.

Commonwealth, 2224 Mission St., Mission, San Francisco, CA 94110; (415) 355-1500; www.commonwealthsf.com; American; $$. Hip and trendy, Commonwealth is a newcomer to San Francisco and is on the rise in popularity. The food is good, but the portions are small. While the menu, and in some respects the prices, read like they would be normally sized appetizers and entrees, this restaurant subscribes to the small plates theme, and even with 3 orders per person (to share with your dining companion), you most likely will not be full. The tasting menu offers 6 courses for $65. The cooking is creative and noticeably full of local ingredients. Chef Fox combines ingredients like quinoa, broccoli, garlic, carrots, and a poached egg to make a meatless but truly flavorful dish. A wonderful pork jowl dish was offered, cooked with fava beans, trumpet mushrooms, Idiazábal cheese and drizzled with an onion consommé. The cooking is 100 percent San Franciscan and unique; you may be offered something different on your visit, but rest assured, the meal will be interesting and creative.

Da Beef, 300 W. 7th St., SOMA, San Francisco, CA 94103; (760) 815-4856; www.dabeef.com; Twitter: @dabeef; Hot Dogs, $. Popular for lunch, and even more popular for late-night drunken eating, Da Beef Hot Dog stand serves up Chicago-style Vienna Beef hot dogs and the popular Chicagoan Italian beef with a few other selections like Frito pies, which is chili and cheese piled atop a bunch of Fritos. The Vienna Beef is succulent and might be the juiciest hot dog you will ever have; Da Beef serves it up on a poppy-seed bun with mustard, relish, tomato, onions, celery salt, and a pickle on top. The Italian beef is served on a bun that is dipped directly into au jus, with thin, juicy slices of beef topped with hot and sweet peppers. Be forewarned: It's messy and dripping wet within 30 seconds, but so worth it.

Delfina Restaurant, 3621 18th St., Mission, San Francisco, CA 94110; (415) 552-4055; www.delfinasf.com; Italian; $$$. This modern and hip restaurant serves up some outstanding appetizers as well as pasta dishes. Some notables on the appetizer menu are the grilled calamari, served atop cooked white beans that complement the calamari so perfectly, accompanied with greens; the Little Gem salad with blue cheese and a sieved egg on top; and chard with garlic and lemon—so simple, yet so massive in flavors. From the pasta menu, definitely try the spaghetti with a surprisingly robust tomato sauce, plum tomatoes, garlic, and olive oil, or the short rib

Wine Culture

Wine paired with good food can often propel good cooking into great territory. San Francisco has known this forever.

Every year, wine events are hosted within city limits, some bigger than others. Rhone Rangers hosts a dinner and tasting at Fort Mason, where winemakers will bring their creations for all guests to taste, and lots are sold in a live auction after a multicourse dinner. It's a great way to end up spending a lot of money on entirely too much wine from one winery—I know, because I bought the entire Syrah lot from Qupé winery one year (and it was absolutely beautiful for years). There are numerous wine and food pairing classes throughout the city, and many restaurants will host RSVP dinners with private winemakers, providing food that pairs perfectly with each bottle offered.

With Napa so close, many San Franciscans are members of their preferred wineries. The membership is usually free, and they will

cappelletti, which are triangular ravioli-like pasta concoctions filled with meat and sauce and cooked perfectly al dente, drizzled with a meat reduction sauce with a hint of orange that enhances every single ingredient used. Check the website for 3 additional locations, including the well-known **Pizzeria Delfina** (p. 117).

El Farolito, 2779 Mission St., Mission, San Francisco, CA 94110; (415) 824-7877; www.elfarolitoinc.com; Mexican; $. I'm usually not ship you 1 to 3 bottles per month and charge your credit card. For wines you love, this is the ideal way to keep your favorite wines in stock. Memberships also come with certain privileges with tastings, and with wineries like Joseph Phelps, they allow you and 5 friends to taste for free on any visit. Members will also be the first to be invited to private dinners featuring their own wines, and these events usually offer decadent food that is ideal for each varietal offered.

For some excellent wine pairings with dinner, try out the following higher-end restaurants in San Francisco: **Acquerello** (p. 56); **Spruce** (p. 200); **Saison** (p. 121); **La Folie** (p. 70); **Gary Danko** (p. 33); and **Prospect** (p. 118).

The sommeliers at these establishments have always been most knowledgeable and talented at making each ingredient in your course shine. They not only understand wines but fully understand the menu they serve, and pairing wine with your meal here is guaranteed to elevate your dining experience to new heights.

impressed with *carne asada* (beef) at Mexican restaurants as often it's too dried out, but at El Farolito, you stick with *carne asada*. In fact, there are two things here you must order: the super *carne asada* burrito and the super quesadilla *suiza*. The burrito is larger than some infants, and it's heavy. What I love about El Farolito's burritos, aside from the great flavors, is that almost every bite consists of all the ingredients because of the masterful way the staff wraps these monsters. The quesadilla is enormous as well, and can easily feed 3 or 4 regular female appetites; filled with cheese, sour cream, steak, and everything else that normally goes only into a burrito, this quesadilla hits the spot each time. With late-night hours until 3 a.m. on weekdays and 4 a.m. on weekends, El Farolito is the king of San Francisco burritos. There are 9 locations throughout the Bay Area—check the website for all listings.

El Metate, 2406 Bryant St., Mission, San Francisco, CA 94110; (415) 641-7209; www.elmetate.webs.com; Mexican; $. When you combine relatively easy parking with outdoor seating options, a huge dining room, every kind of hot sauce imaginable, a salsa bar, great service, and a good menu—you end up with El Metate. Try the *lengua* (tongue) burrito here; the size isn't big but the ingredients are fresh and packed tightly into the tortilla—you'll never eat a messy burrito here. Also great are the tacos. The fish tacos have received the most publicity, being featured in *Check, Please! Bay Area* and *SF Weekly,* but my preference is for the shrimp tacos, where instantly grilled huge shrimp adorn your tacos and bring massive amounts of texture and taste to each bite. If you're really hungry or have a large appetite, you may need to order double what you'd normally get at other restaurants as the portions are a bit on the smaller end of things.

Esperpento, 3295 22nd St., Mission, San Francisco, CA 94110; (415) 282-8867; www.esperpentorestaurant.com; Spanish; $$. When you have a hankering for fresh, tasty tapas, Esperpento should be at the top of your list. This unassuming, casual, and friendly restaurant offers what could be the city's best tapas for minimal price. I will often call the restaurant just to order the *patatas bravas* for take-out, which are crisply fried potatoes, cut like home fries, and drizzled with what can only be described as the most addictive and flavorful sauce—a strangely orange aioli with a huge spicy kick and flavors of peppers, sweetness, and saltiness that catapult basic potatoes to the level of *foie gras*. The garlic shrimp dish is packed with flavor, and the shrimp is never overcooked. The *repollo salteado* is a cabbage dish, sautéed to crunchiness and flavored with garlic, salt, pepper, and paprika—and while the thought of ordering sautéed cabbage doesn't sound appealing, this dish really is noteworthy. Order the paella at Esperpento. I've tried both the meat paella and seafood, and it's just a matter of preference. You simply order for the number of people you have in your party, and the restaurant will prepare enough to feed all of you and then some.

Espetus Churrascaria Brazilian Steakhouse, 1686 Market St., SOMA/Hayes Valley, San Francisco, CA 94102; (415) 552-8792; www.espetus.com; Brazilian; $$$. When in the mood for all-you-can-eat meat, very few choices will compare to Espetus. This popular restaurant is a *churrascaria* where a large variety of meats on a large skewer are brought table side by servers with a knife; whether or not you accept a slice with your tongs is your choice. All side items like fresh vegetables, salads, paella, white rice and other hot entrée items are available at a separate buffet area where you can eat to your heart's content. All meats are barbecued Brazilian-style with heavy use of salt, and the offerings from the buffet stand, like the fresh heart of palms, fresh mozzarella, couscous, and rice, help to balance out the saltiness. Filet mignon, braised ribs, garlic beef sirloin, juicy chicken legs, plump chicken hearts, bacon-wrapped filet, pork loin, and lamb riblets are some of the many offerings. Most are offered medium to medium-rare, but if you want rarer, the gaucho-servers will usually bring you a less cooked piece quickly. Until you call out mercy, the food keeps coming. But save some room because the desserts here are nothing short of dreamy: Definitely order the papaya crème with cassis liqueur (ask for it without the sorbet), and prepare to fight for the dulce de leche ice cream—it is one of those dishes that make you wish all of your dining companions would disappear so you can have it all to yourself!

Farina Focaccia Cucina Italiana, 3560 18th St., Mission, San Francisco, CA 94110; (415) 565-0360; www.farina-foods.com; Italian; $$$. The location is bright and beautiful, and the layout is as modern as you could want in any trendy restaurant—which is totally unexpected in the Mission neighborhood. One of the best dishes on the menu—not to be skipped here—is the octopus salad; it's a perfect mix of hot and cold on one plate, with crisp and cold greens served with just-grilled octopus. Also excellent is the *burrata* and prosciutto focaccina (little focaccia), served with fried sage that lends an amazing herbal fragrance to the already great combination of meat and cheese. Their award-winning pesto sauce is indeed delicious and best combined with the focaccia di Recco, which consists of two crispy dough "sheets" with Stracchino cheese oozing in the middle. Order whatever fish entree they are serving—both the tai snapper and the John Dory entrees were excellent.

Flour + Water, 2401 Harrison St., Mission, San Francisco, CA 94110; (415) 826-7000; www.flourandwater.com; Italian; $$$. The restaurant is modern and minimalist in decor, and it's perhaps one of the hardest reservations in town, despite its relatively recent entry into the San Francisco restaurant scene. Known for its pizza (and it's good), I find their pasta offerings to be even more impressive. Freshly made pasta is paired with unique partners like rabbit sausage and covered in just enough sauce to bring both the flour and meats to life. The farro radiatore with roasted hen, pancetta, arugula, and rosemary was particularly flavorful, with the hen meat in this dish tasting better than any roasted hen that is served sans pasta. The contrast between this and the stark flavors of arugula and rosemary make for an outstanding order. That said, the portions are astoundingly small for the price, so prepare to order a couple for yourself if you won't be sharing a pizza. What you order for your pizza depends on your preference, but the crust is a beautiful blend of chewy, thin, and crispy. The Margherita Pizza with an addition of *burrata* cheese, while a bit on the plain side, was given great acidic accents by the tomato sauce that made each bite bring your taste buds to life.

Foreign Cinema, 2534 Mission St., Mission, San Francisco, CA 94110; (415) 648-7600; www.foreigncinema.com; American; $$$$. Romance is in the air at Foreign Cinema. With a nightly film projected onto the large back wall of the huge patio area, you're whisked away to a different time and land for at least the duration of your meal. The menu changes nightly so it's impossible for me to recommend a particular dish, but they do have a spectacular array of fresh oysters to choose from as an appetizer. If offered, do try the smoked salmon with crème fraîche as well as any scallop

 offerings, which have always impressed. Weekend brunches are really popular here, with a line forming by 10:30 a.m.—and they don't even open until 11 a.m. All of their egg dishes have been stunningly simple with a few ingredients, like the cardamom french toast with bananas; it's one of those dishes where each bite makes you a bit sad, because your entree is coming that much closer to the end. With a full bar, they make actual Bloody Marys here—an essential component of a perfect brunch.

Goat Hill Pizza, 300 Connecticut St., Potrero Hill, San Francisco, CA 94107; (415) 641-1440; www.goathill.com; Pizza, $$. Any pizzeria that uses a sourdough to make their crust earns automatic kudos in my book. Goat Hill Pizza does just that, keeping it thin

and crunchy (though not to the NY-style pizza level) while piling a generous amount of ingredients and cheese on top. Nothing ruins pizza like an overabundance of sauce, and at Goat Hill, the ratio of sauce to cheese to ingredients is always just right. The chicken Florentine pizza, with huge chunks of grilled chicken, spinach, and mushrooms, is always a huge hit, as is the Portuguese pizza, with heaping amounts of linguiça sausage, garlic, black olives, and green onions—it's everything a pizza should be. Monday nights are Neighborhood Nights here, with an all-you-can-eat pizza and salad offering for only $10.95; servers will bring prepared pizzas around for all the tables to enjoy at will. Goat Hill has pastas and sandwiches for those not in the mood for a slice.

Hog & Rocks, 3431 19th St., Mission, San Francisco, CA 94110; (415) 550-8627; www.hogandrocks.com; American/Gastropub; $$$. A relative newbie on the San Francisco restaurant scene, this has quickly become one of my favorite restaurant hangouts in the city. With a full bar, a good wine list, and a stated focus on pork and oysters (hog and rocks, respectively), what's not to love? The ham and prosciutto selection is impressive and served with fruits like strawberries, pineapples, or figs in compote or jam form; the great variety of oysters is exemplary in freshness and taste. While the restaurant has a full dinner menu, Hog & Rocks is the perfect place to gather with a few friends to share appetizer after appetizer, mix in an entree or two to share, along with a few bottles of wine—and call it a meal. Don't miss out on the beet salad, served with golden beets, arugula, prosciutto, and bologna. Open late and serving food until late hours, Hog & Rocks is definitely worth a visit.

Incanto, 1550 Church St., Noe Valley, San Francisco, CA 94131; (415) 641-4500; www.incanto.biz; Italian; $$$. While most commonly known as "the pig offal place," something Chef Chris Cosentino has become a master of, Incanto is so much more than that. Their regular menu offers more commonplace pork parts like the shoulder or loin nowadays. Lightly breaded calf brain is offered—and each bite is about as rich as you can handle. This is served in one generous chunk, and I highly recommend you share it unless you know you are a big fan of eating brain. This is the only place that I'm aware of that serves a lamb tartare; the freshest raw lamb is ground up and blended with light herbs, and each bite offers citrus notes that dance wonderfully with the meat. In addition to *salumi* platters from their offshoot store, Boccalone at the Ferry Building, and other good appetizers, Incanto shows you why they are, after all is said and done, a true Italian restaurant. The pasta offerings are of the utmost freshness, and prepared with absolutely amazing partners like cured tuna heart (and the recipe for **Spaghettini with Cured Tuna Heart and Egg Yolk** is included in this book on p. 266) and a squid ink with fresh squid and spicy red peppers. Forget the offal; I go here when I am craving the best pastas!

La Boulange Bakery, 685 Market St., SOMA, San Francisco, CA 94199; (415) 512-7610; www.laboulangebakery.com; Bakery; $.

With a variety of locations throughout San Francisco, La Boulange is a staple of sorts in the pastry and bakery world of this city. But this place offers more than just breads and sweets; it offers some truly delicious brunch and lunch options as well, with fresh soups changing daily. For breakfast, try the ham and cheese croissant, served hot with fresh ham and cheese oozing out—it's true comfort food in the morning. But my personal favorites are the open-face sandwiches. The goat cheese sandwich with portobello mushrooms, red peppers, and a pesto sauce is as decadent as you can expect from a vegetarian sandwich; the tuna melt with cheddar is scrumptious with bits of apple, shallots, and tomatoes mixed within the tuna and topped with aioli. See the website for additional locations throughout the city.

La Ciccia, 291 30th Church St., Noe Valley, San Francisco, CA 94131; (415) 550-8114; www.laciccia.com; Sardinian; $$$. This is precisely what all neighborhood restaurants should aspire to be. The owners, Massimilano and Lorella, personally go to great lengths to ensure that you enjoy your experience at La Ciccia. Offering Sardinian cooking, La Ciccia is a more adventurous and decadent experience compared to typical Italian restaurants, and each dish seduces your senses. The calamari was very lightly cooked in a clear broth of olive oil that made you moan at first bite. The entire point of this dish is to give the squid center stage, and that's exactly what happens. The octopus stew is fascinatingly comforting and on the heavier side of things (compared to the squid)—it's packed with combinations of flavors and spiciness, jolting your palate awake for what's to come with the pastas. Offering sea urchin and tuna heart fettucine as a special one night, or their signature dish, the *bottarga* (fish roe) spaghetti, every night, the quality of the pasta combined with the freshness of the ingredients and depth of the sauces makes La Ciccia one solid choice when craving pasta or seafood.

La Corneta Taqueria, 2731 Mission St., Mission, San Francisco, CA 94110; (415) 643-7001; www.lacorneta.com; Mexican; $. For every person who says the best Mexican food in the city is at **El Farolito** (p. 98), you will find another person who claims they're wrong—they say La Corneta is. At La Corneta, opt for the tacos, which are piled so high that you can't even see the tortilla, or the super quesadilla, which is so good and enormous enough to fill up two average people. The plated meals are also really large portions. The open kitchen concept allows you to watch while the staff expertly puts your food together. Always consistent, this neighborhood staple serves up food fast, fresh, and no matter how long the line is during mealtimes, it moves rapidly. There is a second location in the Glen Park neighborhood at 2834 Diamond St., San Francisco, CA 94131; (415) 469-8757.

Live Sushi Bar, 2001 17th St., Potrero Hill, San Francisco, CA 94103; (415) 861-8610; www.livesushibar.com; Japanese; $$$.

The main reason to run to Live Sushi is their Chef's Special Oysters. A live oyster is shucked, and a fresh piece of *uni* is placed inside the half shell next to the fresh oyster. Then, some *ikura* (salmon roe) is placed on top of the *uni,* and a delicious ponzu sauce of sorts is drizzled into the entire shell. Lastly, a quail egg is cracked into this concoction. Just looking at the masterpiece can make you happy, but when you tilt it into your mouth and noisily slurp it all in, you experience a moment of ecstasy. It's not uncommon for us to go to this restaurant and consume almost two dozen of these. At $4.50 a piece, combined with a bottle of Masumi sake from their excellent sake menu, the price of this meal can rise rapidly even before you order any sushi at all. There are better places for sushi in the city, but none that have come close to mastering Chef's Special Oysters the way Live Sushi does.

Local Kitchen & Wine Merchant, 330 1st St., SOMA, San Francisco, CA 94105; (415) 777-4200; www.sf-local.com; Italian; $$$. It's a beautiful space with outstanding wines and good food. Lately, they've added a full bar to the lineup, and now Local provides a little bit of everything for San Francisco. Their award-winning open-face shrimp and egg sandwich is absolutely worth trying for lunch or dinner; it's a nice size to share as an appetizer. They have revamped the restaurant with more Italian flair and now are known for their thin-crust pizzas. Combined with their massive wine list, the beautiful decor of this location makes for a nice place for dinner with friends. Drop in and order some truffle and Parmesan fries and an antipasto platter to enjoy with your wine; once your hunger dissipates, order any of the pizzas to finish off the meal. They offer happy hour specials and an all-you-can-eat pizza night on Sunday, which are definitely worth checking out.

Marlowe, 330 Townsend St., SOMA, San Francisco, CA 94107; (415) 974-5599; www.marlowesf.com; American; $$$. There's rarely a "best burger" list created in San Francisco that doesn't include Marlowe's signature burger. It's a mostly beef patty mixed with some lamb that lends a bit of flavor and earthiness to the meat; it's placed inside a good-size bun along with cheddar cheese, caramelized onions, bacon, and an aioli sauce that adds a nice accent to the burger. Within a city that offers burgers ranging from $3 to $100-plus, this $13 burger is a bargain, and it's adequately sized to fill most appetites. But Marlowe does more than just burgers and is grossly underrated when it comes to their other offerings. The steak tartare with a lightly poached egg and served with crostini, is among the city's best raw-beef dishes; the brussels sprouts chips are deep-fried to a crisp and nicely coated with lemon and sea salt; and the polenta dish with wild mushrooms, truffled pecorino, and a poached egg on top is about as decadent as can be for a meatless dish. Marlowe has a good wine list, and service is friendly.

Maverick Restaurant, 3316 17th St., Mission, San Francisco, CA 94110; (415) 863-3061; www.sfmaverick.com; American; $$$. In a city where *burrata* cheese is on almost every single menu, Maverick's *burrata* cheese with *boquerones,* shaved asparagus, and pine nuts, served with crostini, is perhaps one of the best. Another popular item on the menu is the Chesapeake Bay soft-shell crab fluffs, which are their take on the crab cake. Crabmeat is made into little balls and quickly deep-fried for a crunchy exterior and a soft interior that is packed with flavor, served with a remoulade and a pile of sliced and slightly pickled English cucumbers. Their pasta offerings are excellent (despite this not being an Italian restaurant) with an outstanding ragu. The juicy fried chicken is served with dirty red rice, broccoli rabe, and a light gravy. The brunch offerings to try are the pecan-crusted french toast and the andouille sausage Benedict. The restaurant gets a couple points just for even offering a beef cheek hash. Every Tuesday, they offer their Juicy Lucy Butter Burger, made of 30 percent butter; only 17 are made for the first 17 customers who want to try the delicious but suicidal offering for $20, which includes fries and a glass of wine.

Mehfil Indian Cuisine, 600 Folsom St., SOMA, San Francisco, CA 94107; (415) 974-5510; www.mehfilindian.com; Indian; $$. Good Indian food is hard to find in San Francisco. Some places offer tasty food, but it's so Americanized that it's really no longer Indian. While the food in India may use lots of fat, I am certain that they do not use the amount of butter that these Indian restaurants use; you can't taste much else past the butter with other Indian restaurants! At Mehfil, though, the spices and flavor shine through, and the heat and fragrances that should be associated with Indian food are alive and well. The chicken tikka masala is moist with bright, piquant notes and smokiness, and the vindaloo is spicy, as it should be, though you can request less heat should you need to. The naan is fresh and readily available, and dipped into the vindaloo sauce or the raita (cucumber and yogurt), it's delicious. Most impressive here was the dhal; it was as close to home-cooked Indian cooking as I have found to date. They offer wonderfully priced lunch specials at only $5, but be prepared to stand in line to order. Mehfil has a second location at 2301 Fillmore St., Pacific Heights, San Francisco, CA 94115; (415) 614-1010.

Mission Beach Cafe, 198 Guerrero St., Mission, San Francisco, CA 94103; (415) 861-0198; www.missionbeachcafesf.com; American Brunch; $$. Brunch is the word here, and while Mission Beach Cafe (MBC) is open for dinner, too, and the food is good, the brunch here is second to none. Try the braised short ribs with potato-apple hash; it comes with 2 eggs any style, topped with a flavorful horse-radish crème fraîche. Also good are the fluffy pancakes, adorned with fruits and a vanilla crème. The mushroom Benedict sits upon house-made English muffins and is piled high with caramelized onions, spinach, and a truffle mornay sauce (a béchamel sauce made with cheese and infused with truffle oil) drizzled all over the plate. If not in the mood for breakfast items, order the grass-fed Beach burger with aged Gouda; it's served with caramelized onions, sautéed mushrooms, and an order of fries—and it's definitely one of the city's top burgers. Definitely order the Blue Bottle Coffee served here.

Monk's Kettle, 3141 16th St., Mission, San Francisco, CA 94103; (415) 865-9523; www.monkskettle.com; Gastropub; $$. The love affair that San Francisco has with wine notwithstanding, there's a new mistress on the scene named "beer." Slowly but surely, the city has created many beer fanatics who study beer as many winemakers study wines, and one of the first to ride this wave was Monk's Kettle. With pages and pages of their menu dedicated to bottled beers, and an easy 20-plus beers on tap that you won't readily find elsewhere in the city, Monk's Kettle is always busy. The food here used to be true gastropub food, with the best fresh-baked pretzel in town, a burger that paired beautifully with good beer, and a pulled pork sandwich fit for royalty. With a recent chef change, the food has evolved into something that may be of higher quality, with a focus on using sustainable ingredients—but it has decreased in appeal and taste. The pretzel has been "upgraded" into something different—and while not bad, the city is waiting for them to bring back the pretzel we loved so much. In the meantime, it still offers an exquisite beer list from all over the world with a huge emphasis on Belgium, with good reason.

Mr. Pollo, 2823 Mission St., Mission, San Francisco, CA 94110; (415) 374-5546; Latin American; $$. This is the only place in the entire city, and perhaps the entire state, where you can get a fantastic "tasting menu" dinner for $15. It's impossible to predict what Chef Manny will be serving—I can only say that he will greet you like family and prepare 4 small courses that will undoubtedly be tasty, freshly made, locally bought, and always imaginative. With only one sous chef assisting him, it's a two-man operation, and the wait can be long, but the loyal following that Mr. Pollo has built over the years is testament to the great food he serves here, which represents cuisines from all parts of Central and South America. Most appetites won't be full from the tasting menu, and luckily, you can always order additional arepas, which are like *pupusas,* which are thick corn-based tortillas filled with shredded meat or cheese. Order some of their freshly blended drinks, and for a little over $20 per person, you will undoubtedly enjoy a fun and delightful meal in this really small restaurant.

Nihon Whisky Lounge, 1779 Folsom St., Mission, San Francisco, CA 94103; (415) 552-4400; www.nihon-sf.com; Asian Fusion; $$$. The food at Nihon is imaginative, served much in a Japanese small-plates style, but the 400 single-malt scotches that Nihon stocks is what catapults this restaurant into the noteworthy category. They serve creative rolls, heavy on the sauces and clearly geared toward the American palate, with many of the dishes leaning toward a sweeter rather than a savory taste. Try the roll called 1974, which consists of a generous amount of fresh, spicy scallop with salmon and a thin sliver of lemon, or the Dr. Octopus, which consists of thin slices of octopus with ponzu sauce and a habañero-infused *tobiko* to give it some kick. Uni on a Spoon is a must-try: a piece of *uni* laid in a spoon with *tobiko*, scallions, ponzu sauce, and a raw quail egg on top—but that spoonful costs $7. With some happy hour offerings, it's ideal to come here to snack on appetizers, then perhaps head elsewhere for dinner if cost is a consideration.

Old Jerusalem Restaurant, 2976 Mission St., Mission, San Francisco, CA 94110; (415) 642-5958; www.oldjerusalemsf.com; Middle Eastern; $$. It's not easy finding good Middle Eastern cooking in San Francisco, but Old Jerusalem has made a name for itself serving up as authentic a shawarma platter as you will find in this city. Halal lamb, rice, vegetables and 2 dipping sauces—a tomato-based sauce and a hummus-like cream sauce—is presented on a platter with pita bread for $12.95, and all are prepared with the right spices to result in great taste. Definitely order a baklava for the end of your meal; it's extremely moist and juicy without being overly sweet. Parking can be difficult at this location, but the restaurant is cozy, and service is friendly.

One Market, 1 Market St., SOMA, San Francisco, CA 94105; (415) 777-5577; www.onemarket.com; American; $$$. Chef Mark Dommen runs a tight kitchen, and things work like clockwork in there. I know, because I tried the Chef's Table dinner here, and it was spectacular from beginning to end. For seven courses, items from both on and off the menu are presented beautifully, including a salad course, poultry, fish and beef entrees, plus a dessert, all presented to your group while you are seated inside the main kitchen. The portioning is generous and the wine pairings are sensational. One of the most rewarding parts of this experience is when one or two members from your dinner party put on chef jackets to go prepare and help cook one entree to serve to your party. Off the regular menu, the hand-picked Dungeness crab is excellent; with large chunks of crabmeat in a citrusy soup, served with hearts of palm and cilantro, it's a refreshing and cooling mix of sweet meat and fiery acidity of the citrus notes that just works! The shaved beef tongue is about as much tenderness, flavor, and juiciness as you can handle, served with a slaw of cabbage and a horseradish sauce that enhances the meat. The location and ambience of the restaurant is first-rate and One Market is one of the most spacious restaurants in San Francisco.

Pazzia Restaurant & Pizzeria, 337 3rd St., SOMA, San Francisco, CA 94107; (415) 512-1693; Italian; $$$. Pazzia is a casual Italian restaurant serving up some of San Francisco's finest Italian food. Everything is simple yet so flavorful, and every ingredient used in these dishes retains its full flavor in the cooking process. None of their sauces drain out or overpower the subtle tastes, yet all enhance the taste of the pasta. Most notable of their pastas are their lasagna, gnocchi, and their taglierini with salmon. Much like pasta served in Italy, the flavor of the pasta shines through regardless of the sauce that accompanies it, or perhaps because of the sauce. Definitely order the pizza as Pazzia arguably makes one of the most authentic pizzas in San Francisco. Diavola and Margherita are both excellent choices.

Pizzeria Delfina, 3611 18th St., Mission San Francisco, CA 94110; (415) 437-6800; www.pizzeriadelfina.com; Pizza; $$. Not all thin-crust pizzas are created equal, and Pizzeria Delfina is San Francisco's king of thin-crust pizzas. While they have a wealth of ingredients to put on top of your pizza, the must-try item here is the Margherita pizza. It's simplicity at its best with a crunchy and delicious thin crust, smothered in a light tomato sauce, with plenty of thin slivers of mozzarella piled on top, and a fresh chiffonade of basil leaves. With no meat or any fancy additions, it sounds rather plain, but it best exemplifies all that a good pizza should be: simple in ingredients but huge on taste, framed by a fantastic crust that acts as the base flavor. The prosciutto pizza is served with a savory tomato sauce and fresh arugula, but also worth trying is the Napoli, a pizza with a Mediterranean twist with capers, olives, and anchovies, which pairs beautifully with some of Delfina's wines. This is the pizzeria sister restaurant of **Delfina Restaurant** (p. 97), and there is a second pizzeria location at 2406 California St., Pacific Heights; San Francisco, CA 94115; (415) 440-1189.

Primo Patio Cafe, 214 Townsend St., SOMA, San Francisco, CA 94107; (415) 957-1129; www.primopatiocafe.com; Caribbean; $$. San Francisco doesn't offer a lot of Caribbean food, but Primo Patio does offer you a wonderful glimpse into the cuisine. From the outside, you would barely notice there's a restaurant here, but once you walk into and through the restaurant, it opens onto a charming patio with plenty of seating, reminiscent of eating outside on a tropical Caribbean island. The upside-down chicken and the jerk chicken, which are available both as a sandwich and plate lunch, are the highlights at this cute restaurant. The fries that come with the jerk chicken are phenomenal—perfectly crispy and accompanied with a spicy mayo-based sauce that is addictive. (This sauce is so good that the restaurant has started to sell it!) Otherwise, the plate lunches come with a side of vegetables, beans and rice with a plain salsa, with some of the city's juiciest chicken you will find, substantially seasoned with Caribbean spices. The hamburgers and steak sandwiches are also worth trying, especially en route to a baseball game.

Prospect, 300 Spear St., SOMA, San Francisco, CA 94105; (415) 247-7770; www.prospectsf.com; American; $$$$. Prospect is one of the most popular new restaurants in San Francisco, and rightfully so, as it's located in prime real estate with one of the fanciest interiors in San Francisco. My favorite dish at Prospect has been the octopus and calamari presentation, served with garlic roasted potatoes. Grilled with mild seasonings, it was the ideal appetizer, showcasing two seafood items that may be considered similar but contrast significantly in taste and texture. Another great dish on the menu is the pig trotters, which consist of the chopped meat of pig's feet, which is then mounded together and deep-fried. It's paired with a slightly pickled cucumber concoction with capers and herbs, which successfully breaks up the fattiness of the meat. Order any of the *crudo* or carpaccio offerings, which change often. From the entrees, the braised beef cheeks were unbelievably flavorful, and the meat simply fell apart; the Marsala-type sauce was almost too rich and heavy for one person. When available, opt for the dayboat scallops with *uni* risotto—not many dishes will rival this one in creating superstars out of two ingredients with very distinct but complementary flavors.

Rhea's Deli & Market, 800 Valencia St., Mission, San Francisco, CA 94110; (415) 282-5255; Deli/Korean; $. It's a neighborhood store, but what you need to know is that the Korean steak sandwich at the deli portion of the store is incredible. Tender cuts of rib eye beef, marinated in soy sauce, garlic, and honey are grilled and piled high on an organic Acme bun. Almost anything is good on Acme bread, but pile it high with what is basically *kalbi* and with your choice of aioli, lettuce, pickled red onions, jalapeños, and other ingredients, you have one fantastic Korean sandwich. If you bring a friend, have one order the chicken *katsu* sandwich and share. The chicken *katsu* is nicely breaded and fried, piled high with slaw and pickled onions with a spicy aioli spread; at first bite, as you hear the crunch of the slaw and the chicken, you feel a bit of ecstasy that continues with each bite.

Rosamunde Sausage Grill, 2832 Mission St., Mission, San Francisco, CA 94110; (415) 970-9015; www.rosamundesausagegrill .com; German/Hot Dogs; $. Some of the tastiest things in life are the truly simple things. At Rosamunde, they have a multitude of sausages available, and some are unique and interesting (like the wild boar sausage), but stick to a bratwurst. Two juicy sausages are put into a toasted bun with spicy mustard, then piled high with hot sauerkraut—and that's it, but it's more than enough. The only thought left in your mind is ordering one more, but with the beef chili, which is about as flavorful and sinful as you can handle. Or, you can try the lamb and beef sausage on a toasted bun, and opt for the hot peppers and grilled onions if you need some spice. There are only a few chairs against the wall here, so the tradition is to take your dog next door to Toronado, which coincidentally carries an enormous selection of beers—this might be a sausage's best accompaniment. It's also worth heading to Rosamunde on Tuesday for Burger Tuesday; this sausage joint makes one mean hamburger, but only in limited supply; get there by 5 p.m. to try one of these juicy and freshly grilled burgers. There's an additional location at 545 Haight St., Haight, San Francisco, CA 94117; (415) 437-6851.

Saison, 2124 Folsom St., Mission, San Francisco, CA 94110; (415) 828-7990; www.saisonsf.com; French; $$$$$. At the time of this writing, Saison now has the most expensive tasting menu available in San Francisco. Originally starting off as a pop-up restaurant concept opening just a couple of nights a week at this location, it has quickly established itself on the culinary scene as a real contender with some top-notch creations pumped out of this kitchen, and is now open every night from Tuesday to Saturday. Chef Joshua Skenes pairs together seemingly incompatible ingredients, but with the first bite, you can't help but be amazed at how the combination works! For instance, pairing abalone with artichoke, you end up with a beautiful balance of earth and sea; pairing coffee with *uni* (sea urchin) brings out flavors never before associated with *uni;* or the flavors mixed in with organic asparagus makes you rethink the value of meat. While at Saison, opt for the wine pairing because it takes the already outstanding courses to new heights, course by course. Sommelier Mark Bright personally explains the pairings to you with each course—and he continues to keep your glass filled with some of the best wine I've ever had, which makes each dish's already good flavors soar. The additional cost of the wine pairing is absolutely worthwhile at Saison.

Salt House Restaurant & Bar, 545 Mission St., SOMA, San Francisco, CA 94105; (415) 543-8900; www.salthousesf.com; American; $$$. Any restaurant that decides to lightly boil an egg and then bread it prior to deep-frying earns automatic kudos in my book. While this dish (crispy egg) is not regularly offered on the menu, the crispy shrimp is, and it's a culinary delight. Wonderfully tender shrimp are deep-fried in breading and served up with lightly fried and subtly spicy string beans with serrano ham and some greens with almonds. Every flavor in this dish dances in your mouth. Salt House also has a *poutine* that rivals any offering in Canada: french fries topped with dark gravy and melted cheese. Whatever health risks this may pose are well worth it once you take a bite of this dish. For your entree, opt for the steak of the evening; Salt House prepares it exactly as requested, and if you ask, they will split it for you in the kitchen. The New York steak was placed atop mashed potatoes with corn and was as simple and full of flavor and juices as can be.

The Sandwich Place, 2029 Mission St., Mission, San Francisco, CA 94110; (415) 431-3811; Deli; $. More commonly known as "Juan's" rather than the Sandwich Place, this little restaurant makes mean sandwiches that take effort, creativity, and time. Juan himself will customize it as much as you wish, but the quality of the ingredients used, from the meats to the vegetables to the buns, are top grade, and it shows in their taste. Even meat lovers will agree that Sophie's Delight, a completely vegetarian sandwich with basil leaves, portobello mushrooms, roasted bell peppers, onions, cheese, olive oil, balsamic vinegar, and mayonnaise is so tasty that you don't miss the cold cuts. But it's a constant battle deciding between this or the ridiculously tasty pastrami sandwiches, made of meat that is seriously marbled and seasoned, piled generously high inside toasted rye, with mustard, pickles, and onions.

The Sentinel, 37 New Montgomery St., Financial District, San Francisco, CA 94105; (415) 284-9960; www.thesentinelsf.com; Deli; $. Combine fantastic breads, creative meats, fresh vegetables, and memorable sauces together and you end up with what the Sentinel serves for lunch. Their corned beef sandwich is the most popular and is always available on the menu—and it's good, served on toasted Dutch crunch bread with Russian dressing, cabbage, onions, and gruyère cheese. But I find their other creations to be even more interesting and somewhat daring—like when Chef Leary decided to try a yellowtail ceviche sandwich; or the shrimp salad sandwich with olive, cucumbers, spinach, and mint; or one of my favorites, the pork loin sandwich that balanced spice and sweetness, wrapped inside a freshly toasted bun. The lunch line is long and can be slow-moving as the sandwiches take some time, but you can also call in your order for pickup.

Serpentine, 2495 3rd St., Potrero Hill, San Francisco, CA 94107; (415) 252-2000; www.serpentinesf.com; American; $$. This Dogpatch/Potrero Hill restaurant is a staple in the neighborhood. With a sleek interior that's both industrial yet sexy, plus great service, it also serves up some tasty dishes like the bone marrow and the famous burger with grass-fed beef—as juicy as you want from a burger as it drips cheese and meat juices with each bite. Also notable is the brunch service here during the weekends. Get the red flannel hash, which can only be described as the best of all worlds on one plate: perfectly poached eggs with toasted *levain* bread are served with crispy home fries, juicy beef brisket with—get this—roasted beets, all topped with a dollop of crème fraîche. Do include an order of their homemade biscuits with gravy to complete the ideal brunch meal.

Skool Restaurant, 1725 Alameda St., Potrero Hill, San Francisco, CA 94103; (415) 255-8800; www.skoolsf.com; Asian Fusion; $$$. The concept is a bit all over the place, but Skool somehow makes it work. Even their menu is printed on yellow legal pads, on a clipboard with a No. 2 pencil, and the only thing missing is servers in schoolgirl uniforms. But then from the kitchen come some amazing dishes that are entirely too sophisticated to come from a place called "Skool"! The *uni* flan is at the top of the list, and if it's within budget, order one per person. It's a custard-consistency flan made with sea urchin, topped with *ikura* (salmon roe) and *fleur de sel* (type of sea salt) served in a little mason jar with crostini on the side. Also delicious were the risottos (one mushroom variety and the other a shrimp risotto), which was odd because the restaurant claims to be Japanese fusion; it was nonetheless some of the best risotto I've had in this city. Not to be missed on this menu is the black cod seasoned with cumin, which gives this extraordinarily moist fish a wonderful twist, and served with bok choy.

Slow Club, 2501 Mariposa St., Mission, San Francisco, CA 94110; (415) 241-9390; www.slowclub.com; American; $$. "I'm going to Slow Club," is usually met with an instant, "Have you tried the burger?" There's a reason for that, as this aged burger makes your heart stop for an instant. California's Prather Ranch beef retains its juices during the cooking process and is put atop a bun that holds its own despite the size of this beast. Topped with greens, tomatoes, balsamic onions, Dijon mustard, your choice of cheese (get the Jack cheese!), and a rather spunky aioli with a kick, the first bite will release all kinds of flavors, and the proportion of meat to bread to condiments is ideal. The Caesar salad is very refreshing, especially split between two people, and if you're in the mood for pasta, the fresh egg fettuccine with peas, chanterelle mushrooms, and other lightly cooked vegetables topped with lemon crème fraîche is heavy on the vegetables and big in flavor, but devoid of anything that might be considered unhealthy. (Crème fraîche is not unhealthy, is it?)

Source, 11 Division St., SOMA, San Francisco, CA 94103; (415) 864-9000; www.source-sf.com; Vegan; $$. Given my affinity for meat and fish, my visits to vegan restaurants are infrequent at best. I tried one other restaurant in San Francisco, and to say I abhorred it would be an understatement. For me to actually like one is unheard of—until Source. If this is vegan, I'm up for this every once in awhile! Aside from the faux-meat type dishes, which were also surprisingly tasty, Source offers up creative cooking with top-quality vegetables. Unlike some other places, they do use real cheese when it's required in a food item. The Oink Bits Avocado Burger was actually delicious and flavorful; given the usage of faux bacon bits and pita, this felt healthier while giving up only the pork oils—which I'm willing to part with occasionally. The falafel sandwich (with large and tasty chickpea patties) was also served with pita, drizzled in a yogurt dressing with tomatoes and cucumbers; now this, I can devour every other day. Sharing the magic mushroom pizza is also a good idea—this thin-crust pie is topped with various types of fresh mushrooms, slivers of creamy goat cheese, a sprinkle of thyme, tomatoes, and truffles. It's actually a fantastic vegetarian pizza.

Spork Restaurant, 1058 Valencia St., Mission, San Francisco, CA 94110; (415) 643-5000; www.sporksf.com; American; $$. While Spork became well-known for their regular burger, the new addition of the Champagne of Burgers is spectacular. It offers the ideal ration of meat to bun and is slathered in truffle-studded cheese and bacon, with fresh condiments and a punchy aioli dressing. The burger itself is enormous and requires a really big mouth and extraordinary effort to take a bite. Prepared to the medium end of medium-rare, with each bite, juices are dripping out of the creation. They offer an inside-out burger with two patties and one slice of bread in the middle for those counting their carbohydrates. The goat cheese croquette is the most exemplary combination of sweet and savory, with deep-fried, lightly breaded goat cheese, combined with roasted beets and a port-balsamic reduction. If you like vegetarian dishes, do try the risotto: with slow-cooked fennel and lentils combined with a variety of vegetables, you won't miss meat at all while eating this.

Taqueria Cancun, 1003 Market St., Mission, San Francisco, CA 94110; (415) 864-6773; Mexican; $. This is a typical hole-in-the-wall Mexican joint, but it's open late and prepares fresh food into the wee hours of the night. When they claim it's a "super" burrito, don't think they are kidding: The burrito is as big as some men's forearms and can be more than plenty for two people to share. It's filled with guacamole, sour cream, rice, beans, and your choice of meat; they don't even pretend to make it fancy with vegetables—this is a true carb, fat, and protein-based beast. The salsas offered are plain with a typical tomato-based salsa and an avocado-based one, and while neither is spicy, both go well with the tortilla chips offered here. Taqueria Cancun becomes more popular as it gets later, and on weekend evenings, it's not unusual to find a line out the door of the drunken San Francisco partiers who develop a massive hankering for burritos in the middle of the night. If you're not in the mood for tacos, this restaurant makes a hefty nacho dish and has freshly made soft tacos—a much smaller, lighter, and perhaps wiser choice.

Ted's Market, 1530 Howard St., Downtown, San Francisco, CA 94103; (415) 552-0309; Grocery, Deli; $. I'm always thrilled when I find an unassuming storefront leading to one of the best meals of my life. This tiny store has been around for decades, and it's doubtful that they invested any money into upgrades, only repairs. What also has stayed consistent is the extraordinarily tasty sandwiches offered here at surprisingly cheap prices, not just by San Francisco standards but anywhere. From my experience, the tri-tip sandwiches doused in cheddar cheese are the epitome of comfort food; the turkey, cranberry sauce, and cream cheese rivals any Thanksgiving dinner but is a hundred times lighter; the Caribbean Chicken is an explosion of flavors; the egg salad sandwich, as plain as it sounds, is so good you feel like ordering two; and the meatball sandwich, slathered in provolone cheese, requires you to admire the beauty of it for at least a minute before you devour it. Ted's is best-known for the New York steamed pastrami, and when you watch the staff make it, you see why. The beef slices are piping hot as the staff piles it generously onto rye bread. It's anyone's dream come true.

21st Amendment Brewery and Restaurant, 563 2nd St., SOMA, San Francisco, CA 94107; (415) 369-0900; www.21st-amendment.com; American/Brewery/Gastropub; $$. Three words: Watermelon Wheat Beer. When it's available, that is what you order here. When it is out of season, you hope to God they have the Irish Red Ale, which has more flavors than should be legally allowed in beer. With their own beer lineup, it's vital to serve excellent beer food, and 21st Amendment does just that with spicy chicken wings, creamy ranch sauce, and celery sticks, or a make-your-own-burger option served with steak fries. Another great dish to have with the microbrewery beer is the 21st Amendment fish taco, lightly breaded and served in tortillas.

Urbun Burger, 581 Valencia St., Mission, San Francisco, CA 94110; (415) 551-2483; www.urbunburger.com/index.html; Burger; $$. Urbun Burger is one of the few places in the city that offers a truly customizable burger. You can include or exclude at will, but even the menu items result in one outstanding burger. Quality ingredients are used here, including top quality meats and fresh produce, and while the price is a bit on the higher end of things for burgers, one bite of one and you are convinced it was worth it. All the meat is cooked to order. If you like eggs, you have to try the Breakfast Burger with an all-beef patty, applewood smoked bacon, what seems like a few slices of American cheese, a slathering of the slightly spicy Tabasco mayonnaise, and a softly fried egg atop a toasted bun. Or, for a healthier alternative, try the California Sensation Burger; it offers the same patty and bun with Swiss cheese in lieu of American cheese, but piles on the sprouts and avocado slices, leaving you with a definitively healthier feeling. The sweet potato fries are good, but Urbun Burger offers the option of going "half and half"; try half sweet potato fries and half onion rings. Urbun Burger is open until 3 a.m. on weekends and 10 p.m. on weeknights.

✓ **Yank Sing Restaurant,** 101 Spear St., #A1, SOMA, San Francisco, CA 94105; (415) 957-9300; www.yanksing.com; Chinese/Dim Sum; $$$. This is, hands down, the most expensive dim sum restaurant in San Francisco—or perhaps the entire Bay Area. But before you let that turn you off, Yank Sing also offers the best *xiao long bao,* also known as Shanghai dumplings. The dumpling skins here are amazingly thin; filled with plentiful pork and a slightly gelatinous soup that melts to a liquefied form when steamed. The dumpling pops at first bite spilling hot soup into your mouth. Be careful as it will scald your mouth without any mercy! Gently pick up one of these dumplings and place into your spoon, and pour on a couple spoonfuls of the red vinegar and ginger concoction that is served with it. The *siu mai* (pork dumpling) and the *har gow* (shrimp dumplings) are both exemplary. Yank Sing makes its own hot sauce, offered at each table, and mixed with some soy sauce and Chinese mustard, this sauce enhances all of the food. While your check will surprise you, you'll find that as you leave, you're planning your next visit nonetheless. A second, older location is at 49 Stevenson St., SOMA,

San Francisco, CA 94105; (415) 541-4949; the Spear Street location is much more popular and offers more variety.

Zero Zero, 826 Folsom St., SOMA, San Francisco, CA 94107; (415) 348-8800; www.zerozerosf.com; Italian; $$$. The eating experience here impresses from start to finish. For appetizers, try the blue crab with fennel, which offers a beautiful blend of sea and earth; the polenta with poached egg and chanterelle mushrooms was extremely savory, especially after the egg yolk oozes over the polenta. Zero Zero has great homemade pastas. The offerings change often, but I'd be comfortable ordering anything they have. The best *pici* (a hand-rolled fresh pasta that is a thicker version of spaghetti) I've had to date, including in Italy, was offered here, mixed in with a short rib ragu that made you space out and think of nothing else while eating. The pasta is perfectly al dente, and the deep flavors of the ragu were noteworthy. A tortellini pasta filled with mascarpone cheese, beef, and organic egg, topped with slivers of fresh Parmesan cheese, balanced out the distinct flavors of flour, meat, and cheese masterfully. The portions are surprisingly small; large appetites might find themselves placing more than one order of pasta per person to even begin feeling full. Dessert is always fun; you can cus-tomize your soft-serve ice cream with anything from waffles, sea salt, caramel, and about 15 other toppings.

Specialty Stores, Markets & Producers

Heart of the City Farmers' Market, 1182 Market St., SOMA, San Francisco, CA 94102; (415) 558-9455. Located at the border of the prestigious SOMA and the Civic Center area, this market has some organic offerings, and a few seafood trucks offer fresh seafood. The prices are significantly cheaper than its cousin market on Embarcadero. Visit the mushroom stand for some amazing choices; it's as if you're plucking them out of the ground. Definitely drop by the falafel stand for a generous sample of hummus—you will undoubtedly buy an order to take home! While the market offers lots of fresh produce, fruits, and flowers, the herb selection here seems to be most impressive. Food trucks visit this area on Wednesday and Sunday, when this farmers' market comes to life.

Mi Tierra, 1000 Howard St., SOMA, San Francisco, CA 94103; (415) 553-6333. The selection here is not vast, but what they do have is fresh and offered at unbelievably low prices. Produce and fruits are fresh, though with a limited selection of organic choices.

Most importantly, Mi Tierra offers halal meats. With the exception of pork (for obvious reasons) there is an excellent selection of meat: beef, lamb, chicken, and seafood, including large and succulent shrimp. Given that this area is mostly delegated to Whole Foods for overpriced groceries, Mi Tierra is a welcome treat to the neighborhood. Due to space limitations, you won't be able to find your entire grocery list here, but Mi Tierra does offer a global/international selection of foods, spanning the Middle East, Asia, and even Europe.

Noe Valley Bakery & Bread Company, 4073 24th St., Noe Valley, San Francisco, CA 94114; (415) 550-1405; www.noevalley bakery.com. If you have a sweet tooth, this is the where you want to be. The Most-est Cupcake filled with Bavarian cream and the traditional red velvet cupcake with cream cheese frosting are the classics here. But, the strawberry-hazelnut cupcake, also filled with Bavarian cream, and topped with buttercream icing and strawberries, is a real treat. The moistness of the hazelnut sponge cake is enough to make your eyes roll to the back of your head. This bakery also sells a variety of cakes, pastries, and pies, and their bread selection is baked daily. But the real attractions are these addictive cupcakes. It's no wonder each weekend morning, there's a line forming at the door!

Philz Coffee, 201 Berry St., SOMA, San Francisco, CA 94158; (415) 875-9943; www.philzcoffee.com; Coffee Shop, $. Philz Coffee has rapidly grown throughout the city, and once you have a sip of their coffee, it's no wonder why. This location is newer and larger. There are several tables outside with patio seating at the intersection of 4th and Berry; inside, they have comfortable couches with other table-and-chair combinations. For a great hot cup of coffee, order Jacob's Wonderbar Brew; for the best iced coffee, don't miss the Iced Coffee Mojito with fresh mint leaves. There are several additional stores in the city, and the list continuously grows throughout the Bay Area. Check the website for details on other locations.

Central SF: Marina, Pacific Heights, Western Addition, Japantown, NoPa, Haight, Hayes Valley & the Castro

While this area is not officially called "Central San Francisco," we'll do so for the purpose of this book, because the neighborhoods that this chapter covers are all located centrally within San Francisco. To the west of this area, you have the large neighborhoods of

Richmond and Sunset; to the east, you have the touristy and active areas of North Beach, Nob Hill, SOMA, and other more happening areas of the city, which makes the neighborhoods covered in this chapter extremely central.

Central San Francisco is an equal mix of homes, apartments, and businesses. The rather small but distinct Japantown is located here, as are the affluent areas of the Marina and Pacific Heights. Also included in this neighborhood are other smaller areas like NoPa, Cole Valley, Hayes Valley, Haight, the well-known Castro area, and Western Addition.

Marina & Pacific Heights

These are two of the most desirable neighborhoods in San Francisco. An address in the Marina means that you pay a premium to be in reasonably sunny weather, surrounded by eateries on Chestnut Street and high-end shopping on Union Street (not to be confused with Union Square), another great shopping district located adjacent to the Financial District. Walking around the Marina on any given weekday, you can't help but wonder if anyone in this area works, because it's commonplace to see a full house at restaurants, with people ordering bottles of Champagne while eating brunch or lunch. Patio seating is more prevalent in this area with its better weather (for San Francisco). Much of the area is populated with 20- and 30-somethings. On the weekends, the area is crowded with residents and visitors alike.

Just below the Marina neighborhood is the classy Pacific Heights. Almost any street in this area has beautiful Victorian homes with a truly residential feel. The main bustling street in this neighborhood is Fillmore Street, filled with luxurious shops and cafes as well as some newer eateries offering great food. The bar-hopping scene is toned down in this area, and understandably so, given that the residents of this area are usually more established, and many will just go a bit north to the Marina to party.

Western Addition/NoPa & Japantown

It's difficult to classify Western Addition, which sometimes will include the Japantown district of San Francisco, and sometimes not. It's also commonly referred to as NoPa now, which stands for "north of the Panhandle," a 0.75-mile-long park in the city. While not a large area of San Francisco, it is extremely diverse: One area has multiple-dwelling homes referred to as "the projects," another area is home to many younger folks who work and play in San Francisco, and in yet another area the Japanese and Korean influence is higher.

Japantown used to span across more than 20 blocks in San Francisco, but throughout history, the Japanese have twice been pushed out of the area. First was during World War II and the infamous Japanese internment, and the second time was during the 1950s, when in an attempted revamp of the rundown areas of this neighborhood—called "urban renewal"—the area was declared a slum. Today, while

Japantown is significantly smaller, spanning across only 6 city blocks, active efforts continue to ensure its revival. Still, some of the most traditional Japanese eateries and stores are located in this area, (including the largest Japanese supermarket, Nijiya Market), randomly intertwined with Korean businesses.

Haight & the Castro

Without a doubt, these are the two most colorful neighborhoods of San Francisco, both unique in their own way.

The Haight was once the quintessential hippie area, with color abounding through the neighborhood with brightly painted build-ings, murals and graffiti on the walls. Liberal and relaxed, to this day this area is lively and fun with a starkly different style of living and hanging out compared to SOMA or the Marina. The types of restaurants and bars throughout this neighborhood reflect the cli-entele, with many casual brunch and toned-down restaurants and bars that remain active through the night, serving up great fare at reasonable prices.

A little to the east lies the Castro, which is best-known for its large gay and lesbian population. From business owners to resi-dents, the Castro is home to many good restaurants, and while the nightlife is predominantly geared toward the gay community, lots of folks from all over San Francisco visit the Castro for the lively and fun bar scene. In addition to the large number of gay and lesbian residents in the area, visitors are always welcomed by local busi-nesses. Being centrally located in San Francisco, the area also offers moderate housing costs and proximity to the freeway. Touted as the most openly gay district in San Francisco, if not the world, it's also a hot spot for tourism as people from all over the world come to see the neighborhood freely graced with adult stores and lively bars, and to witness firsthand the developments that the well-known city supervisor Harvey Milk put into play. Slowly but surely, the food scene in this area is beginning to grow.

Foodie Faves

A16, 2355 Chestnut St., Marina, San Francisco, CA 94123; (415) 771-2216; www.a16sf.com; Italian; $$$. I love every single thing I have tried on the appetizer menu at A16 (and I think I've tried it all); getting a table here, however, remains difficult and still requires a long wait on any given night of the week. It's no surprise, considering the scene is exactly what

San Francisco loves. The restaurant offers a great wine list, and the bar in the front of the restaurant is always packed with patrons who want to open up a bottle with a good friend and share in many courses of appetizers, pastas and pizzas.

One of the best octopus salads I've ever had was at this restaurant, served lukewarm and drizzled only in olive oil with some garlic and mixed in with arugula. All the *salumi* options on the antipasti section are worth trying, and ask the sommelier for a wine pairing recommendation; the best prosciutto is served up with variations of pork belly and head cheese with olives. Pizzas are simple with a crisp, thin crust and generous toppings. The *funghi* pizza is classic, and the Margherita is one of my favorites, topped with fresh home-made mozzarella slices and fragrant basil. If you have room, opt for one of the ever-changing pasta dishes as A16 combines fresh pasta with *bottarga* or oftentimes a homemade cheese like mascarpone, propelling good pasta into great territory.

Absinthe Brasserie and Bar, 399 Hayes St., Hayes Valley, San Francisco, CA 94102; (415) 551-1590; www.absinthe.com; French/ Italian/Contemporary; $$$. Absinthe is a great go-to spot for brunch and happy hour. While they do lunch and dinner well, and the burger is well-known in San Francisco, the cocktail menu here makes it the ideal location for happy hours with great starter selections like the soft garlic pretzels with a Vermont Cheddar Mornay, or a cheese platter from their vast selection of cheeses. In fact, the bartenders at Absinthe wrote the book *Art of the Bar* in 2006. For brunch, definitely order the Breakfast Burrito, filled with scrambled eggs, perfectly fried pork belly, potatoes, cheese and a chipotle salsa; if you like Bloody Marys, choose the "Red Snapper," which is the gin version of the drink with Absinthe's own Bloody Mary mix. For special occasions, order a bottle of Champagne and opt for the caviar service with warm blinis and Osetra caviar, along with a nice selection of raw oysters, The coq au vin is always a savory choice for dinner: it's chicken that is infused with notes of bacon and red wine.

Baker and Banker, 1701 Octavia Blvd., Pacific Heights, San Francisco, CA 94109; (415) 351-2500; www.bakerandbanker.com; American; $$$. This husband-and-wife duo of Executive Chef Jeff Baker and Pastry Chef Lori Baker presents a hip and cool restaurant space that is dimly lit, offers great service, and puts a fresh spin on San Franciscan cooking focused on using local produce and ingredients. Start the meal with the trout and potato latke—served with horseradish cream and beets, it's a great blend of textures and flavors, ranging from sweet to creamy, sea to earth. Their take on the octopus salad came with small bits of octopus served with melon, cucumbers, and mint—and was so refreshing as a starter and a pleasant combination of tastes. But nothing compares to the black cod braised in soy sauce and mirin—it's served atop a sticky rice cooked with *foie gras* and shiitake mushrooms, along with some fresh, slightly cooked bok choy. The flavors are enormous and present a wild mix of the Eastern and Western hemispheres. Definitely try Chef Baker's bread—and for dessert, the strawberry shortcake is, in one word, awesome.

Bar Crudo, 655 Divisadero St., Western Addition/NOPA, San Francisco, CA 94117; (415) 409-0679; www.barcrudo.com; Seafood;

$$. What's not to love about a place that focuses on serving all seafood as fresh and raw as possible? It can cost an arm and a leg to try and fill up for dinner at Bar Crudo; I tend to use it as my first stop in the evening, and order a bottle of Champagne or some beer (of which they offer many good varieties) to pair up with an exciting variety of seafood. The Arctic char dish consists of thinly sliced sashimi topped with a horseradish cream and wasabi *tobiko,* taking an ordinarily good fish to new heights. Definitely order the butterfish with blood orange, which is a savvy play between the deep flavors of the butterfish and the great citrus notes. The selection of oysters at Bar Crudo is not huge, but what they do offer is always top-notch in freshness and quality—especially the Kusshi oysters; request the fresh horseradish as they tend not to offer it otherwise. If at the end of your meal, you want something more filling and warm, try the seafood chowder, a creamy blend of seafood, bacon and potatoes.

Bistro SF Grill, 2819 California St., Pacific Heights, San Francisco, CA 94115; (415) 409-6410; www.bistrosfgrill.com; American; $$. For the most interesting take on burgers, Bistro SF Grill has it. With unique meat offerings like ostrich and alligator, and vegan options like curry lentil patties, this restaurant makes one fine burger. The best ones on the menu have been the lamb or the lamb/veal burger, which provided a slight hint of gaminess that made the burger even better. The well-known "geisha burger" consists of a grass-fed Idaho Kobe beef patty topped with caramelized mushrooms and onions, grilled peppers, and Gorgonzola cheese and served on a Kaiser roll. It had extreme meatiness, with a lot of depth provided by the cheese and mushrooms, and the peppers and onions adding that last bit of sweetness to perfect each bite. Order some crinkle-cut sweet potato fries as a nice complement to any burger order. The buffalo burger was also delicious, the lean meat patty full of flavor despite the lack of fat. The meat is loosely packed and tender, and the fixings are all fresh. This restaurant came to be after Bistro SF's food truck became wildly popular at the **Ferry Plaza Farmers' Market** (p. 52).

Blue Barn Gourmet, 2105 Chestnut St., Marina, San Francisco, CA 94123; (415) 441-3232; www.bluebarngourmet.com; Deli; $$. By the time you factor in tax, Blue Barn just misses the cut off for the single $ price range in this book, with most sandwiches hovering close to or just going over $10 per order. But even at double the cost, the sandwiches here would be worth it! They offer a wide variety of sandwich options, including a grilled cheese with your choice of Havarti, Manchego sheep cheese, *burrata,* or other cheeses. The pressed sandwiches are filling and so well made; combined with one of Blue Barn's enormous fresh salads, they're big enough to share between two regular appetites. Try the *burrata* panini, with heirloom tomatoes, a flavorful pesto aioli, and *burrata* cheese oozing over a fresh bed of arugula, or the pressed sandwich with turkey and melted goat cheese—each flavor stands out, along with the bread, and you begin to appreciate what fresh, organic, and local ingredients do for taste. You can opt for any of the salads on the menu or pick the ingredients to build your own, with proteins (like chicken, steak, shrimp, etc.) costing additional.

Boboquivari's, 1450 Lombard St., Marina, San Francisco, CA 94123; (415) 441-8880; www.boboquivaris.com; Seafood/Steakhouse; $$$$. This place is perfect for those who are undecided between steak and seafood. Bobo's, as locals call this restaurant, serves up impressive examples of both. The Dungeness crab crostini is a great starter—crostini served up with crabmeat, smoked salmon, avocado, and *burrata* cheese. Another appetizer, the *burrata* with heirloom tomatoes, is also a great choice to share. When opting for meat here, order the bone-in filet mignon; at Bobo's, it's so tender, and one bite convinces you that properly aged meat that is cooked with the bone does indeed taste better. If this smaller cut is not enough for you, order the porterhouse consisting of a large filet and NY steak cut, cooked medium-rare; each bite is so juicy and tender, and the New York strip steak portion is nicely marbled throughout. If you have an inclination for seafood, not to be missed on this menu is the whole crab; it's a given that the crab is cooked perfectly with a nice whiff of garlic, but one dip into the accompanying butter sauce will make you realize why Bobo's is the number-one choice for those wanting "surf and turf," which is also an option on their menu.

Boxing Room, 399 Grove St., Hayes Valley, San Francisco, CA 94102; (415) 430-6590; www.boxingroomsf.com. Cajun/Creole/Southern; $$$. Newly opened in 2011, Boxing Room is a welcome addition to the Cajun cooking scene in the city. It's a beautiful and big space that's hip and modern, with good service and a simple but pleasant menu. Begin with the thick cut of head cheese on the starter menu, served with really crunchy pickled okra that balances out the heaviness and density of the head cheese. The deep-fried alligator is a safe choice; the meat is breaded and fried, and presented with lemon and a Creole remoulade. The taste is subtle and nothing you'd expect alligator to taste like, and the meat is lean and tender. Most notable on this menu are the huge flavors presented in the **Chicken & Andouille Gumbo** (recipe on p. 268), with strips of chicken, andouille sausage with a significant kick, a deep and powerful broth, and rice—and somehow, all the ingredients retain their original flavors and hold their own. Chef Justin Simoneaux offers the ultimate partner to fried chicken with the corn *maque choux* (a salsa of sorts) that is served alongside buttery mashed potatoes for a truly Southern meal. .

Cha Cha Cha, 1801 Haight St., Haight, San Francisco, CA 94117; (415) 386-7670; www.cha3.com; Caribbean/Cuban/Tapas; $$. The one place in the Haight where you will almost always see a line outside the door is Cha Cha Cha. It's no surprise, once you taste the sangria and freshly prepared cooking, you can see why people wait in line for an hour plus to be seated here. The appetizer to start with is the Cajun shrimp, with large pieces of shrimp cooked expertly in a spicier cream sauce that is even more appealing as a dipping sauce for the bread served at Cha Cha Cha; the fried new potatoes that come with an addictive chile-pasilla aioli is good for just about anything. While I am not normally a fan of mussels, I do tend to order them here because of the amazing saffron broth that they're cooked in; mixed with onions, tomatoes, and heavy on the garlic, it's also a great dipping sauce for the bread! For the entree, the Jamaican jerk chicken is always a hit, juicy with a nice blend of Jamaican spice. There is a second larger and slightly fancier location at 2327 Mission St., Mission, San Francisco, CA 94110; (415) 824-1502—it serves up the same menu but is better for larger groups.

Chotto, 3317 Steiner St., Marina, San Francisco, CA 94123; (415) 441-2223; www.chottosf.com; Japanese; $$. Relatively new to the San Francisco restaurant scene, this Japanese *izakaya* spot is sleek and modern. Izakaya, by definition, is a pub-like eatery where small bites are offered to accompany after-work drinks in Japan; the objective is to allow many orders of small plates per person and all are designed to work well with beers or sake. The dishes are creative and a nice blend of authentic Japanese food and fusion style. The calamari at Chotto is a must-order item—served with a chile-based aioli sauce, it's lightly breaded in a tempura batter that highlights the fresh and subtle taste of squid but provides a slight crunch to each bite. The *kara-age* is delicious, with crispy fried chicken thighs that have marinated in a ginger soy sauce. The *tontoro* consists of juicy and minimally fatty pork jowls, served on skewers; also try the duck breast skewers, which are lightly grilled to retain moistness. At the end of the meal, plan to share a bowl of ramen; the spicy ramen with roasted pork always makes for a warm and comforting end to the meal. With interesting dishes like Avocheezu—an avocado and fresh mozzarella dish—or bacon mochi, Chotto is a culinary experience that is best enjoyed with one of their Japanese beers served in a frozen pitcher and frozen glasses. I don't know any other location in the city that serves colder beer. *Kanpai,* indeed!

Chow, 215 Church St., Castro, San Francisco, CA 94114; (415) 552-2469; www.chowfoodbar.com; American; $$. Perhaps my only reason to consistently visit the Castro, Chow is one of those restaurants that cooks a large variety of items on the menu really well. From soup to pasta to meat dishes, Chow always offers amazing taste, organic ingredients, and fair prices in a casual yet quaint atmosphere that pleases everyone. The French onion soup is so comforting with mozzarella bubbling over on top. The linguini with clams is so simple and seasoned just enough to bring the seafood flavors to life, and the burger with blue cheese is also as simple as it gets, but unusually good. The superstar of this menu, however, is the pot-roasted short ribs, which are decadent and fall off the bone completely; served with mashed potatoes and mushroom gravy, this dish will satisfy anyone. When at Chow, you must always end your meal with an order of the ginger cake with pumpkin ice

COOK WITH JAMES

While it started as an underground restaurant, **Chef James Stolich** now runs a full-fledged eating experience—Cook with James—out of his gorgeous home and kitchen. Suitable for intimate groups of up to eight people, the chef invites you to join in the cooking experience while learning all about the fresh, local ingredients that are used to prepare dinner. Guests are welcome to ask questions, slice and dice, or "cook with James" while he puts together course after course of decadent food. Learn to hand-make gnocchi or fresh pizza dough; you'll see how a fresh Bolognese sauce is made from scratch, or reserve your seats for paella nights. The experience can be customized to meet your needs, and the chef is truly accommodating to personalizing the experience for you and your guests. Included in this book is Chef James' dessert recipe for **La Quesada** (p. 278), brought from the coastal city of Santander, Spain. 1373 Masonic Ave., Haight, San Francisco, CA 94117; (415) 425-3444; www.cookwithjames.com.

cream—their signature dessert dish. I have yet to meet one person whose eyes don't glaze over at first bite.

Dosa on Fillmore, 1700 Fillmore St., Pacific Heights, San Francisco, CA 94115; (415) 441-3672; www.dosasf.com; Indian; $$$. The majority of the menu at Dosa, inspired by south Indian cuisine, is contrastingly different from the typical northern Indian cuisine that I am more used to—the flavors are geared toward the American palate and the usage of the often pungent and uniquely Indian spices are noticeably toned down. That said, the flavors are good and there's a lot of creativity put into each dish—one highlight features the enormous *dosa,* a crepe made of rice and lentils that is rolled into a cone shape, perfect to dip into the creamy sauces. Order the prawn Masala with coconut rice and use the *dosa* to dip into the coconut milk and yogurt curry sauce. Other worthy dishes at Dosa are the paneer and peas *uttapam,* which is like a pancake of sorts with the paneer (cheese made from curdling milk with lemon juice) and peas mixed into the rice batter—very filling—and the Chennai chicken, which consists of crisply fried but moist chicken that is served with a yogurt dipping sauce; I recommend ordering the lemon rice with your non-curry dishes. Order cocktails here—the bar makes some truly delicious ones! There's another Dosa location at 995 Valencia St., Mission, San Francisco, CA 94110; (415) 642-3672; it serves beer and wine only.

Ella's Restaurant, 500 Presidio Ave., Pacific Heights, San Francisco, CA 94115; (415) 441-5669; www.ellassanfrancisco.com;

American; $$. On any given weekend morning, you will find a line here from 10 a.m. until closing time. The most popular thing on the menu is undoubtedly the chicken hash, consisting of potatoes with shredded chicken, served with gravy and eggs. Or, if hash is not your thing, you can opt for robust flavors with their special scrambles, which will change often—but, for example, the ham, mushroom, and Gouda combination with moist and fluffy eggs was quite memorable. Brunch at Ella's should always include a glass of their fresh orange juice, pulp included, and often made with blood oranges when in season. The blueberry pancake with mascarpone cheese is everything a pancake should be: fluffy with strong blueberry presence and scents and mascarpone cheese just melting off the top, or try the strawberry ricotta pancakes, which delivers sweet and savory flavors that linger!

Frances Restaurant, 3870 17th St., Castro, San Francisco, CA 94114; (415) 621-3870; www.frances-sf.com; American; $$$. Any chef that makes it okay for you to start the meal with what should be a dessert—applewood-smoked bacon beignets—is good by me. Pair it with a crème fraîche infused with maple and chives as a dipping sauce, and Chef Melissa Perello qualifies for deity status. Frances may be a newcomer, but it's not often a restaurant become so popular so quickly—and it's well-deserved. When offered, try the white corn soup, which is a bowlful of goodness, mixed in with dill, crème fraîche, and bits of red onions for some bite. The Parmesan and ricotta gnocchi were large, pillowy potato puffs, paired with deeper notes from the pancetta and chanterelle mushrooms that accompanied this dish. The entrees continue to shine here long after the starters have dimmed. The sweetness of the northern halibut was forced out by the English pea ragout and mushrooms; the addition of onions and bacon raises the bar for fish entrees everywhere. The red wine–braised Liberty duck leg fell right off the bone, and each bite paired with the butter beans that came with the entree made music in my mouth. The menu changes often, but rest assured, anything you order at Frances will be good.

Grove Cafe on Fillmore, 2016 Fillmore St., Pacific Heights, San Francisco, CA 94115; (415) 474-1419; American; $. What's there not to love about Grove on Fillmore? Tasty cafe-style sandwiches and other food items with good coffee in generous portions? Check. Patio seating and Chimay beer? Check. I'm there. I used to visit Grove for a cup of Americano, freshly brewed, with a bagel and cream cheese (and they never skimp on the cream cheese), regardless of the time of day. Then, I spent a year or two only ordering their Florentine steak sandwich which is basically a panini with juicy cuts of flank steak, arugula, tomatoes, and fresh mozzarella; it's one of those perfectly portioned sandwiches that leaves you feeling sated. Once I found the chicken potpie, I ordered nothing else. With the creaminess of the pie filling, chock-full of chicken, carrots, and peas, covered in a flaky and buttery crust—all you need is a bottle of Chimay to wash it down. Grove also has a lavender ice tea that is as fragrant and refreshing as can be. Grove Cafe has additional locations throughout San Francisco at 2250 Chestnut St., Marina, San Francisco, CA 94123; (415) 474-4843; and 690 Mission St., SOMA, San Francisco, CA 94105.

Harry's Bar, 2020 Fillmore St., Pacific Heights, San Francisco, CA 94115; (415) 921-1000; www.harrysbarsf.com; American/ Gastropub; $$. It's a restaurant, and they do serve food, but I can't recommend this place for the food. There are two reasons one goes to Harry's, in my opinion: one is for the city's best Bloody Mary, including the celery stick, olive, and the great blend of spices used. This could literally replace coffee in my morning ritual if drinking it in the morning wouldn't get me intoxicated; it has a real kick to it, and awakens all of your senses immediately. The second reason to go to Harry's is because they have a nicely priced wine list, and on Tuesday all wines are half off. The place gets busy and the food is decent for "bar bites," but as mentioned, the main reason to go here is for the aforementioned attractions.

Hukilau Hawaiian Restaurant, 5 Masonic Ave., Western Addition/ NoPa, San Francisco, CA 94118; (415) 921-6242; www.dahukilau .com; Hawaiian; $$. Very few things in life are as comforting—or filling—as Hawaiian food. If you go on the weekends, Hukilau will also have live bands playing Hawaiian music—and with a piña colada in hand, you almost feel like you're on the beautiful island of Hawaii—if you ignore the brisk wind and cloudiness of San Francisco. The menu is a great blend between Japanese, Korean, and true Hawaiian food; the most impressive items are the Pele chicken *katsu,* aloha chicken adobo, or one of my favorites, the Hukilau breakfast: 2 eggs, rice, Portuguese sausage, Spam, and toast, piled high on a plate. All of this is served up with what I consider to be the best macaroni salad; creamy without the tartness, it's so incredibly addictive that I sometimes drop by just to order it. See Hukilau's recipe for **Classic Poke** on p. 263.

Ike's Place, 3489 16th St., Castro, San Francisco, CA 94114; (415) 553-6888; www.ilikeikesplace.com; Deli; $$. Fresh bread, secret "dirty" sauce, tasty ingredients, and a terribly long wait is what Ike's is all about. The place is so popular that the line usually extends down the block during peak hours. Ike himself bakes the bread daily, and with his family, including his lovely mother, he serves up some fascinatingly good sandwiches from a small shop. The prices are on the higher end of things, but the sandwiches are huge; one half is sufficient to fill most appetites, and the other half can be eaten later. Ike's also offers mega-sandwich orders, perfect to order if two or more are sharing lunch. For instance, the Kryptonite sandwich, costing near $20, is a foot-long Dutch-crusted bread filled with—well, just about everything. It includes not just your ham, bacon, turkey, pastrami, salami, and roast beef, but pesto sauce, Pepper Jack cheese, avocado, and lest you still want more—it also includes fried mozzarella sticks and jalapeño poppers, along with crispy fried onion rings, all *in* the sandwich. It goes without saying that the regulars like onions, pickles, peppers, and tomatoes, which are, of course, included. If you and your friends can't enjoy this—then you probably just don't like sandwiches. Check the website for additional locations throughout the Bay Area.

Ino Sushi, 22 Peace Plaza, Japantown, San Francisco, CA 94115; (415) 922-3121; Japanese; $$$$. Those in the know are well aware that Ino Sushi is as authentic and traditional as sushi will get outside of Tokyo. The secret to great sushi is not just fresh fish; the secret is having amazing sushi rice, and that is where Ino Sushi delivers time and again. The chef, Inoue-san, prepares his own *ankimo* (monkfish liver) here, which puts *foie gras* to shame, and the *ikura* (salmon roe) is also exemplary with none of the fishiness commonly associated with it. The *engawa* (an area adjacent to the fin on the flounder), *toro* (belly of the tuna), *uni* (sea urchin), and even something as plain as *ika* (squid) tastes remarkable when prepared by this chef. Don't miss out on the *saba* (mackerel), which he wraps in pickled white seaweed that will—I promise you— make you close your eyes to relish the taste, or the *unagi*—a steaming hot piece of eel with a small amount of sauce, put atop the ideal amount of sushi rice. You will find no specialty California rolls and such here—and I suggest you not even ask. Just reserve a seat at the bar and tell the chef, "Omakase, kudasai" (which means "Chef's choice, please"), and let him take your palate on an unforgettable journey. A sushi experience like this is hard to find outside of Japan!

Isa Restaurant, 3324 Steiner St., Marina, San Francisco, CA 94123; (415) 567-9588; www.isarestaurant.com; French; $$$. Isa offers up cooking that truly delights all the senses. The crab salad at the beginning of the meal consists of large chunks of crabmeat offering the taste of the sea, combined with earthiness offered by the avocado chunks—but just when you think you need one more addition, you get a bite of some apple and the perfect trio is created. As an entree, the duck is seared to a nice crisp on the skin while retaining all the moistness in the meat; paired with a huckleberry sauce, beets, chèvre, and arugula—the combination is enough to make you guard your plate so you won't have to share. Also wonderful is the halibut, crisp on the outside and so buttery on the inside—and this dish is served with roasted beets, which let the flavor of the fish dance with their sweetness. All of the dishes at Isa are served family-style and are meant to be shared by the table, and many will come pre-sliced to make sharing easy.

Jake's Steaks, 3301 Buchanan St., Marina, San Francisco, CA 94123; (415) 922-2211; www.jakessteaks.net; Deli; $. Take a soft and fresh submarine roll and slice it in the middle, almost all of the way through. Grill plenty of well-marbled, thinly sliced beef with some juicy onions and fresh mushrooms. Mix in a heaping amount of Cheez Whiz until it's a thoroughly cheesy mix and pour the entire piping-hot concoction onto the bread, and top with some pickled jalapeños. Toss some just-cooked waffle fries (also scalding hot) into a basket, salt, and serve them up to the customer. That is what eating at Jake's is about. You can easily order for takeout, or within the area, you can even request delivery. Whether you're watching the game at Jake's, or chowing down in front of your own television, this is the ultimate cheesesteak in San Francisco, and it's better than some places in—well, Philadelphia. Always request the "Whiz," not the real stuff—and don't skip the grilled onions and mushrooms!

Little Star Pizza, 846 Divisadero St., Western Addition/NoPa, San Francisco, CA 94117; (415) 441-1118; www.littlestarpizza .com; Pizza; $$. If you like Chicago-style pizza, you'll find a never-ending debate in San Francisco between **Patxi's** (p. 160) and Little Star. Both use a cornmeal crust and are deep-dish pizzas (though both offer thin-crust options as well), but there are subtle differences. Little Star Pizza is preferred by those who want a heavy dose of sauce compared to cheese and toppings. The sauce is on the chunkier side with massive tomato flavors pervading throughout. They use fresh ingredients and take a little less time than Patxi's (25 minutes compared to 40 minutes at Patxi's), and generally, Little Star Pizza is much more crowded on weeknights. Like most Chicago-style pizzas, a couple slices are usually enough to satiate most appetites. Most interesting at Little Star is the garlic bread; lightly toasted and heated bread is served with an interesting butter concoction, and half a garlic head is completely roasted in its skin. You can then spread the amount of butter you prefer, and take a soft chunk of roasted garlic out to spread on your bread. Combined with a salad, it makes for a nice start to a large pizza meal. A second location is at 400 Valencia St., Mission, San Francisco, CA 94103; (415) 551-7827.

Lucca Delicatessen, 2120 Chestnut St., Marina, San Francisco, CA 94123; (415) 921-7873; www.luccadeli.com; Deli; $. Hands down, Lucca offers some of the most delicious sandwiches in San Francisco. All sandwiches are custom-made when you walk in, or you can even order your sandwich via their website—and the online ordering system actually works well. The quality ingredients that they use—from the meats that they slice once you order to the huge array of cheese and breads—make it incomparable to most delis in the city. While the latest rage is greasy and saucy sand-wiches dripping in butter, Lucca Deli offers classic sandwiches on great bread with fresh ingredients that deliver in taste and flavor. My favorites are the prosciutto, head cheese, and fresh mozzarella on Acme bread, or the pastrami sandwich, filled to the rim with perfectly marbled slices of meat stacked high and seasoned to perfection, always a safe choice for meat lovers. Lucca Deli enables San Franciscans to leave this city for one meal, and step into a small but well-stocked deli in Italy—where the sky's the limit as far as sandwich, salad, and pasta choices go. Do try the homemade ravioli—there's more filling than pasta in these beauties!

Marina Submarine, 2229 Union St., Marina, San Francisco, CA 94123; (415) 921-3990; Deli; $. Order the turkey—with avocado. Or the pastrami—with avocado. Or meatballs—with avocado! Watching Kyu, the owner, slice avocado makes a visit to Marina Submarine worthwhile as he's elevated it to an art form, so whatever I order here, I include avocado. In turn, he seems to put a full avocado into each sandwich that requests it! The cold cuts are fresh, and the bread is baked daily and toasted immediately before the sandwich is prepared. With sandwiches like pastrami on rye, or an awesome meatball sandwich with cheese and the fixings, Marina Submarine doesn't skimp on the ingredients and offers much more than the low cost of each sub. Whatever you order, it will be the biggest and best sandwich in recent history. The secret sauce here is slightly tangy with a kick, and all sandwiches come with mustard and mayonnaise unless you request otherwise. Instead of lettuce, fresh sprouts are used, which are crucial in my book to make a truly gourmet sandwich. Don't forget to order the avocado.

Mojo Bicycle Cafe, 639 Divisadero St., Western Addition/NoPa, San Francisco, CA 94117; (415) 440-2370; www.mojobicyclecafe .com; American; $. This is one of those restaurants I found purely by chance—and what a treat it is to eat here. The front of the store is a cafe and small eatery, and the back end of the store is a spacious bike shop. Outside on the street are a few tables with plenty of bike racks so customers can tie down their bikes while getting a fresh cup of coffee and some food. Le Marocain is a turkey and gruyère cheese sandwich that is topped with roasted bell peppers, cucumbers, tomatoes, and lettuce, served on a toasted bun; it's warm but fresh with the ideal amount of cold and crunchy from the vegetables, and a nice kick is delivered through the harissa aioli. Also delicious is an open-faced sandwich called Le Croque Mojo— the main difference is it uses thinly sliced cuts of French ham in lieu of turkey, and it is served open face with gruyère cheese melted perfectly all across the 2 open faces of the sandwich.

On the Bridge, 1581 Webster St., Japantown, San Francisco, CA 94115; (415) 922-7765; www.sfonthebridge.com; Asian Fusion; $$. This small restaurant serves up a large fusion Japanese menu with everything from *don-katsu* (pork cutlet) to Japanese noodle dishes. But it's best known for the Japanese curry, and even then, this restaurant offers the option of increasing spice to level 18X for those who really like things painful. You can custom-order your curry with the ingredients you want, then choose a level of spiciness. I've tasted up to 9X here, which was hard to manage even for me; I usually stick to 6X now, and most people can't even have one bite of my curry. I recommend opting for onions, tomatoes, chicken, pork, broccoli, and an additional fried egg. The order comes with a plate of rice, which you will need. You'll sweat, hallucinate, and drool while eating anything above 4X at this restaurant, but you'll also become strangely addicted to the heat. Also great on the menu is the *mentaiko* spaghetti, which is standard pasta noodles, butter, topped with cod roe—much like the Italians' *bottarga* spaghetti. With seaweed and green onions as garnish, this dish also serves as a nice break between the incredibly spicy bites of curry. On the Bridge also offers a very simple *natto* (fermented soybeans) spaghetti.

Patxi's Chicago Pizza, 3318 Fillmore St., Marina, San Francisco, CA 94123; (415) 345-3995; www.patxispizza.com; Pizza; $$. I admit I wasn't a big fan of Chicago-style pizza in Chicago, so I have rarely searched for it elsewhere. But Patxi's is my exception to the rule. The deep-dish pizza here is quite remarkable—the cornmeal crust is thick around the edges and crispy while maintaining enough oils to keep it moist and chewy; the bottom of the crust is significantly thinner, holding the pizza well; the cheese is creamy and plentiful with a good balance to the great tomato sauce. Order the "favorite"; it sounds minimal with just pepperoni, black olives, and mushrooms, but the way Patxi's piles it all into the bottom layer of the pizza, topped with cheese, then sauce makes every single ingredient shine. Very few things are as delightful as when they lift a slice of pizza from the pan to serve you, when the mozzarella extends in cheesy strings for at least a foot as it's lifted. It's also quite impressive how the pizza doesn't get soggy like other deep-dish pizzas;

even the day after, the leftovers are delicious. Check the website for 2 additional locations in San Francisco; the original location is in Hayes Valley—but the Marina location is larger and newer.

Paul K Restaurant, 199 Gough St., Western Addition/Hayes Valley, San Francisco, CA 94102; (415) 552-7132; www.paulkrestaurant .com; Mediterranean, $$$. This restaurant usually tops my list as the ideal date restaurant that is fair in price, great in ambience, impressive in food, and fantastic in service. While definitely Mediterranean in influence, a lot of their menu is distinctly rooted in American cuisine. The brunch features bottomless mimosas or Bloody Marys and includes options like a duck confit hash consisting of duck meat braised until it barely needs a knife, with grilled potatoes and onions, and topped with two poached eggs. Or for dinner, start with the mezza plate consisting of grilled lamb kebabs, braised lamb riblets that are both sweet and savory, olives, pita bread, feta cheese, yogurt, cucumber salad, and a tasty baba ghanoush. The hummus here is not to be missed—it's just enough to get the juices flowing. Try the Syrian-spiced duck; it's served completely devoid of sauce while retaining all the depth of duck, served atop spelt, and sprinkled with dates and hazelnuts. This dish is such a creative play of flavors and textures, exemplary of the flavors that abound at Paul K.

Playground, 1705 Buchanan St., Japantown, San Francisco, CA 94115; (415) 929-1471; www.playgroundsf.com; Korean; $$. While this restaurant tends to get packed with young and loud Koreans feasting on delicious food and *soju,* there's a reason it's always packed. This is one of the few places in San Francisco that serves good Korean food. While the menu is far from representative of the best of Korean cuisine, Playground does offer all of the more casual and fun dishes that are popular with Korean culture. The *jja-jang myun* (noodles with black bean sauce) is mixed with jalapeños here that offer a nice spicy kick to this dish; it's one of only two places in this city where I would order this. They also offer "cheese corn" (heated corn with melted mozzarella on top) that is strangely addictive, and a fried chicken dish that pairs with beer as beautifully as a Cabernet and steak. People also love the *boodae jjigae* here, which is a classic Korean dish, rooted in the days of the Korean War, where whatever was leftover by the US military was cooked into a spicy broth. It's a tasty large pot of soup that is on the spicier side of things, with ingredients like hot dogs, Spam, vegetables, ramen noodles, and bits of rice cakes. While it may have had odd origins, it's one of the favorite dishes with which to drink *soju.*

Pork Store Cafe, 1451 Haight St., Haight, San Francisco, CA 94117; (415) 864-6981; www.porkstorecafe.com; American; $. If you mix chunky home fries, green peppers, chunks of bacon, tomatoes, and garlic, melt an insane amount of cheese on the creation, top it with two poached eggs (or your preference), and serve it with heavily buttered toast on the side, you have Pork Store's Eggs in a Tasty Nest. It might be the only time I pop the egg yolk, let it ooze all over the concoction, and then mix it all up to eat, with a heavy dose of Tabasco for punch. If you wake up on a weekend morning feeling like a glutton, nothing beats the pork chop breakfast. Two large pork chops are served up with eggs prepared any way you like and crispy yet soft hash browns—and opt to order a side of the fresh biscuits, and don't forget the gravy. You won't be hungry again until midnight, but you will also consider going the next morning to do it again. The second location at 3122 16th St., Mission, San Francisco, CA 94103; (415) 626-5523, offers a larger location with a full Bloody Mary bar; they give you a glass of vodka and you prepare it any which way you want to drink it.

Rose's Cafe, 2298 Union St., Marina, San Francisco, CA 94123; (415) 775-2200; www.rosescafesf.com; French; $$. This charming restaurant offers plentiful patio seating on the sidewalk, totally reminiscent of eating on the streets of Paris, though you're on a street corner in San Francisco. Order a fresh ice tea to start. For brunch, don't miss out on the breakfast pizza; it's a thin and delicate pizza crust topped with eggs (opt for sunny-side up) topped with fontina cheese and thin slices of smoked ham placed all over. It makes you want to just fold it up to devour whole. It's generous in portion, so you can order some french toast (which is exemplary, but it's only a small portion) and share between two people. For lunch, start with the polenta with Gorgonzola—it's served with a soft-poached egg on top that you pop to let it drizzle over the perfectly baked polenta. For your entree, order the Wild King Salmon Cozy—a flatbread sandwich with fresh grilled salmon piled high with watercress, red onion, and cucumbers with an herbal aioli; the toasted flatbread fish is juicy and hot, and together with the cold vegetables, this is one sandwich you will come back for time and again.

The Sandwich Spot, 3213 Pierce St., Marina, San Francisco, CA 94123; (415) 829-2587; www.sandwichspotsf.com; Deli; $. Pair awesome, friendly service with fresh-baked breads and a world of creative sandwich choices and you have one of the best sandwich spots in the city. Right before lunch, you can whiff fresh bread in the air, and even if your stomach was craving something else, you start thinking, "Sandwich!" Try the Mother Clucker on Dutch crunch bread; this concoction is piled high with marinated chicken, ham, and swiss cheese, smothered in both honey mustard and spicy mustard, and topped with crunchy fried onions. While I'm inclined to think that almost anything on this menu is good, the Naughty Nannie is one of my favorites. How can anything with massive amounts of fresh turkey, avocado, and cream cheese be bad? The sandwich comes with the Sandwich Spot's famous Bomb Sauce—a spicy ranch that balances the creaminess of the avocado and cream cheese pop.

Shabusen Restaurant, 1726 Buchanan St., Pacific Heights, San Francisco, CA 94115; (415) 440-0466; Japanese; $$. With the recent invasion of numerous shabu-shabu restaurants in San Francisco, Shabusen is a classic. It paved the way in San Francisco for this Japanese method of cooking your own meat and vegetables and dipping them into ponzu or sesame sauce—and today, while there are more popular places serving up creative broths or higher-grade meat, Shabusen remains popular with the traditional and classic shabu-shabu. Like others, they offer an all-you-can-eat option, and a large bar with many burners is available for each person's individual use. But the sukiyaki option is becoming more popular at Shabusen. While shabu-shabu is dipped into sauces, sukiyaki has the seasoning already mixed into the soup base, and the meats and vegetables are simmered in the pot. Typically, as you lift each piece out, you dip it into a mixed raw egg, both to cool down the meat and impart the creaminess of egg yolk to the cooked items.

Sophie's Crepes, 1581 Webster St., #275, Pacific Heights, San Francisco, CA 94115; (415) 929-7732; Creperie; $. There really isn't a way to beat a Nutella-filled crepe with generous portion of bananas and strawberries with whipped cream—until you put a scoop of vanilla gelato in the hot crepe. The crowd that is always outside this store is testament to how popular this creperie in Japantown is—and it's the crepe batter. Thinner, lighter, and more delicate than other typical creperies, this store offers all kinds of optional items for your crepe for an additional cost. One can easily make a $10 crepe here! For a different twist from Nutella, try the

Japanese crepe filled with green tea gelato, matcha sauce, and red bean—it's the ultimate dessert, or if you can have more than one, a very naughty meal. I don't recommend this store for savory crepes; stick to the sweet here.

Sushi Zone, 1815 Market St., Hayes Valley, San Francisco, CA 94103; (415) 621-1114; Japanese; $$$. This restaurant is truly small, and starting at 5 p.m. (opening time), it's a full house every night. Sushi Zone is a neighborhood favorite with loyal patrons that have been coming for years. The fish is fresh, and though the variety doesn't compare to some others, the menu offers an interesting array of choices when it comes to rolls and even sushi items. The appeal here is to get fresh fish in creative rolls and sashimi in relaxed surroundings. The *hamachi* is buttery, and the albacore tuna can only be beat by something just caught at sea. The chef makes a spicy albacore roll that brings out intense flavors in the chopped tuna and packs some heat,. Of the rolls, the Alaskan roll with chunks of with fresh and fatty salmon, creamy avocado, and scallions is fabulous, even though I'm not a fan of rolls in general. The cooked items are flavorful, including a baked seabass with mango, or savory baked mussels. When at Sushi Zone, you can order sashimi to your heart's content and still expect to pay less than at other sushi restaurants in the city without sacrificing quality. You'll feel a bit guilty while you savor your fish and sake slowly, wanting it to last, despite the crowd waiting outside—but just when you think of getting up, you'll undoubtedly opt for one more piece.

Suzu Noodle House, 1825 Post St., Japantown, San Francisco, CA 94115; (415) 346-5083; Japanese; $$. I will declare this the best ramen in San Francisco for the time being. The Bay Area has better bowls of ramen, but none are in the city—not to my knowledge anyway. The chicken and pork broth is rich and savory, and on the many cold nights we have, very few things are as comforting. But the noodles are what catapult this ramen place over others: Thick, chewy, and perfectly al dente, each bite of the noodles remains perfect through the entire bowl. A bowl of ramen is served with a thick slice of *chashu* (fatty pork slow-cooked in soy sauce, ginger, and other spices), seaweed, bamboo shoots, green onions, and half a hard-boiled egg. For larger appetites, you can order the combination meal served with your choice of ramen, along with a side plate of rice plus one ingredient (like a pork cutlet or the tuna sashimi), or for those who like chicken, the chicken *kara-age,* small chunks of chicken that are breaded and deep-fried, is absolutely tasty and particularly moist at Suzu.

1300 on Fillmore, 1300 Fillmore St., Western Addition/NOPA, San Francisco, CA 94115; (415) 771-7100; www.1300fillmore.com; Soul Food; $$$. Very few restaurants in the city offer the ambience and aura that this classically beautiful restaurant does. Located a few doors down from **Yoshi's** (p. 169), patrons who have tickets for a jazz concert there will often dine here first, or at least have a drink. Bar bites in the lounge are popular, and with large, plush seating areas, it's an ideal location at which to enjoy a glass of wine or scotch while eating the lamb sliders that are usually on the bar menu. Most notable on the menu are the short ribs that are cooked thoroughly and barely need a knife, and when offered, do try the sweetbreads, which have always been good here. The fried chicken with creamy cheese polenta and wilted greens is also quite decadent.

Woodhouse Fish Company, 1914 Fillmore St., Pacific Heights, San Francisco, CA 94115; (415) 437-2722; www.woodhousefish.com; Seafood; $$. There are four things you can't miss out on when you visit Woodhouse Fish Company—a seafood haven of San Francisco. First is the grilled artichoke with shrimp and crab—it's the most succulent appetizer with awesome deep notes of the artichoke and high notes provided by the fresh seafood. Then, the lobster roll, with large chunks of lobster meat on a toasted sourdough bun. The lobster mixture is light on the mayo; there's just enough to highlight the sweetness of this delicate shellfish, and it's adorned only with chives—but what else do you need with this much lobster on great bread? Then, you have to order the fish tacos, with lightly breaded cod placed inside a soft tortilla and covered with sliced cabbage, avocado, and fresh pico de gallo—it's so fresh and juicy, dripping with each savory bite! Finally, finish off the meal with the apple pie a la mode that provides all the creaminess from the scoop of ice cream and fruitiness from the large chunks of apple in the pie— completing a well-rounded meal. Very little in San Francisco will be as satisfying as eating these dishes, in this order, for a two-person meal. A second location is at 2073 Market St., Castro, San Francisco, CA 94114; (415) 437-2722. Neither location takes reservations, so be prepared to wait.

Yakini-Q, 1640 Post St., Japantown, San Francisco, CA 94115; (415) 441-9292; Korean/Barbecue; $$. This is a welcome addition to San Francisco. Without a lot of (good) Korean options in the city, Yakini-Q offers a tasty and economical option to Korean barbecue. For a little bit over $20, you're offered an all-you-can-eat menu with pork belly, intestines, pig skin, chicken, brisket, as well as other choices to cook on your table grill. The only item that is available in limited portions is the *kalbi* (short ribs)—only 2 per person at the table, though this has never been a problem for most folks. They also serve the barbecue with unlimited amounts of egg casserole and other cooked items like kimchee stew, some with additional cost. They offer *dduk-bossam* here: Vegetables are mixed with cooked meat, dipped in sesame sauce, and wrapped in sticky rice paper. This meal goes perfectly with cold beer or *soju*—but don't plan to go anywhere afterward as you will be in a food coma and undoubtedly reeking of barbecue smoke.

Yoshi's San Francisco, 1330 Fillmore St., Western Addition/ NOPA, San Francisco, CA 94115; (415) 655-5600; www.yoshis.com/

sanfrancisco; Japanese; $$$. Gindara (black cod) is the item you must order when at Yoshi's. On second thought, get the Lobster Blossom, too, as both these items are stellar. The black cod has always been cooked perfectly and so moist and flavorful, served in a mushroom-and-soy broth that brightens every flavor note in the cod. Request it with rice to make a fantastic entree. The Lobster Blossoms are actually a chopped lobster and scallop filling, wrapped in nori (seaweed), then dipped into batter, and deep-fried. The slight crunchiness on the outside, mixed with the soft sweetness on the inside, makes this one of the tastiest appetizers in the city. It's with creative creations like this that Yoshi's continues to delight its patrons, who frequent the venue for the great concerts here—and while I don't recommend Yoshi's for sushi, per se, their cooked items have always delighted all palates.

Zazie, 941 Cole St., Cole Valley, San Francisco, CA 94117; (415) 564-5332; www.zaziesf.com; American Brunch; $$. One of the city's favorite brunch spots, Zazie doesn't disappoint with its offerings. The New York Scramble is one of my favorites. Fluffy scrambled eggs mixed with chunks of smoked salmon and intertwined with whipped cream cheese makes this dish so creamy and comforting; it's all the taste of a bagel with lox except the salmon is cooked lightly, and you get no carbohydrates—until you taste the piping hot crunchy home fries that accompany this order. Or, try the La Mer Benedict: 2 poached eggs served with a hefty portion of crabmeat, avocado, and green onions, slathered in rich hollandaise sauce. Significantly lighter than the Scramble, this particular Benedict tastes luxurious and fresh to the last bite, with the high notes of crabmeat blending beautifully with the deeper notes of the egg and hollandaise sauce. The most popular item on the menu is hands-down the French Toast Tahiti—a thick slice of french toast stuffed with caramelized bananas and bits of walnut; this dish hardly requires maple syrup (though that was delicious, too).

Zuni Cafe, 1658 Market St., Hayes Valley, San Francisco, CA 94102; (415) 552-2522; www.zunicafe.com; American; $$$. Zuni is synonymous with great food in San Francisco. Everyone raves about the chicken for two, which is indeed quite fantastic: A whole chicken is roasted in the brick oven, cut into pieces for easy consumption, and served up with a warm sourdough bread salad that is steeped in the chicken drippings and mixed in with pine nuts, greens, and currants. But dreams are made of the bowl of polenta at Zuni Cafe—it's basically grits mixed in with mascarpone or Parmesan cheese; usually the server recommends opting for both.

It's so rich and so creamy that one bite of it and, quite literally, your worries fade to the background as all of your senses revel in the taste and texture. For your appetizer, don't miss out on the Caesar salad; with the scent of anchovies balanced by the creaminess of the dressing, it's as crisp and fresh as one can expect of a terrific salad. Anything you order at Zuni is excellent, and with the great service and space, it's one of the best date locations in the city.

Zushi Puzzle, 1910 Lombard St., Marina, San Francisco, CA 94123; (415) 931-9319; www.zushipuzzle.com; Japanese; $$$$$. "Roger, you are a God." I have said this countless times while eating at Zushi Puzzle. I have yet to see one sushi restaurant stock 7 different types of salmon (along with at least 50 different types of fresh fish) and lay them all out on a plate before you as nigiri—with each of the 7 varieties tasting distinctly different! Also, outside of Tokyo, I haven't seen anyone bring out the entire carcass of a 300-pound tuna from the kitchen to the sushi bar, to scrape out the cheek to make something Chef Roger lovingly calls "ocean beef" (and it does taste amazingly like filet mignon!). I highly recommend sitting at the sushi bar and having Roger serve you omakase-style ("chef's choice"); course after course, your taste buds will be titillated from start to finish. Not to be missed is what the chef calls, "the best hand roll" which is usually Roger's first course for his sushi bar omakase patrons. Also amazing are all of the *toro* (tuna belly) varieties including the albacore tuna; the Kobe beef nigiri topped with *foie gras* and a drop of truffle oil; the platter of all his white fish and then the platter of all his red fish; and finally, marvel as

he fillets a flying fish, pencil fish and whole mackerel to make into nigiri for you right on the spot. Cost is high; with a bottle of great sake (about $80), I have never left here with a bill less than $300 for two people. Ever.

Chile Pies and Ice Cream, 601 Baker St., Western Addition/ NOPA, San Francisco, CA 94117; (415) 614-9411; www.greenchile kitchen.com/chilepies. Thinking about Chile Pies makes me sigh. Even though I don't usually have a sweet tooth, this place often makes me think of feasting on just pies and ice cream and skipping lunch and dinner to have as much of it as possible. Thoughts of throwing your whole face into one of the buttermilk lemon pies will haunt you—and their well-known Green Chile Apple Pie a la mode with cheddar crust is so fresh and sweet that even someone like me will give up a juicy steak for another order of this. With pies baked fresh daily, Chile Pies makes pies cool again—forget the cupcakes; give me a good ol' pie any day. Another menu item to try is the "pie shake": you pick a pie, pick an ice cream, and a few minutes later, a miracle is produced in front of you.

DeLessio Market and Bakery, 302 Broderick St., Western Addition/ NOPA; San Francisco, CA 94117; (415) 552-8077; www.delessio market.com. For breakfast, you come into this store for some *rabanada* (a Brazilian take on french toast) and a fresh cup of coffee. For lunch, you come in here to get their roast beef sandwich—perfectly rare cuts piled high on a Kaiser bun with all the fixings. While there, you pick up dinner because eating the hot items available in this store is a bit like going home to your mom's kitchen. The baby back ribs and the meat loaf are the favorites here, and paired up with a serving (or four) of mac and cheese, you and your family can be set for the evening. But then you might as well devour their tres leches cake; it very well may be the best cake in San Francisco, with the creamy sweet milk flavors paired with the meringue on top and tiny pieces of kiwi and pineapple. I could conceivably live in this store. There is a second location at 1695 Market St., Hayes Valley, San Francisco, CA 94103; (415) 552-5559.

Nijiya Market, 1737 Post St., Japantown, San Francisco, CA 94115; (415) 563-1901; www.nijiya.com. You don't come to Nijiya for cheap prices. You do come to Nijiya for sashimi-grade fresh fish, fresh *natto* (fermented soybeans), and access to all kinds of Japanese goodies imported for the San Francisco residents. The space is creatively packed in to make as much shelf-space as possible, and maneuvering around the aisles can take some patience. But it's the one place in San Francisco where you can shop for fresh *uni, maguro,* and even mackerel—and bring it all home for a fraction of the price you'd pay at a sushi restaurant. While they do sell pre-packaged *natto* here, you definitely want to try the fresh variety imported from Japan—if you can handle it.

Richmond & Sunset

Both the Richmond and Sunset districts have an "inner" and "outer" designation to split up an otherwise large area that makes up most of the western part of San Francisco. For both districts, the inner areas are to the east, heading toward downtown, and the outer districts are the western parts of the districts, heading straight to the Pacific Ocean.

Richmond

The Richmond district includes all of San Francisco north of the Golden Gate Park and west of Arguello Boulevard (also known as 1st Avenue). Originally, the area had a heavy Russian and Irish immigrant population. To this day, the Richmond district has quite a few Irish bars, but it is heavily populated by the Chinese. In fact, Clement Street, between Arguello and Park Presidio, is also referred to as "New Chinatown"; many people will claim the food here is better than San Francisco's original Chinatown near North Beach, which has become more a tourist attraction than the hub of great Chinese food. Many of the Asian restaurants are also located in this district. Other than the major streets like Geary Boulevard and 19th Avenue, much of this district is residential with duplexes and flats. Home prices, compared to the rest of San Francisco, are considered moderate; it's cheaper to live here than SOMA or other popular neighborhoods, but your commute to the freeway or the other side of town can occasionally take an exorbitant amount of time, depending on traffic.

Sunset

The first thing that comes to mind when one thinks of the Sunset district is the famous (or infamous) fog of San Francisco. It tends to make for dramatic postcard photos of the city, but honestly, very few of the residents really like this fog. With the Pacific Ocean coastline serving as the western border of the "outer Sunset," the residents of this beautiful area commonly cannot even see the ocean due to the heavy fog. This area has some well-known city landmarks like the San Francisco Zoo, but the "inner Sunset" is better known today for good food options. Like Richmond, the Sunset is also heavily inhabited by the Chinese population, and naturally, Asian cuisine abounds in this area, ranging from good Indian and Thai restaurants, along with well-known Chinese restaurants, usually on Irving Street or Taraval Street.

Sunset is the largest district of San Francisco, and of all the major neighborhoods of San Francisco (excepting the outer, less-popular ones), it is most economical to live in this area, compared to San Francisco standards anyway. While it's close to the I-280 leading south, commuting to most other parts of San Francisco is toughest when you live here, and a drive across the city has been known to take over one hour in heavy traffic.

Foodie Faves

Bella Trattoria, 3854 Geary Blvd., Inner Richmond, San Francisco, CA 94118; (415) 221-0305; www.bellatrattoriasf.com; Italian; $$. Romantic and cozy, this small Italian restaurant serves up some fine Italian fare. Without being too pricey, the location is ideal for dates and sharing good food while enjoying a bottle of delicious Italian wine. While all of their pasta dishes have been good, I never visit this restaurant without ordering the baked polenta with Gorgonzola and shiitake mushrooms; this appetizer ranks up there as one of my favorite dishes in San Francisco. Also notable are their gnocchi choices—especially the duck gnocchi with its deep flavors and the ideal chewiness one wants from a well-made gnocchi. Service is friendly, and the staff goes out of their way to ensure a smooth experience here. The restaurant is quickly becoming a popular place for larger groups to dine, too, with prior reservations, of course. Groups with 10 to 15 in their party should be able to have a nice dining experience here, and you can request a prix-fixe menu that will delight all in your party

Burma Superstar, 309 Clement St., Inner Richmond, San Francisco, CA 94118; (415) 387-2147; www.burmasuperstar.com; Burmese; $$. This place is always bustling with a long wait out the door during peak meal times. If you haven't tried Burmese food, it's an interesting blend between Indian and Thai cuisines that is ideal for lunch or dinner. Burma Superstar doesn't take reservations, so your visits just have to be planned during off-peak hours, or go expecting a long wait. The tea leaf salad is a combination of lettuce, tomatoes, and fermented tea leaves, mixed together with nuts, sunflower seeds, and sesame seeds, and tossed with fried garlic slices and fried chickpeas. Extremely refreshing, this appetizer brings your palate to life for the entrees. The curries are all creamier than one would expect of Indian curries and less spicy in comparison. I recommend the pork curry with potatoes. Make sure to try the coconut rice here as it's fragrant and enhances whichever dish you order. Also notably good is the chicken dhal and braised pork belly, which tastes as good as it sounds.

Chapeau!, 126 Clement St., Inner Richmond, San Francisco, CA 94118; (415) 750-9787; www.chapeausf.com; French; $$$$. Located on the innermost area of Clement Street, Chapeau is an unexpected gem amongst primarily small, casual Asian restaurants and neighborhood bars on this street. Formal and beautiful, with a full bar and outstanding wine list with both Napa Valley and French wines, Chapeau is a quaint and formal French restaurant serving up what might be considered San Francisco's finest French cooking. With a customizable prix-fixe menu served nightly, Chef Philippe Gardelle greets you personally before your culinary excursion begins, and every lady's evening will end with a farewell kiss from the chef himself. Not to be missed at this restaurant are the veal sweetbreads and seared *foie gras;* everything you order off of this menu will rival the best you've ever had of that specific entree. For dessert, do not miss the french toast with hazelnut ice cream; even if you think you're stuffed, make sure you order this. Trust me—you will find room in your stomach for this one.

Craw Station, 1336 9th Ave., Inner Sunset, San Francisco CA 94122; (415) 682-9980; www.crawstation.com; Cajun; $$$. It opened in February 2011, and quickly it became the Sunset district's sweetheart. The food is excellent, but the owners really make your visit here worthwhile, personalizing everything to you. It's one of the few places in the city that will actually deliver the level of spice you request, and when I requested "dynamite—but make it double dynamite" for the crawfish, that was exactly what they delivered. The seafood is combined with the sauce into plastic bags and cooked inside the bag, and placed into a bucket to be served to you in the steaming plastic bag. The quality of ingredients here is superb, with huge shrimp, crawfish that are actually pretty meaty, and even the habañero they use to spice up the sauce was first-rate; I have never found as much flavor in habañero peppers. Their proprietary sauce is simply delicious, full of garlic and spices, and it works so beautifully with the seafood. Order some rice to mix in, and you will end up dreaming of that sauce for weeks to come. The cost is relatively economical for fresh seafood, and when the steaming hot "bag" of seafood in sauce is presented to you, you'll quietly vow to yourself to return monthly for an amazing dose of spices.

Curry Village, 1386 9th Ave., Inner Sunset, San Francisco, CA 94122; (415) 731-2388; Indian; $$. If you're going to do a buffet-style restaurant, this is the way to do it. On a nightly basis, Curry Village offers up some good Indian cooking in a long buffet line, with fresh nan, mango lassi, samosas, and a variety of other great Indian fare available for the taking. The dhal I had here was good, as were the several types of curries they offer. When I first went to review this restaurant, they offered me a bunch of freshly prepared a la carte menu items from the kitchen—and I will say that the owner-chef in the kitchen can put together one mean Indian dish. If you are ordering a la carte, definitely try the tandoori salmon, which was exemplary and came out sizzling on a hot plate. Free chai tea is served generously throughout the meal.

D&A Cafe, 407 Clement St., Inner Richmond, San Francisco, CA 94118; (415) 668-7882; Chinese; $. What a fun place this is! The food here is prepared fast and fresh, and the prices are unbelievably cheap, with happy hour pricing intermittently throughout the day during nonpeak times; items are priced as low as $2 per order for full-size servings. Some impressive things on the menu have been crispy tofu, deep-fried stomach (if you like pork belly, you will love this!), Chinese greens, abalone porridge, and sautéed oysters with vegetables. Combine these with the enormous menu, fast preparation time, late-night hours (until 1 a.m.), and the really friendly service that abounds here, and this is easily the one of the top choices for late-night dining in San Francisco.

El Burrito eXpress, 601 Taraval St., Outer Sunset, San Francisco, CA 94116; (415) 566-8300; www.ebxsf.com; Mexican; $. In a city where there are plenty of choices when it comes to Mexican food—especially burritos—there has to be something special for one particular restaurant to stand out. EBX does this by using quality ingredients that are freshly prepared, and wrapping it all up in a warm, comforting tortilla. They make their own tortilla chips and also offer a fascinatingly delicious selection of salsas. The *carnitas* burrito is about as rich as one can handle, jam-packed with rice, black beans, guacamole, a refreshing tomato salsa, sour cream, and loads of steak, all firmly wrapped inside a large tortilla. As big as this is, it's surprisingly not messy, and the meat is tender and juicy; with the right balance of creaminess in each burrito, the meat and salsa take center stage. My favorite is the surf and turf burrito with a mouthful of steak and shrimp in each glorious bite. Also worth tasting is the Norcal Burrito with tofu; vegetarian as it may be, it's quite a tasty beast—and the breakfast burritos with scrambled eggs, cheese, sausage, and potatoes, topped with fresh salsa, are always a huge hit. A second, newer location is at 1812 Divisadero St., Pacific Heights, San Francisco, CA 94115; (415) 776-4246.

Good Luck Dim Sum, 736 Clement St., Inner Richmond, San Francisco, CA 94118; (415) 386-3388; www.goodluckdimsum.com; Chinese/Dim Sum; $. If I had $8 left in my wallet and I needed to eat with it for two days, I'd run to Good Luck Dim Sum and splurge there. Most of the time, when the staff (who probably won't even greet you and just nod at the menus) tells you how much your order will be, you wonder if you should have them recalculate because it's entirely too cheap. Every time I go to this tiny hole-in-the-wall restaurant, I quickly place my order, hand it to the ladies behind the counter, and they pile everything you ordered into a take-out box. The box hardly shuts, and then they tell you, "$4." The food is freshly made on an almost hourly basis, and each basket is steaming hot with quite a big array of dim sum choices. I particularly like the *siu mai* (pork dumplings with shrimp), with the *har gow* (shrimp dumplings) coming in a close second; I also like the sticky rice in lotus leaf. With most of the items, I prefer to bring them home and reheat one more time to make sure they remain piping hot when being eaten.

Gordo Taqueria, 2252 Clement St., Inner Richmond, San Francisco, CA 94121; (415) 387-4484; www.gordotaqueria.com; Mexican; $. It really depends on whom you ask, but some people will leave the Mission, an area full of Mexican restaurants, to drive out to the Richmond for a Gordo's burrito; others will claim that this isn't a real burrito, and will travel to the Mission to eat at a Mexican joint. What Gordo's offers is a truly customizable burrito and/or quesadilla option, and you can pick and choose what you want, or don't want, in your own burrito. It's wrapped right, not that messy, and overall the ingredients are fresh and properly prepared to make for a good meal. Having been to Mexico, I will say that this is not quite what a burrito tastes like in Mexico, but it's good nonetheless, and it won't require you to drive clear across town to go to the Mission. Open until 10 p.m.; check the website for additional locations throughout the western section of San Francisco and new stores in the East Bay.

Halu, 312 8th Ave., Inner Richmond, San Francisco, CA 94118; (415) 221-9165; Japanese; $$. Combine a tiny location with a pack of hungry San Franciscans wanting to eat good food, and you end up with Halu. Much like the typical yakitori joint, the highlight of

their menu is the grilled items, like beef tongue, pork jowl on a skewer, bacon-wrapped scallops, or grilled chicken skewers, which are all must-try items while here. Their regular scallop yakitori, called the *kushikatsu* scallop, features a scallop breaded with panko bread crumbs, pan-seared, and served with a tangy dipping sauce; the delicate sweetness and tenderness of the scallop is top-notch. They serve a pretty mean and relatively spicy bowl of ramen, too; if you like it spicy, request the lava ramen, order it extra spicy, and it will be provided for you. The location is tiny, so unless you are arriving at opening time, expect a wait. Fortunately, there are plenty of bars in the neighborhood where you can begin drinking until your table at Halu is ready.

Hanuri Korean BBQ, 4217 Geary Blvd., Inner Richmond, San Francisco, CA 94118; (415) 221-5227; www.hanuribbq.com; Barbecue/Korean; $$$. This is, hands down, one of the nicest Korean barbecue restaurants in San Francisco. The layout is such that large groups can be accommodated, and the husband-and-wife team tend to your every need. Their barbecue meat items are first-rate; in particular, always order the *kalbi,* which are short ribs marinated in soy sauce, sugar, garlic, and spices, and the pork belly. The *kalbi* offers the ideal amount of saltiness and sweetness each time, and the pork belly is absolutely delicious, slathered thickly with soybean paste that really melds nicely with the fattiness of the pork. Become a regular here and you will find that the owner takes

TODAY'S FORECAST . . .

Let's be honest—the weather in this city is pretty unusual.

Just 25 miles south of San Francisco, it might be 100 degrees; 13 miles to the east, it might be equally hot—but in this city, it might be a crisp 65 degrees. Don't think of this as your usual 65 degrees either, because it's unusually cold when you realize your neighbors just miles away are swimming, while you bring out your coat and boots in August—which is one of our particularly cold months. Normally, the warmest months in San Franciso are not the summer months but as we head into fall—perhaps September and October; I've seen warmer days in November than I have in August.

But this is also one of the only places in the world where you can don your boots and scarves when the remainder of the world complains of heat waves and electricity bills. Most people don't appreciate the cool weather here, but it really is one of my favorite things about living in this city.

The fluctuation in temperature is really not that severe for most of the months of the year; we rarely get below 50 and rarely go above 75 on warm days. Naturally, due to this weather, most of the city isn't equipped with central air—and on those rare days (about a handful per year) when the heat wave rolls in and the city hits 99 degrees, San Franciscans panic.

great care of you and treats you like family. The *banchan* array is tasty and plentiful. In the summertime, I order *naeng myun* here (cold noodles in beef broth), but otherwise I stick to the grilled meats and might order a stew. Ideally, always order a bottle of *soju* to accompany your meal; that's the Korean way. See Hanuri Korean BBQ's recipe for **Kalbi** on p. 275.

Hard Knox Cafe, 2448 Clement St., Outer Richmond, San Francisco, CA 94121; (415) 752-3770; www.hardknoxcafe.com; American; $$. Hard Knox is synonymous in San Francisco with true soul food. Interestingly enough, this place is owned by an Asian family, with chef-owner Tony Hua at the helm. The Southern cuisine that is pumped out of this kitchen at an alarmingly fast pace is nothing short of outstanding. I've been known to order extra sides of the grits here, as they're so addictive; the fried chicken is crispy and spicy; and the braised short ribs fall apart at the touch, leaving you wanting more even after your stomach is filled over capacity. The macaroni and cheese is spectacular, and the collard greens should not missed. Their breakfast options, available until 3 p.m. daily, are also delicious and as hearty (and heavy) as you would want and expect of Hard Knox. Their original location is in the Dogpatch district of San Francisco at 2448 Clement St., Richmond, San Francisco, CA 94121; (415) 752-3770. Their Richmond location is bigger and newer—and perhaps better, especially with easier parking. Hard Knox feeds not only our stomachs, but our souls on a regular basis.

Izakaya Sozai, 1500 Irving St., Inner Sunset, San Francisco, CA 94122; (415) 742-5122; www.izakayasozai.com; Japanese; $$. The cost of this meal will depend entirely on your appetite. What Izakaya Sozai offers is a large selection of Japanese tapas, or small plates, most costing under $10 and all tasting wonderful. Where else can you go where you can start your meal with a small bowl of raw octopus marinated in wasabi sauce, eat a couple skewers of pork jowl and short ribs cooked beautifully, then have some braised pork belly while munching on freshly garlic-sautéed shishito peppers, while dreaming about the creamy and perfect ramen that would be coming at the end of the meal? How about a heartier, spicy tuna concoction served atop crispy rice? Or a *hamachi* carpaccio that can make you swoon? With a top-notch selection of sakes available, the prices for food and drinks are fair and the service is efficient. You can order as much or as little as you want, and despite it being a Japanese restaurant, you can easily eat for under $25 per person—or the sky is the limit.

Kabuto Sushi, 5121 Geary Blvd., Inner Richmond, San Francisco, CA 94118; (415) 752-5652; www.kabutosushi.com; Japanese; $$$$. This tiny little Japanese-owned restaurant is a gem in the Richmond. Like a few other restaurants in San Francisco, it takes the traditional and gives it a whirl, and while not offering fusion, per se, the chef at Kabuto uses his imagination for menu offerings. But most important is that Kabuto has very fresh fish, and while not all the creations hit a home run, you do give points for effort. The 1849 is worth one try, and I say "one" due to its extraordinary cost at $7.50 per oyster: It's a freshly shucked oyster with *uni, tobiko,* quail egg, and ponzu sauce, garnished with gold flakes. Other creations include a lamb-apple sushi, *foie gras* sushi with a raspberry reduction, and a couple of varieties of crepe sushi. This is all in addition to the traditional lineup of sushi that Kabuto offers. Reservations are highly recommended because the restaurant is small and fills up rapidly past 6 p.m. While they have a substantial dinner menu, I suggest you stick to the sushi here and let the chef challenge your taste buds.

Koo, 408 Irving St., Inner Sunset, San Francisco, CA 94122; (415) 731-7077; www.sushikoo.com; Japanese; $$$$. Koo has been a popular sushi restaurant in San Francisco for some time. The Japanese owner, Chef Kiyoshi Hayakawa has put together a creative yet authentic menu offering some truly interesting combinations. Definitely, start your meal with Spoonful of Happiness; for $10, you get one spoonful of *uni, tobiko,* and a quail egg in ponzu sauce along with another spoonful of *ankimo* (monkfish liver) wrapped in whitefish and doused in truffle oil. A good selection of the popular rolls is available at Koo, including the dragon roll, but the true highlight at Koo is the sushi and sashimi (like the *uni*), with much of the fish flown in from Japan that day. As such, the price of a meal at Koo is also considerably high, especially compared to other neighborhood joints. Whenever possible, sit at the bar with the sushi chefs, and let them serve you omakase ("chef's choice"), their freshest and best at their discretion.

Mayflower Seafood Restaurant, 6255 Geary Blvd., Outer Richmond, San Francisco, CA 94121; (415) 387-8338; www.may flower-seafood.com; Chinese/Dim Sum; $$. This is my go-to restaurant for dim sum, as it meets all the requirements and expectations one has of dim sum. It's tasty, cheap, fast, and filling. On weekends, this dim sum restaurant can fill up fast and require a significant wait; weekdays are usually much better. The *siu mai* (pork dumpling with shrimp) offered here is large and topped with fresh roe and a small shrimp; the *har gow* is filled with fresh shrimp and served extraordinarily hot. While dim sum is their main fare during the day, the kitchen is opened for special orders. I will usually order a seafood pan-fried noodle, which is absolutely delicious, if not sinful, with crispy fried egg noodles with fresh scallops, squid, shrimp, and freshly sautéed vegetables on top, drizzled in a clear gravy—it is so savory! Even with many servings of dim sum and a special order, the cost per person rarely, if ever, goes over $15 or $20, at most. The restaurant also offers takeout, and it's the perfect food to pick up when you're about to start a short road trip as much of dim sum can easily be eaten with your fingers. For the evenings, this place turns into a regular Chinese restaurant, serving up fresh seafood and other Chinese dishes a la carte. The majority of its clientele seems to be Chinese folks, which is always a good sign.

My Tofu House, 4627 Geary Blvd., Inner Richmond, San Francisco, CA 94118; (415) 750-1818; www.mytofuhouse.com; Korean; $$. This Korean restaurant serves up tofu soup in a clay pot that comes to your table bubbling over from being almost at full boil. You can opt for vegetarian tofu soup, or include seafood (like oysters, shrimp, and clams), or opt for meat instead by ordering tofu soup with beef, pork, or a combination of the above. You can also pick your level of desired spiciness; a nonspicy version is available as well for those with less adventurous palates. With your order comes a select array of *banchan,* or side dishes, and unlike most places, included in the side dishes is one fried yellow corvina per customer—which is a popular fish in Korea. My Tofu House also offers barbecued Korean meats like *kalbi* (short ribs), *bulgogi* (marinated beef) and *dwae-jee bulgogi* (spicy marinated pork). While there may be a wait during peak meal times, the turnover rate is relatively quick. You can always go shopping at the Korean market next door while you wait your turn to be seated.

Namu, 439 Balboa St., San Francisco, Inner Richmond, CA 94118; (415) 386-8332; www.namusf.com; California/Asian Fusion; $$$. One thing that California does well is create a mishmash of cuisines and call it "fusion." While not all fusion food is good, Namu is exemplary in that it takes a foundation of Korean cooking, and spins it into masterpiece that can only be called "classic California cuisine." You don't come here to eat real Korean food; you come here to find out to what heights one can take Korean food. Offering creative combinations like loco moco–kimchee fried rice, or short rib *(kalbi)* tacos wrapped in nori, Namu hits a homerun with the classics like the hamburger, too, that is served with additions like daikon and aioli; it's one of the most popular things on Namu's menu. A must-try dish at Namu is the shiitake dumplings served in a dashi broth, which is out-of-this-world delicious. While they allegedly serve ramen here, the story goes that they limit it to only 6 bowls per day, so I have not yet had the honor of having tried it.

Pacific Catch, 1200 9th Ave., Inner Sunset, San Francisco, CA 94122; (415) 504-6905; www.pacificcatch.com; Seafood/Asian Fusion; $$. Not only does Pacific Catch offer fantastic food, but it also has one of the nicest lounges available in the Sunset area. Whether it is happy hours with friends or a nice dinner date, Pacific Catch is good for virtually any occasion. Very fresh seafood is served here. The trio ceviche presentation is always fun to taste as a starter with ceviche from Mexico, Hawaii and Peru represented on one platter. The deep-fried oysters served with tartar sauce are one of my favorite deep-fried dishes in the city, with plump, large oysters battered and deep-fried to a nice crisp. Served on newspaper and in a basket, don't skip this! The wasabi bowl with Hawaiian poke is a bowl of rice (brown or white) served with daikon, wakame salad, and ginger, sprinkled with soy sauces; you mix it up and it's like eating a sashimi salad with rice—fresh and tasty. If you have the room, try the traditional Baja tacos; the fish is deep-fried and served with fresh cabbage, avocado-tomatillo salsa, a jalapeño tartar sauce, and lime— the combination is packed with fresh ingredients and a great combination of texture and flavors. Check the website for other locations in the city.

Pho Clement, 239 Clement St., Inner Richmond, San Francisco, CA 94118; (415) 379-9008; Vietnamese; $. The pho here is what we typically expect of pho restaurants: a hot bowl of beef broth with perfectly cooked noodles, and a side dish of fresh sprouts, basil leaves, jalapeños, and lemon. Service is friendly and fast here, and when on a time crunch during lunch, you can easily enter and exit within 30 minutes. They offer a small, medium, and large pho, and even I, with a typically large appetite, could not come close to finishing the large. With a vast menu, they offer all varieties of pho as well as a wide array of other entrees like banh mi (Vietnamese sandwiches) and pork chop and rice with fried egg. All the dishes are under $10 and freshly made. Quick, tasty, and delicious, Pho Clement has a second location at 5423 Geary Blvd. in San Francisco, also in the Richmond.

The Pot's, 2652 Judah St., Inner Sunset, San Francisco, CA 94122; (415) 682-7889; Chinese/Japanese; $$. This is a newer addition to the otherwise saturated all-you-can-eat hot pot and shabu-shabu choices in San Francisco, but it's a notable one in that the Pot's has taken the best of Chinese hot pot and Japanese shabu-shabu and mixed them up into one. While shabu-shabu tends to offer only meat and vegetables, with some noodles, the Pot's includes typical hot pot offers like pork, shrimp and lobster dumplings, stomach, tripe, coagulated blood, at least five different kinds of noodles, and a slew of different vegetable options like bok choy, and prime rib slices in addition to lamb and pork. Unlike most shabu-shabu restaurants, the Pot offers a large selection of soup-base choices and allows you to pick 2 soup bases that they will serve divided in one pot. The cost of the meal is also really economical, especially given the vast amount of choices; week-ends cost a little more per person than weekdays, but compared to other options, it's still a bargain. Service is friendly. At this time, they do not have a liquor license, and it's unknown whether they will have one in the future.

PPQ Beef Noodle House Restaurant, 1816 Irving St., Inner Sunset, San Francisco, CA 94122; (415) 661-8869; Vietnamese; $. Everyone tends to have their favorite pho joint in the city, and PPQ ranks among the top five on that list for most people. The typical southern-style pho is served here, with your regular choices of rare beef, beef balls, tendon, and more; my experience at PPQ is that the broth is very good, full of flavor and always fresh. The noodles are always well-cooked. PPQ offers other noodle dishes and rice plates, but is primarily known for their pho. This restaurant is generally packed during mealtimes and is relatively busy during off-hours as well. Expect a short wait if you go, and you will be rewarded with a generous bowl of pho for a really economical price. Also in the Richmond you will find their sister location, **PPQ Dungeness Island Vietnamese Cuisine** (below), which serves pho but is better-known for their delicious crab offerings.

PPQ Dungeness Island Vietnamese Cuisine, 2332 Clement St., Outer Richmond, San Francisco, CA 94121; (415) 386-8266; Vietnamese/Seafood; $$$. PPQ has a full menu that serves pho in addition to rice plates and other Vietnamese cuisine. But the popularity of this place is entirely due to the crab and garlic noodle combination they serve. PPQ offers Dungeness crab in 5 different ways: roasted, peppercorn, curry, drunken, or spicy. I've tried all but the curry, and while all 4 were exemplary, my favorites were the peppercorn and spicy, which also came with little bits and pieces of garlic and peppers, stir-fried to a crisp. The atmosphere here is much more casual than its main competitor, **Thanh Long** (p. 202), and the prices reflect that, too, as everything is priced slightly lower. Between the two, Thanh Long is more ideal for dates, if eating crab with your date is your thing, and PPQ is ideal for big gatherings with friends.

Q Restaurant and Wine Bar, 225 Clement St., Inner Richmond, San Francisco, CA 94118; (415) 752-2298; www.qrestaurant.com;

American; $$. Offering true American comfort food for brunch, lunch, and dinner, Q Restaurant is a cozy, small restaurant that is quintessential San Francisco. It exudes a neighborhood restaurant feel, but people from all over the city come out to dine here. While they have plentiful salad choices on the menu, the real appeal of this restaurant is in the hearty entree choices, like the macaroni and cheese with Tater Tots, which should not be missed, along with the meat loaf, or pork ribs with beans. They serve beer and wine, with a good array of both. Service is always friendly, and while they do not take reservations, and it usually requires a substantial wait to get seated, there's plenty of bar options in the area at which to kill time.

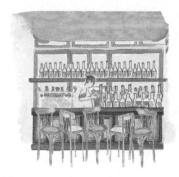

The Richmond, 615 Balboa St., Inner Richmond, San Francisco, CA 94118; (415) 379-8988; www.therichmondsf.com; American; $$. The atmosphere here is warm and quaint. This might be the only place in San Francisco where I have found an $11 bottle of Chilean wine, and it was actually delicious. The Richmond strives to remain a neighborhood restaurant offering reasonable, if not surprisingly low, prices for their food, all in an atmosphere that rivals many bigger and fancier restaurants. The short ribs with mashed potatoes and greens offered here were so savory and decadent, it left me wanting more of the heavily braised meat and the buttery potatoes!

The pork loin is tender, and served with a creamy macaroni and cheese. The soft-shell crab salad on the menu must be tasted—the freshness of this dish pops out—and if you like *foie gras,* their seared version was delicious. Walk-ins are welcome, but to ensure prompt seating, reservations are recommended.

San Tung, 1031 Irving St., Inner Sunset, San Francisco, CA 94122; (415) 242-0828; www.santungrestaurant.com; Chinese; $$. This long-time Chinese establishment was put on the map for their Dry Fried Chicken Wings; I know people who salivate at the thought of these wings. They are fried to a crisp, and a sweet and tangy sauce is slathered all over them. Don't even try to eat them with utensils—just use your hands, as everyone else will be, too. Their hot-and-sour soup is consistently good, but even better is the sizzling rice soup, which I always order at the start. Served in a large bowl, one order is enough for a small bowl of soup for about four people. Unlike many other Chinese restaurants, they serve *jja-jiang myun* (black bean sauce over noodles) and *jjam bbong* (noodles in a spicy seafood soup), which are Cantonese-Korean dishes. Accordingly, they also serve a Chinese version of cabbage kimchee, which is quite potent in garlic flavor, though not too spicy. Definitely try the dried string beans; the string beans retain a fascinatingly good crunch even after being sautéed, and they're always seasoned perfectly. The cost is reasonable, but because of the good food and good cost, the wait is almost always long. I've been here at 4 p.m. on Sunday and was shocked at how many people were already waiting.

Shabu House, 5158 Geary Blvd., Inner Richmond, San Francisco, CA 94118; (415) 933-8600; www.myshabuhouse.com; Japanese; $$. At Shabu House, you can combine thinly sliced cuts of American Kobe beef and fresh vegetables with a hot soup, dipping and swirling to your heart's content; virtually no other cuisine is more comforting on the cold San Francisco nights. Based on the crowd here most nights—with a line out the door—it's safe to say many San Francisco residents agree. At the time of this writing, this is the best shabu-shabu restaurant in San Francisco. For those who have never tried shabu-shabu, a soup base is placed in front of you over a burner, along with a plate of thin, quickly cooking meat and a plate of fresh vegetables and udon noodles, all meant to be cooked in the boiling soup, then dipped into the ponzu or sesame sauce prior to being eaten. You can order by the plate; one order of meat (small or large) comes with one plate of vegetables/noodles, or you can opt for the all-you-can-eat option for $29.95, which gives you a limitless amount of meat and vegetables, perfect for hearty appetites. For an additional $10, you can include the all-you-can-drink option that includes the house hot sake and a good choice of Japanese beers. While these all-you-can-eat options are widely popular in San Francisco right now, there are very few places that can hold a candle to the quality and taste of Shabu House. Service can be slow, and they do not take reservations for parties smaller than 4 people. Walk-ins are accepted on the waiting list, but the wait can be ridiculously long. They have a bigger location in Burlingame, just a short drive south of the city, at 1150 Paloma Ave., Burlingame, CA 94010; (650) 558-8800.

Shimo Sushi, 2339 Clement St., Outer Richmond, San Francisco, CA 94121; (415) 752-4422; Japanese; $$$. Shimo is a tiny sushi restaurant located in the Outer Richmond that has been around for a long time. The sushi choices are pretty typical, and this is not really the place to go to try salmon from New Zealand, for instance. It is, however, a classic sushi restaurant that serves really fresh fish, with their *uni,* at least on my last visit, being quite spectacular. Service is basic, but the people who are loyal to Shimo seem to be diehard fans. I'd suggest trying to sit at the bar and befriending the chef, which, in my experience, always enhances the sushi-eating experience.

Social Kitchen and Brewery, 1326 9th Ave., Inner Sunset, San Francisco, CA 94122; (415) 681-0330; www.socialkitchenand brewery.com; American/Brewery/Gastropub; $$$. Social Kitchen is new to the San Francisco food scene, and has a great concept: Brew your own beer and serve it up in a hip and cool location, paired with awesome pub-style food while still offering meal-worthy items! It's a very 21st-century-esque place, located out in the Sunset. The first thing you notice here, from the moment you enter, is that the service is top-notch. With plentiful seating, the vibe is bustling, and hipsters from all across San Francisco drink and eat here—and this is not something all Sunset establishments can claim about themselves. Try the deep-fried brussels sprouts or the salmon burger; the macaroni and cheese is also quite delicious and goes nicely with many of their microbrewery beers.

Sociale, 3665 Sacramento St., Laurel Heights, San Francisco, CA 94118; (415) 921-3200; www.caffesociale.com; Italian; $$$. Stroll down a little alleyway in Laurel Heights and you will find this neighborhood gem with a lovely outdoor patio. Chef Harrison's cooking is simple but delicious, with starters like breaded and deep-fried cheese-stuffed olives. With items like duck meatballs and polenta fries, Sociale manages to serve comforting and hearty cuisine in a romantic and private location that feels secluded from the bustling city. The chef pairs beautifully seared scallops with slices of watermelon and an apple compote, taking the sweetness of the scallops to new heights—fruit and scallops! Be it how she cooks sweetbreads or puts together a carrot soup with prawns, or even better, the mushroom risotto, the chef at Sociale creates food that is synonymous with "flavor." If you like crab, don't miss out on the crab timbale—fresh crabmeat with shallots and chives atop a bed of English-pea puree and drizzled in a vinaigrette; it's a heavenly combination that exudes flavors long after the dish is done. The location is ideal for a romantic date, and on the rare warm night, the charming outdoor patio can't be beat.

Spices, 294 8th Ave., Inner Richmond, San Francisco, CA 94118; (415) 752-8884; www.spicesrestaurantonline.com; Taiwanese; $. Spices is a great restaurant to visit late at night, and for the really adventurous, while I can't be certain, this might be the only place serving up "stinky tofu," a very popular snack in China that is basically heavily fermented tofu that is well-known for the associated stench. I had seen this food item defeat even the daring Andrew Zimmern, the host of *Bizarre Foods* on the Food Network, during the Taiwan episode of the show. A couple of years later, it defeated me after three pieces too, but perhaps you would like to take a shot at it. With interesting items like lip-numbing spicy tendons, intestine casseroles, and other great items on their huge menu, everyone can pick and choose what they want to eat for minimal cost. Many nonspicy items are available on the menu. A second location is available at 291 6th Ave,, Richmond, San Francisco, CA 94118 (415) 752-8885.

Spruce, 3640 Sacramento St., Laurel Heights, San Francisco, CA 94118; (415) 931-5100; www.sprucesf.com; American; $$$$$. Chef Mark Sullivan owns one of San Francisco's finest and most under-rated dining establishments, and in the greater scheme of things, it's also newer on the high-end dining scene. Spruce's contemporary interior is sleek and beautiful, their bar stocks some of the finest spirits, and the food is exemplary of all things high-end dining should be. When at Spruce, always opt for soup as your first course; it doesn't matter what is offered that night—order it, and devour it.

I once had a cauliflower soup with orange oil and rinds that I will never forget. The burger is always at the top of everyone's list at Spruce, and it is quite spectacular with their homemade buns that are most similar to a freshly baked, more delicate English muffin; definitely request it with the duck-fat fries. Everything on the menu is delicious. Definitely try the halibut with asparagus in olive oil, and if they have it, order the fava bean-and-ricotta ravioli; I still remember this dish's intense creaminess! While I don't usually recommend wine pairings at all restaurants, I absolutely urge you to try the wine pairings here; what the kitchen creates, the sommelier makes soar. See Chef Mark Sullivan's recipe for **Chantenay Carrot Soup with Turmeric Dates & Almonds** on p. 264.

Taco Shop at Underdogs, 1824 Irving St., Inner Sunset, San Francisco, CA 94122; (415) 566-8700; www.tacoshopsf.com; Mexican; $$. With 10 plasma screens showing sports for the quintessential sports buff, Taco Shop serves up the tacos that **Nick's Crispy Tacos** (p. 246) has made famous. This place is co-owned by Nick Fasanella, and the tacos are just as good as his own store on Polk Street. The service is very casual, and the bartenders are friendly. The clientele is primarily here to watch the sports, but nobody can resist a taco "Nick's way," especially when it involves deep-frying the tortilla and loading globs of guacamole on the taco. Try the Baja fish taco, Nick's way, of course. Definitely order the sangria while here, but be forewarned: It's not very often you will pay close to $20 for 2 tacos and a pint of beer, and if you order the sangria, your total will go slightly over that amount—but it's worth it.

Thanh Long, 4101 Judah St., Inner Richmond, San Francisco, CA 94122; (415) 665-1146; www.anfamily.com; Vietnamese/Seafood; $$$. The An family began this restaurant over 30 years ago, and some say it was the first authentic Vietnamese restaurant in San Francisco. The atmosphere is more formal than at any of the other Vietnamese crab restaurants in San Francisco with the exception of Crustacean, their sister restaurant across town. With a good wine list and what I've found to be very courteous service, Thanh Long makes one mean roast crab, with secret spices and heavy on the garlic. The garlic noodles here are the best I've had in the city, and they're a must-try when ordering the crab. The crab is large and sold at market price; sharing one crab and an order of garlic noodles between two people is usually enough for most appetites. If you need a little more, their shaken beef with tender cuts of New York steak flambéed in wine is a good choice with some jasmine rice.

Tia Margarita, 300 19th Ave., Outer Richmond, San Francisco, CA 94121; (415) 752-9274; www.tiamargaritasf.com; Mexican; $$. Nowhere else in San Francisco have I found a better piña colada than what Francisco, the bartender at this restaurant, can make. Factor in the full bar, the great food, and warm atmosphere, and it's no wonder that I spend as much time here as I do. With every order comes a generous amount of tortilla chips and a mild salsa along with a strangely addictive spicier salsa. Be careful, though, because the two things not to be missed on this menu are the homemade guacamole as your starter, and the enchiladas *rancheras* with a fried egg on top as your entree; make sure you leave room for this! Request warm tortillas so you can clean off your plate with them.

Ton Kiang, 5821 Geary Blvd., Inner Richmond, San Francisco, CA 94121; (415) 387-8273; www.tonkiang.net; Chinese/Dim Sum; $$. The aura of Ton Kiang is a bit fancier than that of other dim sum locations throughout San Francisco. With the white tablecloths, branded napkins, and more formally trained servers, Ton Kiang caters to a slightly more American clientele, while retaining low prices and serving fresh and authentic food. This venue is more appropriate for business luncheons, compared to the bigger but more rundown location at **Mayflower Seafood Restaurant** (p. 189), but the food portions tend to be smaller and the service slower at Ton Kiang. Basically, I run to Ton Kiang only when Mayflower's line is too much, and I don't have the time or patience to wait there but must satisfy my dim sum craving. Ton Kiang also serves dim sum to 4 p.m., whereas Mayflower only serves it until 2:30, so definitely, if the other isn't available, Ton Kiang is a strong second choice in the neighborhood. Be sure to try the deep-fried oysters, *har gow,* and the pan-fried turnip cake, which is quite delicious at Ton Kiang.

Toyose, 3814 Noriega St., Outer Sunset, San Francisco, CA 94122; (415) 731-0232; Korean; $$. Imagine my shock when I discovered something akin to San Francisco's best Korean cooking inside a garage in the outer, outer Sunset. This place is so far out there that other than my infrequent visits to the Pacific Ocean, there was no other reason to come out this far. However, once you enter this garage space (it was literally a garage to an apartment building prior to its renovation into a restaurant), you feel like you stepped into a small restaurant in the outskirts of Seoul, Korea. The food here is actually quite delicious, and the menu is everything you'd expect of a small *soju* and beer joint. There's a large selection of what you'd consider bar food, along with many entrees that make for a good meal. Most notable is their spicy pork *(jae-yook bok-keum)*, kimchee fried rice, and their sizzling broiled eel was absolutely perfect with a hot bowl of rice. The ambience is extremely casual, and the service is friendly and relaxed. This is a good spot to bring a few friends to share some good Korean cooking while taking shots of *soju*. One downer? The restaurant doesn't serve a lot of *banchan* (side dishes), which is one of the main highlights of visiting a Korean restaurant.

Troya, 349 Clement St., Inner Richmond, San Francisco, CA 94118; (415) 379-6000; www.troyasf.com; Mediterranean; $$. It's a cute joint, cozy as can be, filled with friendly servers and offering great Turkish cuisine. Many of the customers are locals to the neighborhood, and it's clear they've been frequenting Troya for years. The selection of food varies from light and fun to heavier and filling so order accordingly. Try the halloumi cheese dish, which is balanced nicely by the tomatoes and cress; definitely order the *beyti,* a delectable lamb dish wrapped in bread and served with yogurt sauce. They have daily specials, and try to leave room for the Turkish coffee that is strong yet not offensive. With happy hour specials where select appetizers are only $5, it would be worth your time to visit Troya for an early evening treat with a glass of wine.

Wooden Charcoal Korean Barbecue House, 4611 Geary Blvd., Inner Richmond, San Francisco, CA 94118; (415) 751-6336; www.kvwcr.com; Barbecue/Korean; $$$. It's a bit on the overpriced end of things for what it is, but this restaurant does serve up pretty tasty Korean food, and they are open until 2 a.m. on weeknights, 4 a.m. on weekend nights. For that alone, given the lack of late-night dining in San Francisco (particularly in this neighborhood), I visit this location often. The *banchan* (side dishes) served with every meal is quite abundant and the menu choices are standard Korean restaurant fare. Where else, though, can you grill Korean barbecue meats at 2 a.m.? Try the *bee jee jjigae,* which, in exact translation, is a "bean curd dreg casserole." The marinated rib and spicy pork are also delicious.

Landmarks

Beach Chalet/Park Chalet, 1000 Great Hwy., Outer Richmond, San Francisco, CA 94121; (415) 386-8439; www.beachchalet.com;

American; $$. Park Chalet and Beach Chalet are both located on the same property. Beach Chalet is upstairs, serving the menu, overlooking Ocean Beach; Park Chalet is downstairs, surrounded by open windows, and the backyard is technically a part of Golden Gate Park. While this is more of a tourist destination on Great Highway, second in popularity only to **Cliff House** (see below), it's a madhouse when the sun finally shines on Ocean Beach. All the San Francisco residents will bring blankets, dogs, children, Frisbees, and lawn chairs to come to Park Chalet for a good beer and pretty decent bites. Besides tourists, I don't know anyone who actually comes to Park Chalet to eat a full meal, but I do know that we all go to grab beers and order the truffle fries, macaroni and cheese (which is quite good!), and perhaps a few other bar bites that all match nicely with the large selection of local beers offered here.

Cliff House, 1090 Point Lobos Ave., Outer Richmond, San Francisco, CA 94121; (415) 386-3330; www.cliffhouse.com; American; $$$. Nowhere else in San Francisco can you get the view that Cliff House offers. This old and classic building used to have dark wood panels, and with an Irish coffee in hand, you could sit in one of the embroidered chairs overlooking the Pacific Ocean, waves crashing against the rocks. While it was a tourist location back then, too, you could just feel the history in those walls. Then they underwent construction and completely rebranded the establishment. Gone are the wood panels and in are the enormous windows with a stunningly modern decor, offering a better view of the same ocean. Some of the mood is lost, but it's replaced with grandiosity. Whether you visit Sutro's, the restaurant within Cliff House, the Terrace Room for brunch, or the bistro for a brew, keep in mind that you're at what is potentially San Francisco's number-one tourist destination, and remind yourself—you did not come here for the food.

Specialty Stores, Markets & Producers

New May Wah Supermarket, 707 Clement St., Inner Richmond, San Francisco, CA 94118; (415) 221-9826. It'll be tough to find a place where you can buy more groceries for less money than New May Wah. From an impressive selection of live shellfish to heads and body parts of all kinds of fish and animals laid out on ice, this grocery is incomparable to any within city limits, and second only to supermarkets like Ranch 99, which would require leaving San Francisco. If something is of Asian origin, chances are likely it's in this store somewhere. But then, so is much of the Asian population in the city, so be prepared for a shoving match to the cash register, or to be pushed over for a head of cabbage. Just keep your sense of humor and know you're buying a lot for a little bit of money.

Y&Y Vietnamese Deli, 661 Clement St., Inner Richmond, San Francisco, CA 94118; (415) 221-5722. It's hard to get cheaper, or better, banh mi (Vietnamese sandwiches) than the one Y&Y serves up. You will think this is a produce store or market, but never would you guess that inside, sweet Vietnamese ladies will make you a banh mi to rival all banh mis, and that noodle soups and plate lunches can be pumped out of here like nobody's business. Go strolling in there for your produce needs, then put your bags down and order to your heart's content; with this menu, it will be hard to top $10 per person unless you practice eating as a sport.

Bayview–Hunters Point, Bernal Heights & Glen Park

As mentioned, San Francisco has a whopping 89 neighborhoods. Some are much smaller than others, but throughout a city that is only 7 miles long and wide, each neighborhood has its own characteristics.

Covering all of them in one book would be difficult—but when it comes to food, not all of them are worthy of inclusion; some smaller neighborhoods barely have one corner store, never mind a renowned restaurant.

I've covered the major neighborhoods in the previous chapters, and am grouping the remainder of the southwestern and southeastern areas of the city into this chapter. Just because they don't get their own chapter has no bearing on the great food that some of these areas offer.

Bayview–Hunters Point

Candlestick Park, home of the San Francisco 49ers, is located here and is perhaps the main attraction of this area. Come time for football games, the traffic in and out of this area can be horrendous. This area is significantly higher in both violent and non-violent crime than the other parts of San Francisco, and there's little industry at the time of this writing, but the San Francisco government has a variety of plans in effect to bring some life to this neighborhood. Despite the lower cost of living, residents opt out of living here owing to the high crime and often dangerous conditions, and they would rather reside outside of the city. It's unfortunate, too, because Bayview-Hunters Point offers some priceless views of the water and is ideally located with close proximity to the city and easy access to the freeway.

Bernal Heights

Surrounded by Bayview–Hunters Point to one side and the Mission to the other side, Bernal Heights is reminiscent of suburbia while technically being a part of the city. In recent years, good eateries have popped up here as the residents expanded outward from the residential and more gentrified Noe Valley to what used to be a more economical area of Bernal Heights. Many younger families purchase their first homes here, and as a result, the area is jokingly referred to as "Maternal Heights"; children and dogs are both abundant here. Accordingly, of the "outer neighborhoods" in this chapter, Bernal Heights is home to the most restaurants.

Glen Park

This is a tiny little "town" within the city limits with a cozy and private feel to it. It's a mostly residential area with a street that has a surprising number of restaurants to serve the locals, and no nightlife to speak of, but then it's only a few minutes from some of the busiest areas for nightlife. With its own BART station and a public library, Glen Park is a nice area that offers the feeling of living outside the city while being close to the center of San Francisco. With good transportation options, it's some city dwellers' dream come true: live within San Francisco with a home, backyard, and great commuting options.

Foodie Faves

Angkor Borei Restaurant, 3471 Mission St., Bernal Heights, San Francisco, CA 94110; (415) 550-8417; www.cambodiankitchen .com; Cambodian; $. Having never traveled to Cambodia and having never tried Cambodian home cooking, it's hard to say whether this food is authentic or not. I can only say that it was a wonderful dining experience. The tiny restaurant offers great service along with some unique cooking, like the fresh spinach leaves served with dried shrimp and toasted coconut with other ingredients like lime wedges, peanuts, and red onions. Wrap the items into the spinach and dip into the tamarind-based sauce for a refreshing bite. The squid salad with lemongrass, cilantro, and spearmint was like an explosion of flavors in your mouth, combined with lettuce and a spicy dressing. For entrees, the duck prik king can't be beat: Large chunks of duck meat with a nice layer of fat under the crispy skin, slathered in curry paste, and served with green beans and rice, this dish is utterly satisfying. For the vegetarians out there, Angkor Borei offers some of the most varied and delicious nonmeat dishes in San Francisco. With mock chicken, duck and beef, along with plenty of tofu options, almost any dish can be customized to include these vegetarian options; do try the spicy tofu as a starter, and the pumpkin curry is a delightful entree full of flavor.

Auntie April's Chicken, 4618 3rd St., Bayview-Hunters Point, San Francisco, CA 94124; (415) 643-4983; Soul Food; $. There are three words/reasons for which you should risk your safety and well-being by driving to Hunters Point to get to Auntie April's: chicken, waffles, and grits. The fried chicken, made personally by Auntie April herself, is so crispy while retaining fat and moisture in the skin, which is a must for fried chicken in my eyes; the meat inside is dripping with juices! For me, waffles are breakfast items or even desserts, so I order the grits to eat with the fried chicken and save the waffles for later. Chicken and grits were a combination made in another world and with perhaps more fat than one person should ever consume in one sitting, but not once did I regret the choice. Once that's done, I tackle the waffles—these thick yet fluffy, gorgeous Belgian waffles with deep pockets throughout that were filled with butter and a maple syrup that's as decadent as can be. Call me bizarre, but that's the ultimate dessert—especially after the fried chicken and grits, the sweetness and richness of the waffles and syrup make for a perfect ending to a decadent meal. The food here is truly as bad for the heart as it is good for the soul; eat up!

Breakfast at Tiffany's, 2499 San Bruno Ave., Portola, San Francisco, CA 94134; (415) 468-0977; American Brunch; $. As far as I'm concerned, breakfast is good anytime of day, and if Breakfast at Tiffany's were open for dinner, I'd be having dinner at Tiffany's, as well as late-night meals at Tiffany's. I'd also weigh 500 pounds, but it might actually be worth it. The portions here are enormous and for minimal cost; all but the largest of appetites will take home a doggie bag. The hash browns have options: You can get cheese, peppers, and other goodies mixed in—make sure you include this in your breakfast. Tiffany's makes hash browns so crispy on the inside while the potatoes retain all the mushiness on the inside of each bite. The Armida's Special is hard to resist; it's an omelet made with 3 eggs, completely fluffy and yellow, wrapping up chorizo, mushrooms, and green peppers, with tomatoes providing acidic accents and the immense amount of cheddar cheese providing the creaminess with a slight sharpness. The amount of fillings they put in this omelet is what's incredible. As if that weren't enough, it's served with sour cream and salsa to mix in, along with the hash browns and toast. Pour some Tabasco in to make the dish shine. I was never a big fan of corned beef hash until Tiffany's, where the concoction comes with tasty chunks of potato and beef, a couple of eggs on the side, and smothered with cheese on top; order it over easy and mash the entire dish together—it's heavenly! The service is nice, and the coffee is continuously refilled. It's a greasy-spoon kind of diner with a long wait on weekends—I doubt anyone would give you a glance if you chose to come dressed in your pajamas.

Broken Record, 1166 Geneva Ave., Crocker-Amazon, San Francisco, CA 94112; (415) 963-1713; www.brokenrecordsanfrancisco.com; American/Gastropub; $. One of the best bacon cheeseburgers in San Francisco can be had at Broken Record—a neighborhood bar that some might call a dive, but the atmosphere and the great selection of beers and alcohol actually make it the ideal location at which to order this delicious burger. You will find no bacon in sight on top of it; the bacon meat is ground into the burger patty, and the end result is an even juicier version of the burger, with its fat content coming from the bacon. Put on a toasted brioche bun, the burger is topped with red onions, lettuce, and Tillamook cheddar that's crispy on the edges and melting all over the burger—you can request avocado on it, too. Also great at Broken Record is the pork tenderloin sandwich, served with honey mustard and cabbage, fennel, and apple slaw—it's a masterful balance between sweet and savory. From a macaroni and goat cheese topped with a cornbread crust, to cheddar crawfish grits and fried chicken offerings, Broken Record is a totally unexpected surprise: A bar doesn't typically serve up food this tasty—not to mention a bar in the Crocker-Amazon neighborhood.

Chenery Park Restaurant, 683 Chenery St., Glen Park, San Francisco, CA 94131; (415) 337-8537; www.chenerypark.com; American/Southern/Soul Food; $$. A classy little establishment in Glen Park, this is a gem of a restaurant. While classified as American cooking, there's a definite Southern flair to everything offered. In addition to the fried chicken and seafood with andouille gumbo, the real highlights at Chenery Park are the pork chop and the salmon. This is one of the few places where I don't do an appetizer course followed by an entree; instead, I will order the baked macaroni and cheese with bacon and the mushroom gnocchi to be served with the pork chop and salmon. The pork chop is huge and cooked to a nice medium; brined for reportedly three days, all the juiciness and moisture are completely retained within the meat. It's served with sautéed greens with bacon and apricot sauce, and Yukon Gold pota-toes; each bite is to be relished with a bite of the macaroni—a match made in heaven! The salmon (request it medium-rare), is served with mashed potatoes and laid atop a bed of lightly sautéed tatsoi, a type of spinach. This particular dish, combined with a bite of gnocchi doused in a creamy mushroom sauce with bits of portobello mushroom in each forkful is as close to bliss as you can get while eating. There's a full bar, so enjoy a couple of cocktails during your meal, and make sure to save some room for the bread pudding.

Emmy's Spaghetti Shack, 3355 Mission St., Bernal Heights, San Francisco, CA 94110; (415) 206-2086; www.emmysspaghettishack .com; Italian; $$. There are lots of places in San Francisco that offer great pasta dishes with all kinds of interesting twists—but when in the mood for just plain, real spaghetti, Emmy's is the place to go. Given the line out the door even on weeknights, I'm not the only who thinks so, either. The spaghetti with meatballs is the thing to have here—and don't stray from it. The tomato sauce is flavorful and so simple, it enhances the dish. But the real highlight is the meatballs that come with each order; these beasts are large and chock-full of flavor! I don't know how they are prepared, but it's a true joy to cut up each meatball into five to six bites, then combine with the already mixed pasta and sauce. Each bite is all one wants and expects from an awesome plate of spaghetti—and the portions are really generous. Go prepared to wait, but be confident in the fact that your patience will be rewarded with the best spaghetti in town.

The Front Porch, 65A 29th St., Bernal Heights, San Francisco, CA 94110; (415) 695-7800; www.thefrontporchsf.com; Southern; $$. The Front Porch offers excellent Southern comfort food and skimps on nothing to make sure you feel better (and heavier) with every order. The sautéed shrimp with garlic, bacon, and mushrooms, served atop a bowlful of creamy and buttery grits, and the baked macaroni and cheese is about as cheesy as you can handle with a good dose of béchamel sauce drizzled throughout; it's not fancy, and it's exactly what mac and cheese should be. When you order a bucket of fried chicken, it's a lightly battered order of crispy fried chicken served in a movie-theater popcorn bucket, with popcorn sprinkled throughout the entire dish. How do you walk away from this not feeling better already?

Giovanni's Pizza Bistro, 3839 Mission St., Bernal Heights, San Francisco, CA 94110; (415) 647-6122; www.giovannispizzabistro .com; Pizza; $$. You can hardly fault a pizza for getting soggy in the middle when it is piled high with ingredients, offers a delectable handmade thin crust, and is so cheesy that you think of it hours after you've left. Giovanni's is just a neighborhood joint with local owners who are friendly and so welcoming—but they make a mean pizza. The ingredients are fresh, and the flavors shine through because the tomato sauce is not overpowering; it's balanced nicely by the crust. Most comforting on the menu, however, is a Philly cheesesteak calzone—a combination of all things wonderful with tender steak and loads of melted cheese wrapped in dough and baked until it can handle no more heat. Another unique to Giovanni's item on the menu is the lamb rigatoni; perfect pasta served with a hefty portion of lamb braised in red wine, and the addition of fresh mint to this dish enhances both the heavier flavors of pasta and meat. It's addictive, and a pleasant surprise to find such great Italian cooking in this neighborhood.

Goood Frikin Chicken, 10 29th St., Bernal Heights, San Francisco, CA 94110; (415) 970-2428; www.gfcsf.com; Mediterranean/Middle Eastern; $$. Sounds like a fried chicken place that would serve Southern cooking but Goood Frikin Chicken (GFC, with deliberate misspellings) is purely Mediterranean/Middle Eastern cooking. The pita offered is thick and buttery with plenty of herbs throughout, and it pairs wonderfully with yogurt or the plain hummus as a starter. The side salad that accompanies all "meal" options (versus a la carte) is refreshing and flavorful; it's tossed with a light herbal dressing that is bottled and sold here. The lamb shawarma is served like a burrito, and the yogurt lamb concoction inside was creamy and tender. The *mosakhan* is a quesadilla of sorts, with thin tortillas encasing shredded chicken, onions, and herbs, and then grilled to a toasted state. Of the entrees, the *mansaf,* a Jordanian staple dish with tender lamb chunks served over a buttery sticky rice, topped with a pile of almonds and pine nuts, served with additional yogurt sauce, was the superstar, followed closely by the kefta kebab, which came with a tomato-based rice pilaf topped with 4 beef and lamb "sausages"—tasty!

Kingdom of Dumpling, 1713 Taraval St., Parkside, San Francisco, CA 94116; (415) 566-6143; www.kingofchinesedumpling.com; Chinese; $. This tiny—and I mean tiny—restaurant in the Parkside area serves up some extremely fresh dumplings. This place is known for their soup dumplings *(xiao long bao),* but I prefer their regular dumplings. Freshly made daily, these dumplings are chock-full of meat and chives, and the wrappers are chewy and light. They are offered steamed, and while the fillings for beef, shrimp, and pork all taste similar, they are also all equally delicious and addictive. For the minimal cost of $6–$7, each plate consists of 10–12 bite-size dumplings, and inevitably, you order more than you can finish. Take caution with every bite as each dumpling is served straight out of the steamer, and the heat can take off the roof of your mouth. The soup dumplings were tasty, though they didn't compare to **Yank Sing** (p. 130), solely because the skin is thicker and chewier than Yank Sing's silky dumpling skin. Barely anyone in the restaurant speaks English, but the menu is pretty self-explanatory. With the dumplings, order some salt and pepper tofu; each piece of tofu is deep-fried with a crispy exterior and a hot, meltingly soft interior—one of the best I've had in the city.

Le P'tit Laurent, 699 Chenery St., Glen Park, San Francisco, CA 94131; (415) 334-3235; www.leptitlaurent.net; French; $$$. This quaint French restaurant pleases all of your senses. It's about the last area in the city you'd expect to find such good French food— and it's Glen Park's little secret. But those in the know realize that Le P'tit Laurent offers truly comforting cooking that is beautifully presented and tastes as good as it looks. The escargot here is not to be missed—the snail meat is flavorful, tender, and buttery, and they slide right out of their shells. The must-try item on the menu is the cassoulet, a fragrant and hearty bean stew with generous chunks of Toulouse sausage, duck leg confit, and pork; the meat just melts in your mouth. Despite the stewed nature, each ingredient holds its own within the creation, and it pairs beautifully with a glass of Sauvignon Blanc. Also notably rich and savory is the lamb shank, slow-braised until it slides off the bone and served with a generous portion of chard. Service is friendly and the staff goes beyond to make the customers feel comfortable. With a prix-fixe option on weeknights—3 courses for $22—it's obvious why Le P'tit Laurent is Glen Park's sweetheart.

Mi Lindo Peru Restaurant, 3226 Mission St., Bernal Heights, San Francisco, CA 94110; (415) 642-4897; Peruvian; $$. Peruvian cooking is about freshness and distinct, stand-alone flavors in my mind, and Mi Lindo Peru offers just that to the residents of San Francisco. Bread is served with a red salsa here; take care not to go overboard with this amazing starter. You spread a layer of butter on the bread, then top it off with spoonfuls of the spicy-ish salsa— and each bite makes you salivate more. Start off with the ceviche: fresh chunks of snapper marinated in lime juice, served up with onion, corn, and sweet potatoes—the way it should be. The *lomo saltado* is so simple and so comforting—strips of marinated sirloin are stir-fried with onions, tomatoes, and garlic, and served on a bed of french fries with herbed rice; request a fried egg on top to complete the masterpiece. The steak strips remain juicy and flavorful, and match perfectly with the fries; the sauce and the rice mix together well, and before you know it, the large plate before you is empty. Another dish to order is the *pescado al ajo,* which is a large snapper fried to a buttery crisp outside and smothered in a light but incredibly garlicky sauce; the garlic is piled onto the fried fish, and the flakes of fish combined with the garlic and skin is a pairing made for the gods.

Mozzarella Di Bufala Pizzeria, 69 W. Portal Ave., West Portal, San Francisco, CA 94127; (415) 661-8900; www.dibufala.com; Pizza/ Italian; $$. With a choice of New York–style pizza crust or a crunchy but moist cornmeal crust, this restaurant has a huge variety of topping choices. Both crusts are good—the thinner New York crust is not as thin as at other Italian restaurants and instead offers more chewiness, and it holds the toppings well without getting soggy. The cornmeal crust is addictive and enhances everything you put on top of it. Try a combination of the cornmeal crust with tomato sauce, ground beef, linguiça, mushrooms, and black olives—or the New York–style pizza with shrimp, boiled eggs, jalapeños, and spinach. Calzones are made-to-order here with your choice of 1 to 6 fillings, and are served hot out of the oven, oozing cheese with each bite. While quite a variety of pastas are offered here, stick to the simple dishes like the meat lasagna or the cheese ravioli; the portions are plenty for one adult or two children to share, topped with a flavorful and fresh tomato sauce.

Parkside Tavern, 1940 Taraval St., Parkside, San Francisco, CA 94116; (415) 731-8900; www.parksidetavernsf.com; American/Gastropub; $$. Any place that offers macaroni and cheese, cheeseburgers, prime rib (Sunday only), and fresh oysters on the same menu, along with a full bar and beer selection, scores itself a secure spot in my world, even if located in the Sunset/Parkside neighborhood that I rarely need to visit. Factor in a different menu for lunch and dinner, late hours, and good service, and it becomes my second home. For lunch, try the smoked salmon and boxty pancake with dill cream and scallions—it's about as savory as you can handle and pairs wonderfully with ice tea, or as I have it, with a creamy pint of Guinness. The flavors of the salmon and the lightness and tartness of the dill cream pair beautifully with the heaviness of the potato pancake, and while heavy for lunch, it is incredibly satisfying. On the dinner menu, this item makes it to the appetizer section and is ideal to share, perhaps with a dozen oysters. For dinner entrees, it's hard to stray from the half-pound Tavern burger with cheddar cheese, pickled onions, and tomatoes; request it medium-rare and wash it down with a pint of Stella Artois for the ultimate combination. They also have chicken potpie with organic chicken and vegetables. From top to bottom, without committing to a certain cuisine, Parkside Tavern offers the ultimate pub food, and comfort food.

Piqueo's, 830 Cortland Ave., Bernal Heights, San Francisco, CA 94199; (415) 282-8812; www.piqueos.com; Peruvian; $$$. Flavors take center stage at Piqueo's. Every dish consists of fresh ingredients that retain their flavors and sparkle amongst their partners in the final creations. The soft sweet potato served with snapper, shrimp, mussel, and scallop ceviche, lightly doused and marinated in lime juice, mixed with red onions and cilantro is, as they say, a party in your mouth; each flavor bounces around taking turns being in the spotlight. Baby calamari stuffed with chorizo sausage, laid on top of green apples and fresh greens, drizzled in a rocoto (type of pepper) aioli is the ultimate starter dish, with the sweetness of the apples and crispness of the greens balancing out the harsher and heavier flavors of the chorizo, which paired nicely with the subtle flavors of the squid. Or for a healthy and delightfully light twist, try the quinoa salad, with well-cooked quinoa grains mixed in with greens, corn, tomatoes, and onions with a light vinaigrette dressing. All of the tapas plates are delicious, but make sure to end the meal with the negra paella—a squid-ink paella with fresh chunks of seafood including halibut and mussels.

Smokin' Warehouse Barbecue, 1465 Carroll Ave., Bayview–
Hunters Point, San Francisco, CA 94124; (415) 648-8881; www
.smokinwarehouse.blogspot.com; Barbecue; $. As many amazing
restaurants as San Francisco has, the one thing that's truly missing
is a real "manly man" barbecue joint. Normally, I'll take a drive to
Oakland to **Everett & Jones** (p. 234) for some great meats, but
then I found Smokin' Warehouse. If you drive all the way down to
the Hunters Point area of the city, there is one place that offers
what can really be called a good ol' American barbecue. The brisket
is brined, then smoked and cooked for 10 hours straight, and
it's fascinating how juicy the meat can still be.
On its own or in a sandwich, this meat can
covert vegans if they'd give it one try. The
ribs require no utensils, and even
princesses will be found eating
this stuff with clenched fists
with their "Q" sauce dripping
all over their chins, paired with a
spoonful of potato salad. Also notably
good are the baked beans, slow-cooked with pork and offering a
hint of sweetness mixed in with the most savory flavors known to
mankind. Also available is an awesome bowl of steak chili that is
both smoky and spicy, with a generous portion of chunky steak
pieces throughout; it redefines what a great bowl of chili should
be. Take it all home, cook up some rice, call over a friend, and
devour while watching a movie—that's the recipe for a fabulous
Friday night.

Superstar Restaurant, 4919 Mission St., Excelsior, San Francisco, CA 94112; (415) 585-4360; Filipino; $. Coming across any restaurant in San Francisco that isn't "fast food" where for well under $5 you can go into a food coma is difficult, if not impossible. Even food trucks cost more than that in this city. The one exception is Superstar Restaurant. In a city where brunch for two can easily top $50, Superstar has been offering the cheapest and tastiest Filipino brunches, lunches, and dinners for years. All rice plate options are served with a plain yet strangely delicious garlic fried rice, your choice of protein cooked, be it Spam, fish, or meat, and an over-easy fried egg with either tomatoes or pineapples. It's simple, cheap, delicious—and filling for the shockingly cheap prices. Best on the menu are the boneless *bangus* and *galunggon*—milk fish and mackerel scad, respectively—which are two of the Philippines' most popular fish varieties. While these choices may have been due to the cheap cost, they are also both extremely flavorful and tender fish. Superstar fries them and lays them out on a plate with your garlic fried rice and egg. Also delicious are the Hong Kong–style pork chops, lightly breaded and enormous in size; it's a true man's meal. All of this is available starting at 9 a.m., and you begin to wonder why anyone else is eating at the fancier brunch spots when fish, garlic fried rice, and a fried egg are available here for a measly $4. You can order 3 plates and still spend only half of what others in the city spend on lunch, nevermind dinner.

Vega, 419 Cortland Ave., Bernal Heights, San Francisco, CA 94110; (415) 285-6000; www.vegapizzasf.com; Pizza/Italian; $$. This cozy and rather romantic little Italian getaway makes a thin-crust pizza that looks and tastes like it came out of some pizzeria in Firenze, Italy, but the appetizers and pastas also make you feel like you've come home to the family. The calamari is unique and is presented free of any batter, lightly grilled with a vinegar-based sauce that makes the flavors of the squid pop. The goat cheese–stuffed artichoke hearts are savory to the nth degree, and the grilled asparagus with Parmesan cheese is as simple and as tasty as one could want from asparagus. The gnocchi *alla boscaiola* is sensational—perfectly pillowy gnocchi with sausage, mushrooms, Parmesan cheese, and a sprinkle of truffle oil—as is the pappardelle with venison ragu—simple and flavorful, it pairs beautifully with a glass of Pinot Noir. Also good is the spaghetti alla carbonara, with al dente noodles and egg, served with smoked pancetta, and a nice hint of pecorino and Parmesan cheese. The fresh fish of the day entree is always a delight—and it is served on a cauliflower-and-potato puree that somehow works spectacularly with whatever fish they lay on it. For the pizza, their Margherita is delicious; always opt for the egg on top for an additional cost.

Specialty Stores, Markets & Producers

Ambrosia Bakery, 2605 Ocean Ave., Lakeside, San Francisco, CA 94132; www.sfbakery.com; (415) 334-5305. This bakery is worth traveling long distances for in order to supply the whole cake to celebrate virtually any occasion. The always-fresh princess cake is always a phenomenal hit at parties; with berries and custard mixed throughout the layers of cake and topped with a marzipan wrap, this cake is just the right balance of sweetness and tartness. The hazelnut buttercream cake is fragrant and beautiful; it's light, and for those who prefer a less sweet cake, this one is sure to please. Almost nothing pairs better with a fresh cup of coffee. My personal favorite is the fruit tart at Ambrosia. Beautiful to look at, the whole tart is filled with a creamy custard topped with big, fresh, and jammy chunks of fruit.

Guerra's Quality Meats, 490 Taraval St., Parkside, San Francisco, CA 94116; (415) 564-0585; www.guerrameats.com. I am always a bit sad that butcher shops are now nearly extinct, but am happy to report that Guerra's is still going strong. It's no surprise, either, as the quality of meat, the prices, and the service here are nothing short of exemplary. When you know what you want, you can go to Guerra's and most likely find it—but even when you don't know what to cook, you can just admire the meats and one of the butchers will make a top-notch dinner selection for you. From lamb to all parts of the pig and cow, to rabbit meat, plenty of sausages and deli meats, as well as some fresh seafood, this one store can satisfy anyone's cooking needs. Long live private butcher shops!

Paulie's Pickling, Bernal Marketplace, 331 Cortland St., Bernal Heights, San Francisco, CA 94110; (415) 285-0800; www.paulies pickling.com. Once you've tried one of Paulie's freshly pickled items, you'll really be loath to ever buy anything pickled from the grocery store again. The cost is considerably higher than store-bought brands, but the freshness, sourness, and the crunchiness of these perfectly pickled items are infinitely better, making the higher

cost more than worthwhile. From garlic-pickled cucumbers to pickled jalapeños and brussels sprouts (seasonal), the little storefront has mastered the art of pickling. The bite of these items is like fresh, as if the pickling process didn't soften them up at all but simply enhanced the flavor of everything. Get some chopped liver while there, and come home to make your own chopped liver sandwich, topped with the pickled peppers, and with a side of the pickles.

San Francisco Meats & Delicatessen, 1330 Ocean Ave., Ingleside, San Francisco, CA 94112; (415) 859-9900; www.sfmeats .com. In Ingleside, this is a neighborhood favorite. In fact, people from all over San Francisco come to this butcher shop for their meat and seafood needs. While some will claim they make a great sandwich, what makes San Francisco Meats special is that with one phone call, they will find you the cut or variety you need. If you

suddenly find yourself in need of
40 pounds of crab by Saturday,
place a phone call and see if Joe,
the owner, can make it happen for
you. Need a whole pig in a week for a luau?
Call Joe. While they have a good array of fresh
meats available, don't miss out on the homemade sausages here;
the spicy Italian sausage can't be beat on the grill, and the flavors
of this sausage reign long after your meal is done.

Outside the City Limits

Living in San Francisco, you can't help but consider yourself lucky. Just across the bridges, you have different climates and scenery. The famous Golden Gate Bridge leads you to Marin County and Northern California, with its scenic beauty, coastal towns, and fresh seafood options. Across the Bay Bridge, you're led into hotter temperatures with a mass of different cultures and cuisines. A few hours to the east is beautiful Lake Tahoe, which provides days of entertainment year-round, whether it be fishing and boating in the summer, or testing the slopes during the winter. A short drive south and you can visit the garlic fields of Gilroy, or relax at a gorgeous spa property in Carmel or Monterey.

But even without venturing as far out as I have described above, you have access to Napa Valley (not discussed in this book), which is incomparable to anything in the United States, and is worth spending lots of time there exploring and experiencing its bountiful offerings. A trip to "wine country" is something all residents do, whether it be for the food or wine—and it's undoubtedly one of the most popular excursions that San Francisco tourists will also take. The experience is not just in Napa, California, but extends throughout Sonoma, Healdsburg, Saint Helena, and other cities around the area; which you choose is determined solely by what you want to visit, taste, or eat.

Right outside the SF city limits are also outstanding restaurants that make a name for themselves by serving up something that can't readily be found within the city of San Francisco, if at all. In this chapter, we cover some of those notable places and the areas surrounding San Francisco, excluding Napa Valley. All are within driving distance, and all will undoubtedly make you wish you lived in this gorgeous city and its access to virtually everything a person's stomach could desire.

Foodie Faves

Chez Panisse, 1517 Shattuck Ave., Berkeley, CA 94709; (510) 548-5525; www.chezpanisse.com; American; $$$$. Chef Alice Waters leads the movement on "slow food," focusing on local ingredients and sustainable farming. Each dish presented at Chez Panisse subscribes to this, and the freshness of the ingredients used shines through the simple presentation and cooking—so long as "simple" isn't confused with "easy," as I am certain I cannot replicate it. The price is on the high side for a 4-course prix-fixe menu, but from the first course onward, each dish is a marvel that only a seasoned professional can put together. The menu varies each evening as the chef uses what is available and freshest, but you can go to Chez Panisse assured that only the greatest local ingredients will be used. Nowhere else will you appreciate the flavors that only organic ingredients can impart as you will by the time you take one bite from the heirloom tomato salad here, mixed with a very light and refreshing dressing. The pork belly braised with a black trumpet mushroom ragout and served with fava beans is so simple, so delicious, and essentially so Californian.

Cowgirl Creamery, 80 4th St., Point Reyes Station, CA 94956; (415) 663-9335; www.cowgirlcreamery.com; Creamery; $$. For a truly fun experience, a trip north is not complete without a visit to the Cowgirl Creamery. If you love cheese, you have to experience this; if you don't love cheese, chances are likely that by the time you're done with the tour and tasting here, you will. There are tours available but just visiting the shop and sampling all the cheeses will be fun enough for most; each person working there is so informed about the characteristics of the individual cheeses, what they're known for, and what pairs well with these wonderfully creamy creations. Mt. Tam is undoubtedly the crowd favorite, and outside of France, it's likely you have never had anything as soft, creamy, and decadent as this triple

cream cheese. Spreading this cheese on top of anything will cata-
pult it into the "wonderful and dreamy" category. As you sample
each variety, you will find yourself requesting a pound of this, a half
pound of that, a little bit of this one, and a lot of that one—and
before you know it, you have more cheese than you can possibly
consume. There's also a picnic area on the premises if you want to
enjoy your cheese experience there. With a deli, quite a selection
of wines, and other food available on-site, it's easy to put together
a fascinatingly fun picnic while at Cowgirl Creamery.

Drake's Bay Oyster Farm, 17171 Sir Frances Drake Blvd.,
Inverness, CA 94937; (415) 669-1149; www.drakesbayfamilyfarms
.com; Seafood; $$. If, as of yet, you're unaware of what "sweet-
ness" in an oyster tastes like, it's probably because you haven't
tried Pacific oysters from Drake's Bay. These plump, rather large,
and incredibly juicy oysters will amaze you when eaten at the oyster
farm. The extra-small ones are the sweetest, but my preference is
to eat the meatier, medium-size ones raw, and to
barbecue the large ones. However, a visit to this
farm will redefine "freshness" for you, and this
family-owned business is the epitome of sustain-
able farming practices. Group tours are available
to teach you and your party the unique and
labor-intensive method of farming their hand-
harvested oysters at Drake's Bay; make sure
you call ahead to make reservations. If you want
oysters for a party at home or a special occasion, call

to place your order and make the short drive up with coolers and ice in tow; your guests will love you forever.

Everett & Jones Barbeque, 126 Broadway, Jack London Square, Oakland, CA 94697; (510) 663-2350; www.eandjbbq.com; Barbecue; $$. You don't go to Everett & Jones expecting good service. You don't even go there expecting a clean table. You go there because you were lucky enough to be passing Oakland, where Everett & Jones has become synonymous with a great brisket. Slathered in Everett & Jones' own barbecue sauce that is a mix of sweet, tangy, and a bit of spice and kick, the brisket is smoky and juicy, and each bite throws you into nirvana. You can start with utensils, but quickly, you'll find that you're eating with your hands and look like a 3-year-old who had a bowl of spaghetti. Simply put, Everett & Jones offers the best barbecued brisket in the Bay Area. Additional East Bay locations are listed on the website.

Fifth Wheel, 898 San Leandro Blvd., San Leandro, CA 94577; (510) 635-7538; www.fifthwheelfood.com; American Brunch; $. This tiny little mom-and-pop restaurant serves up the best breakfast and brunch items in the Bay Area. Huge plates are covered with food for under $10, and the hash browns that come with most meals are addictive. They're browned and crunchy on the outside, with the strips of potatoes soft and near mushy on the inside. Eggs are prepared exactly as you want them—and the omelets here are so big and filling that usually they end up being breakfast and a mid-day snack. Each omelet is created with 2 eggs, and the fluffy egg wrap is filled with everything you ordered whether it be jalapeño-cilantro sausages and good old American or cheddar cheese with mushrooms, or whatever your heart desires. Plate lunches are offered here from opening to closing—with steak and eggs, or chicken-fried steak with a heaping pile of rice with over-easy eggs on top. Or custom-order with hash browns, a bowl of grits, pick your meat choices, throw in 3 eggs the way you want, and ask for a bowl of rice. No matter what you order, you'll be shocked at how good it tastes, and even more shocked at the low price tag. You come here for awesome, greasy, hangover-curing breakfasts; you do not come here looking for a healthy alternative, as no such thing exists here. If they were open for dinner, I'd most likely drive here for dinner, too, but unfortunately, they close at 2 p.m. daily, and the Christian family closes the restaurant on Sunday.

Ohgane Korean Restaurant, 3915 Broadway, North Oakland, Oakland, CA 94611; (510) 594-8300; www.ohgane.com; Korean; $$. In San Francisco, we're hard-pressed to find anything worthwhile when it comes to Korean cuisine, other than a few Korean barbecue places. So when you have a hankering for real Korean food—you hop on the Bay Bridge and drive 20 minutes to Ohgane for some great flavors and well-marinated meats. With an impressive array of complimentary *banchan* (side dishes), your dining experience begins. Order some *kalbi* (short ribs marinated in a soy-based marinade) and *jumuluk* (salted beef rib meats) and grill to your heart's content on the mesquite charcoal grills. Then, order some casseroles or stews to eat with the rice. Particularly good here are the cod roe casserole and intestine casserole (for two or more). The soybean paste stew is also full of thick and deep flavors—a perfect combination with the hot sticky rice that is served. Service is friendly, and the location is huge. With a reservation, Ohgane can easily accommodate really large groups. A second location is open at 7877 Amador Valley Blvd., Dublin, CA 94568; (925) 875-1232; while this location is smaller in comparison, the food is equally delicious, but the wait on weekends is sometimes longer.

Spud Point Crab Company, 1860 Westshore Rd., Bodega Bay, CA 94923; (707) 875-9472; www.spudpointcrab.com; Seafood; $$. The best things in life are usually very, very simple. This small little storefront with only outdoor seating makes the finest crab sandwich I've ever had. Order the creamy clam chowder to go with it; combined with a drink, and you'll be sliding a wee bit over $20. Find a seat, take one bite, and you'll wonder how you lived without it until now. Soft bread is filled with a hefty portion of creamy mayonnaise and that wonderful, slightly sweet crab—every bite is perfection. Don't neglect the chowder; its consistency is not as thick as others and is complemented with chunks of clam and potatoes throughout. It, too, is so good that you may find yourself chasing a mouthful of sandwich with a spoonful of soup. Fresh crab is available to purchase whole here, and there are many more items on the menu. Spud Point is the go-to spot for local crab fishermen as they begin their mornings, as it's located directly in front of the marina. While the cost is not cheap, it'd be a challenge to find fresher crab in California.

Tomales Bay Oyster Company, 15479 Hwy. 1, Marshall, CA 94940; (415) 663-1242; www.tomalesbayoysters.com; Grocery/ Market; $$$. To run up to this area and bring back oysters, Drake's Bay might be a better choice—but if you plan a getaway from the city to go and grill freshly farmed oysters, nothing beats Tomales Bay Oyster Company. This is one of the favorite day-trip locations for city dwellers to visit as it's only a little over an hour's drive away, and it has the setting and major necessities in place to have your "staycation" of sorts. The grill, park bench and table seating, and a great view are already supplied for you at Tomales Bay; you need only buy your oysters here, and bring everything else up with you. Tablecloths, charcoal, alcohol, utensil, napkins, and plates must all be brought, including barbecue tongs and shuckers. I highly recommend you bring grillable meats and vegetables with you, as you'll find that there really is a limit as to how many oysters you can eat in one sitting. But each oyster here is fresh and meaty; the smaller oysters are perfect for eating raw, and medium or larger oysters are usually grilled until they open up. All you need is a squeeze of lemon, Tabasco, and a pinch of horseradish on each one; the water inside the oyster shell provides all the necessary seasoning. It's first come, first served, and you will have to come quite early to secure a seat and grill for your group. It might be wise to bring a cooler to take some oysters with you back to San Francisco. It's considerably cheaper to buy them here, not to mention fresher.

Top Dog, 2534 Durant Ave., Berkeley, CA 94704; (510) 843-5967; www.topdoghotdogs.com; Hot Dogs; $. This shop is an icon around Berkeley and might qualify as a landmark. It's a way of life for Berkeley students, but anyone who has tried Top Dog knows that it's virtually impossible to find a better dog in the Bay Area. Once you've had it, you become a glutton when standing before the cashier, about to place your order. One hot dog is enough, but since you're here, you might as well order two—but then there's the ride home, and heck—I might as well order dinner and my midnight snack while I'm here. (It somehow makes sense when you're standing there; you'll see.) From chicken-apple sausage on buns, to all-beef hot links (Louisiana-style) dogs, which kicks up the spice level with four types of peppers inside the hot dogs. Hot links, lemon chicken, linguiça to bockwurst—each meat choice is placed on a sesame-seed bun and wrapped in parchment paper, then handed to you. It doesn't look like much, but you pile on the onions and sauerkraut at the condiment station, pour on as much mustard, mayonnaise, or ketchup as you care to have, and then take one bite. I dare you to not like it. Then, soon enough, you'll find yourself without a hot dog, and wanting just one more. You look at the ridiculous line, and contemplate—and then you understand why someone (I'm not saying it's me) might stand before the cashier and order an insane amount when it's their turn. Open late and cash only. Top Dog is a must-try item when passing through Berkeley.

The Village Pub Restaurant, 2967 Woodside Rd., Woodside, CA 94062; (650) 851-9888; www.thevillagepub.net; American; $$$. Chef Mark Sullivan of **Spruce** (p. 200) in San Francisco, along with Chef Dmitry Elperin who acts as executive chef, head up this gorgeous Michelin-starred spot, catering to the affluent residents of Woodside along with any foodie who will travel miles to eat here. Pairing ingredients like sweetbreads with lobster, leeks, and mushrooms, 80 percent of the ingredients that are used in the cooking are secured from SMIP Farm in Woodside, which is dedicated to sustainable food and farming practices. The freshness of the ingredients is wholly discernable in each dish. For lunch, try the boneless pork ribs, served with grilled peaches with arugula—it's a balanced mix of savory, sweet, and bitter that you won't forget. For dinner, make sure someone at your table orders the spectacular spaghettini with golden chanterelles and sweet corn; you will be stunned at what the chef accomplishes in a basically vegetarian dish that's creamy, rich, and highlights the depth of the mushroom flavor while enabling the sweetness of corn to dance on your palate.

Foodie
Itineraries

So you finally arrive at SFO, and are mere minutes away from this gastronomically delightful city. It's 11 p.m. already, and you wonder if there's any place to try tonight when you get to the city. This chapter's for you.

Or, you only have a couple of days and intend to stretch out those stomach muscles to fit as many San Francisco eats as possible during your short stay; gluttony is useful sometimes. This chapter's also for you.

Perhaps you brought your significant other and are paralyzed by the realization that you haven't planned a thing for San Francisco, and she's eyeing you, wondering if you got French Laundry reservations for your anniversary—tomorrow. (It won't get you that reservation, but you'll make that part up with other fantastic food!) This chapter, my friend, is for you.

Late Night Eats

It's past midnight, or even 3 a.m.; you've been barhopping and you're insatiably hungry. Fear not; while the pickings are slim compared to some other cities at this time of the morning, there are late-night eateries in San Francisco.

Option 1: North Beach Area

Head to North Beach and pick between **Yuet Lee** or **My Canh,** 626 Broadway, San Francisco, CA 94133; (415) 397-8888, two doors down from Yuet Lee. The service can be excruciatingly slow for Vietnamese noodles, but it is the only late-night pho place that is open late, and the pho offers good noodles in a beefy broth that tends to be a bit salty; request extra tendon, and if you want to try something really tasty, order a raw beef salad. It's a plate of thinly sliced raw beef topped with peanuts, basil leaves, and lemon juice.

If you prefer Chinese food and the line at Yuet Lee is too long, walk to the other corner of the block to **New Sun Hong Kong**, 606 Broadway, San Francisco, CA 94133; (415) 956-3338. While the prices are a bit higher and service is slower, the place is big and the sizzling rice noodle soup is fantastic on those cold nights.

Option 2: Financial District

Globe Restaurant, described in detail on p. 66, Globe has some great late-night eats. It's about the only place in San Francisco where you can get a rather upscale meal at this time of night. Open until 1 a.m., Globe offers their full menu until closing. Their macaroni and cheese is one dish I can't resist, regardless of time of day: large pasta cooked al dente, slathered in Tillamook cheese!

Option 3: Tenderloin or Nob Hill Area

Grubstake, located at 1525 Pine St., San Francisco, CA 94109; (415) 673-8268; www.sfgrubstake.com, is open until 4 a.m. nightly, and their Nugget Cheeseburger is made infinitely better with the addition of crunchy bacon and a fried egg; opt for the onion rings instead of the fries.

Alternatively, you can visit **Mel's Drive-In,** 1050 Van Ness Ave., San Francisco, CA 94109; (415) 292-6357; www.melsdrive-in .com, which is a staple in the neighborhood. While not really a drive-in anymore, and the burgers leave a bit to be desired, the fries are good, and those milk shakes are sinfully creamy. Late at night, especially after a few drinks, this might be exactly what you're wanting.

Tommy's Joynt, at 1101 Geary Blvd., San Francisco, CA 94109; (415) 775-4216; www.tommysjoynt.com, is open until 2 a.m. and serves up roasted meats and other comfort foods until closing, all cafeteria-style. Much of San Francisco adores this place—order a pastrami sandwich or the barbecue brisket dinner plate.

Option 4: Richmond

Red Wings is a small Korean bar and restaurant that offers Korean fried chicken. Any place that deep-fries boneless chicken thighs earns immediate points. Get the original (sauce-less) fried chicken, or opt for one of the sweet, spicy, or soy-based sauces to get the true Korean fried chicken experience. They're open until 2 a.m., and serve *soju* and beer here, bearing in mind that "Korean fried chicken" is normally consumed with beer. If you need soup, try the *budae jjigae,* which is a stew with hot dogs, onions, kimchee, ramen, and all kinds of leftover-type ingredients.

Or, for some hot stews or Korean barbecue meats, you can head to **Wooden Charcoal Korean Barbecue House** (p. 205); the food is good, the price is steep for Korean dishes, but they're open until 4 a.m. on weekends!

And—I hate to admit I have done this, but don't knock it until you've tried it! Desperate times call for desperate measures, and there's a **Jack in the Box** at the corner of Geary and 10th at 4649 Geary Blvd., San Francisco, (415) 752-4916; www.jackinthebox .com, and it's open 24 hours a day, every single day. Walk in and say only these words, "Extreme Sausage meal, please," and pick your drink. About 5 to 6 minutes later, a freshly prepared sausage, cheese, and egg burger comes out on a soft bun with greasy and scalding hot mini-hashbrowns—and I'm not kidding when I say you will never think of breakfast again without conjuring up an image of this burger. I'm not a fast-food fan, but this—at 3 a.m.—is inspirational!

Option 5: Mission

El Farolito (p. 98) has got to be my favorite late-night spot for *carne asada* burritos, or that scrumptious quesadilla filled with the works!

For a burger, go to **Urbun Burger** (p. 129), where you can build your own burger or opt for one of theirs on the menu. Very few things in life hit the spot like their Breakfast Burger does late at night. The restaurant is open until 3 a.m. on weekends, but only until 10 p.m. on weekdays.

For finer dining, check out **Beretta** (p. 94); the kitchen is open until 1 a.m., and dishes such as meatballs, pizza, and lamb chops are available all night.

The Food Tripper

You're here on business, or you have a long stopover—and the one thing you know is that the food in San Francisco is top-notch. Some might spend the day going to the Golden Gate Bridge, and others might visit wine bars, but real foodies will run around town to fit in as much as possible during their stay; you can see the bridge on a postcard at the airport.

Whether it be one, two, or three days that you have, following the itineraries below is guaranteed to redefine "gastronomic pleasure" in your mind, and you'll book your return to San Francisco before you've even left. All of these locations are either available within the book chapters and are described at length under their own listings, or the addresses are listed below for the venues not included within the book.

Day One
Breakfast: Turtle Tower Restaurant (p. 81)
Order the pho ga (No. 9), or No. 10 if you feel adventurous and don't mind having some chicken gizzards with your pho.
Lunch: Ike's Place (p. 153)
Pick any sandwich of your choice and devour; start walking to burn off the calories.
Late-Day Snack: Mo's Grill (p. 42)
Order the Belly Buster with an avalanche of cheese, grilled onions and mushrooms—cut in half. Finish the first half, and then finish the second half anyway.
Dinner: Shabu House (p. 197)
Forgo the all-you-can-eat option to order a large plate of American Kobe beef with the spicy miso soup. Cook the veggies; cook the meat; avoid finishing the rice—and regret not opting for the all-you-can-eat option as you roll yourself out of the restaurant.

Day Two
Breakfast: Mama's on Washington Square (p. 41)
Get the Dungeness crab eggs Benedict at Mama's, or order any one of the omelets here. Run— not walk—around town to work it off.

Morning Snack: Yank Sing (p. 130)

Order just the Shanghai dumplings, and reach new heights in the dim sum world. Nowhere on this coast will you find dumplings this good (or expensive).

Lunch: Hard Knox Cafe (p. 186)

Have the braised ribs with collard greens and a creamy mac and cheese, or try the spicy fried chicken. It's the ultimate comfort food.

Late-Day Snack: Nick's Crispy Tacos (p. 246)

Order one Baja fish taco "Nick's way," which will mean it's a soft taco tortilla with a deep-fried tortilla, and whatever you ordered will come slathered in fresh guacamole; it should be illegal for tacos to be made like this.

Dinner: Zushi Puzzle (p. 172)

Make sure you have a reservation and sit at the bar and tell Roger, "Omakase, please!" ("chef's choice") for an extraordinary trip through sushi, sashimi, and sake.

Or, go to **Acquerello** (p. 56) and order the 4-course meal, but do not miss the ridged pasta with *foie gras,* marsala sauce, and truffles—their signature dish. Drink lots of wine here as the sommelier and wine list are spectacular.

Late-Night Snack: Hog & Rocks, 3431 19th St., San Francisco, CA 94110; (415) 550-8627; www.hogandrocks.com.

Order a cured meat plate or one dozen of the many varieties of oysters they carry; get a single-malt scotch with one cube and reflect on the last two days of eating.

Day Three

Breakfast: Fifth Wheel in San Leandro (p. 234)

Rent a car by 7 a.m. and drive to this tiny restaurant. Order anything on the menu. Leave the location at least 3.5 pounds heavier, recline seat in car, and sleep.

Lunch: PPQ Dungeness Island Vietnamese Cuisine (p. 194)

Order a salt and pepper crab or the spicy crab, and a full order of garlic noodles for yourself. Admire self for eating so well. Ignore waist completely.

Mid-Afternoon Snack: Jake's Steaks (p. 155)

Order a small Philly cheesesteak—"with mushrooms, onions, and Whiz": hot, tender beef strips with Cheez Whiz fried right in, grilled mushrooms, and onions on soft bread—you can't ask for more!

Dinner: House of Prime Rib (p. 83)

This place is a mandatory visit for the King Henry VIII Cut of Prime Rib. The sourdough loaf that comes out in the beginning is addictive; the salad served here is slightly tangy and sweet, but the sliced beets and lettuce concoction is so good, you will finish it. Opt for the baked potato with everything on it (though the mashed potato really is just as delicious), and choose the creamed spinach as your side. Ask for a wheelchair to be taken out to the street because you won't be able to walk anymore.

The Romantic Food Lover

San Francisco, above all else, is a romantic city. This city offers a European flair with classic and old architecture, endless strolling options, and stunning water views with landmark bridges. As such, the romantic culinary options are also plentiful, and depending on your budget and available time, with some dedication, you can easily plan an unforgettable date that will impress and score you points.

So you've wanted to take that certain girl out for a long, long time. She's finally said yes to a date—now what do you do?

Daytime Date

The sun is still out, the day is warm and you need to find a place to have lunch together that will taste great, but also show that you know food, and you aim to please her. Here are some options in the city that will always be ideal for daytime dates.

Rose's Cafe (p.163): Ask for outdoor seating on wicker chairs just like on the street of Paris.

Mission Beach Cafe (p. 112): A modern but small cafe with excellent service and good brunch and lunch options.

Foreign Cinema (p. 104): Weekends only; reserve the patio—order some oysters.

Pier 23 Cafe (p. 44): Sit out on the back deck overlooking the water, sharing seafood delights with great cocktails.

Hog Island Oyster Company (p. 37): Order a couple dozen oysters with a bowl of clam chowder, and split a grilled cheese sandwich while enjoying views of the Bay Bridge, sailboats, and ferries.

The Slanted Door (p. 45): Order a glass of white wine while dining on refreshing Vietnamese fusion dishes.

Zazie (p. 170): Order a bunch of options, including the wild smoked salmon sandwich and the poached egg Florentine, and share everything together with a glass of cold rosé.

Or, run to **Lucca Delicatessen** (p. 157) and grab some sandwiches; drop by **Hukilau Hawaiian Restaurant** (p. 152) and take-out some macaroni salad; go to **K&L Wines** (638 4th St., San Francisco, CA 94107; 415-896-1734; www.klwines.com; Wine Shop) and grab a cold bottle of white wine—then pick her up and go to Golden Gate Park with a blanket for comfortable seating.

Nighttime Date

You're dressed up, the car is cleaned and you're ready for a great night on the town. Here are some iconic San Francisco establishments that will help set the mood and tone for the evening.

This list is far from comprehensive, only a choice few from the massive list of great eateries for romantic dates.

High End

These restaurants are some of the city's finest, offering a dining experience and a level of service that rival any other high-end establishment in the country. The average price here will be above $100 per person, usually including imbibes, making these locations ideal for special occasions, or even first dates if it strikes your fancy and you're aiming to impress.

Alexander's Steakhouse (p. 89): It's a three-level restaurant, each floor offering a different mood. Opt for the top floor where you will look down at the beautiful space below, but you'll be secluded in a more private area with nice ambient lighting and truly sexy cuts of meat.

Post-Dinner: Take a stroll over to **District Wine Bar** (216 Townsend St., San Francisco, CA 94107; 415-896-2120; www.districtsf.com)—a gorgeous wine bar with sofa seating and a nice selection of wines and beers. While crowded in the earlier evening, it tends to be more peaceful and romantic past 10 p.m. Order a cheese plate and try the wine flights.

Acquerello (p. 56): Co-owners Chef Suzette Gresham and Wine Master Giancarlo Paterlini bring you sensational culinary delights in one of the most romantic dining rooms in the city. In addition to every course served, every single person you come in contact with here, from the servers to the sommelier, will take your dining experience to new heights. If your date doesn't swoon over the ridged pasta with *foie gras* . . . find a new date.

Post-Dinner: With Polk Street right around the corner, this neighborhood is hopping on most nights! You have plenty of dive bars and live bands. To hear live music, check out what's playing at **Red Devil Lounge** (1695 Polk St., San Francisco, CA 94109; 415-921-1695; www.reddevillounge.com). For a classier evening, continuing with the wine theme started at dinner, visit **Amelie Wine Bar** (1754 Polk St., San Francisco, CA 94109; 415-292-6916; www.ameliesf.com)—a fun and popular wine bar with a great wine selection and bartenders who are friendly and very European.

Gary Danko (p. 33): If you have enough time to plan it, you can score a reservation here and thoroughly enjoy a multicourse meal of some of the best dishes in San Francisco; opt for the additional cost of the caviar course with a half bottle of Champagne—trust me.

Post-Dinner: Take a quick cab ride to the Marina, and you should find plenty of places to continue the date. Two beautiful wine bars exist in this neighborhood: **Nectar Wine Lounge** (3330 Steiner St., San Francisco, CA 94123; 415-345-1377; www.nectar winelounge.com) and **BIN38** (3232 Scott St., San Francisco, CA 94123; 415-567-3838; www.bin38.com); both places are an ideal location at which to share another bottle of wine. For a nightcap drink, if it's Sunday through Thursday, check out **Matrix Fillmore** (3138 Fillmore St., San Francisco, CA 94123; 415-563-4180; www. matrixfillmore.com)—the fireplace in the middle of the room is exquisite, and the music is always good, though the place is entirely too crowded on weekends.

Saison (p. 121): The decor is rustic but with a modern and spacious twist, and the seats are spaced far apart. Request a corner table and it's easy to forget that you're in a public place as you feast on course after course of beautifully presented and decadent creations.

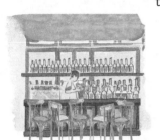

Post-Dinner: Most likely having had your fill of wine at Saison, with their generous wine pairing option, head to **Nihon Whisky Lounge** (p. 114) for a cocktail or a great glass of single-malt scotch. With over 400 choices of scotch, this is a dark and mood-enhancing venue with some great drink options.

Spruce (p. 200): Your choices are varied here: You can have a relatively economical dinner if you opt for the famous (and fabulous) burger here, or you can go for the full shebang and get a multicourse meal prepared by Chef Mark Sullivan and staff. Every soup, salad, fish, meat, and pasta dish served will woo your date's taste buds (and yours), and by the time dessert arrives, she's hooked. There's a full bar, and you'll be delighted to stay here until closing.

Post-Dinner: You just took your date to Spruce—so go all out and take her to **Top of the Mark** (999 California St., San Francisco, CA 94108; 415-616-6940), at the top of the beautiful

Intercontinental Mark Hopkins Hotel in Nob Hill. Definitely cab it there, as the martinis are strong and the parking is awful, but the jazz music and views are incomparable to anything else in the city.

Mid-Range
These are the classic first- or second-date restaurants, when you're getting to know your foodie date but require a nice ambience combined with lower noise level so you can converse. The average price range here will be above $50 per person, and under $100 per person.

Absinthe Brasserie and Bar (p. 140): For brunch or dinner, this is one of those choices where you go, and stay. The food is absolutely savory and rich, and paired with friendly service—you opt for a really long meal. With a full bar, famous cocktail list and an expansive wine and Champagne list, everything you need for your date to enjoy the evening is all here; just provide the good conversation and googly eyes over the table, and you're set. No need to go to another bar afterwards, as Absinthe is open late.

Post-Dinner: While you can stay at Absinthe through the evening, if you feel like moving to a new place that is livelier, you can always check out **Sugar Lounge** (377 Hayes St., San Francisco, CA 94102; 415-255-7144; www.sugarloungesf.com) right across the street. While it can be pretty crowded on the weekends, the drinks are big and strong, and one mojito here will last a long, long time.

Albona Ristorante Istriano (p. 28): With everything from appetizers to desserts being delicious, Albona is a moderately priced, quaint and charming restaurant. It exudes warmth and familiarity even on your first visit—and is reminiscent of bringing the date home to the family, assuming your family is awesome.

Post-Date: If your dinner is on Sunday to Tuesday night, then head to **The Bubble Lounge** (714 Montgomery St., San Francisco, CA 94111; 415-434-4204; www .bubblelounge.com)—a classy Champagne bar that has a location in San Francisco as well as New York City, with comfortable seating and sofas throughout the ground floor. It'll be classy and quiet, but do avoid on the weekends when it draws a more rambunctious crowd and becomes inappropriate for dates.

Tuesday to Thursday, head to **Redwood Room** (495 Geary St., San Francisco, CA 94102; 415-775-4700; www.clifthotel.com/ en-us/clift-san-francisco-redwood-room/) inside the Clift Hotel; the ambience is perfect for a date and the drinks are good, albeit a bit pricey. If your date is during the weekend, it might be a better idea to head to **Rickhouse Bar** (246 Kearny St., San Francisco, CA 94108; 415-398-2827; www.rickhousesf.com) in Union Square; with a rustic atmosphere, cool bartenders, and an ingeniously creative drink menu, there are plenty of seats toward the back of the restaurant in which to hold intimate conversations.

Scoma's (p. 48): The setting is old-school romantic, but once they bring out the fresh seafood platters with lobster, crab, prawns, and oysters with equally fresh pasta entrees, your date will undoubtedly see you in a new light.

Post-Dinner: Fisherman's Wharf is a fun area to walk around and people watch, and with Scoma's right by the water, the atmosphere is ripe for romance. It's not the best area to find a romantic post-drink lounge, though, so a quick ride downtown will get you to **83 Proof** (83 1st St., San Francisco, CA 94105; 415-296-8383; www.83proof.com), one of the best cocktail bars in San Francisco, which also has an impressive selection of scotches and beers on tap. It's usually quieter later in the night past happy hour time in the Financial District, and a cozy table for two should be easy to secure. With friendly bartenders, don't miss out on the basil gimlet. Try 83 Proof's recipe for the **Starry Night** on p. 280.

Zuni Cafe (p. 171): While the ambience is more classy and modern than romantic, something about being on a date at Zuni is classic. It's great food with great service—and with a full bar and a nice wine list, you'll be hard-pressed not to have a great date here.
Post-Dinner: Go right around the corner from Zuni Cafe and you'll find of one of San Francisco's best-kept secrets, **Hotel Biron** (45 Rose St., San Francisco, CA 94102; 415-703-0403; www.hotelbiron .com). It's a wine bar, not a hotel (what did you think I was suggesting?), and it's dark, woody, sexy with dim lighting. The service is phenomenal, and the wines are truly special; share a cheese plate and a bottle of vino to end the perfect date night. Or hail a cab and go to **Martuni's** (4 Valencia St., San Francisco, CA 94103; 415-241-0205; www.dragatmartunis.com/), a predominantly gay bar with fantastic servers, bartenders, and a live piano with some of San Francisco's best voices singing along. It's a one-of-a-kind

experience and always a great time at Martuni's. And yes, you order martinis there!

Mid-to-Low Range

Dates don't have to be so expensive to be fun and romantic!

Here are some places you can visit to eat well, have fun and get to know each other. They are also terrific for established couples wanting to have a date night without a special occasion. The cost will be budget conscious (though not cheap; you can look for those in the next section) without taking away from your "food lover" status. On average, expect the meal to cost under $50 per person.

Bella Trattoria (p. 177): A cozy establishment in the inner Richmond, this location offers what I still call the best baked polenta in town. They also have freshly made pastas with delectable creamy sauces and a moderately priced wine list chock-full of great Italian wines.

Post-Dinner: There's not a lot of date-appropriate, romantic nightlife in the Richmond; the restaurant will call a cab for you and you can head to **Swank** (488 Presidio Ave., San Francisco, CA 94115; 415-346-7431; www.jdvhotels.com/dining/swank), the bar at the Joie de Vivre Hotel only a mile or so away. After a rich and heavy meal at Bella, a classic mojito at Swank with the beautiful fireplace in front of the couches should be a sweet ending to the evening.

Frascati Restaurant (p. 65): A true San Francisco establishment with the cable cars passing by, warm and welcoming staff, and some food that will entice and excite your palate; it's an ideal date location with great prices.

Post-Dinner: Take a quick cab ride to **620 Jones** (620 Jones St., San Francisco, CA 94102; 415-614-9265; www.620-jones.com) for a drink on the rare and fabulous 8,000-square-foot patio, and try to sit near the huge fire. Cabbing it to this location would be best as you have to pass through some shadier neighborhoods to reach this classy establishment.

Pacific Catch (p. 191): It's a more playful location and not quite romantic, but the food is fresh and delicious. With a full bar, you can be pairing a cold beer or a martini with deep-fried oysters or a butterfish entree that melts in your mouth.

Post-Dinner: **Social Kitchen and Brewery** (p. 198) isn't too far from here; head there to sample their microbeers and definitely save room for the brussels sprouts chips.

Patxi's Chicago Pizza (p. 167): The Fillmore location is gorgeous, and the pizzas are so hearty and flavorful. When the deep-crust pie shows up filled to the top with cheese, pepperoni, tomato sauce, and olives, you'll be shocked at how filling each piece is. The cornmeal crust is a marvel. The service is friendly and welcoming; a small pie should be enough for two people.

Post-Dinner: Stroll over to the **California Wine Merchant** (2113 Chestnut St., San Francisco, CA 94123; 415-567-0646; www

.californiawinemerchant.com), and shop around for a bottle of wine. If you're unsure, ask for recommendations, and if they have one open, they will give you a tasting. Buy it—have the staff open it, and you can drink it right there. Awesome.

Q Restaurant and Wine Bar (p. 194): Cozy, casual and rather romantic, too, Q offers comfort cooking in a relaxed atmosphere. With the great food and low prices, it's no wonder that Q is a neighborhood favorite. Picture sharing a baked goat cheese with roasted peppers appetizer, or a hearty and rich meat loaf with mashed potatoes, washed down with a cold beer. It's good ol' American food.

Post-Dinner: Take a quick stroll or cab ride from Q to **Internos Wine Cafe** (3240 Geary Blvd., San Francisco, CA 94118; 415-751-2661; www.internoswinecafe.com), one of the most relaxing and enjoyable wine bars in the city, Great wines from France, Spain, Italy and even South Africa and Napa are represented here, and switched out often; the prices are fair and the atmosphere is ideal for dates. The appetizer menu is perfect as after-dinner bites to pair with wine. See Internos' recipe for White Bean Bruschetta on p. 262 in this book.

All About Business

With the Moscone Center here and all the hottest start-ups and tech companies in the Bay Area, it's inevitable that a lot of business takes place in San Francisco. There are meeting rooms available, and many of the hotel banquet rooms are taken up for these occa-sions—and with as much income as the city generates based on tourism and hotel occupancy, San Francisco is the mecca of busi-ness in the Bay Area.

When you have more than 10 clients who need to be taken out, these are the venues I recommend, especially on short notice. These are also some of the largest restaurants in San Francisco, and most are up there in pricing—best for expense accounts.

Alexander's Steakhouse (p. 89): The space is big, and with three floors, large groups can be accommodated. The high prices for the superb quality meat make it perfect for business expense accounts; the service and atmosphere make it well worthwhile. The meats are presented a la carte, and while they don't make a big show of each cut as they do at Morton's, the flavor is better here. Opt for the Wagyu meats, and splurge on wine. Alexander's is open for dinner only.

One Market (p. 115): This gorgeous venue is ideal for meetings. The noise level is average, and the restaurant is spacious with high ceilings and modern decor. The menu has some outstanding appe-tizers, and many of the entrees make you understand how they got the coveted Michelin star. Chances are extremely high that you will impress your clients here, if you know what you're doing. Contact management if your group will need special treatment. One Market is open for lunch and dinner daily.

Seasons (p. 78): Restaurants of this size and caliber do not get much better than Seasons. Everything I've ever ordered here has been good to perfect—and the items I've had here range from the raw oysters, to salmon, sole, and steaks, of course. The freshness of the ingredients is obvious—but the items come out of this kitchen with magic sprinkled on them; everything tastes even better than it looks. The location is large, elegant, and classy, with a pianist playing live music; it's nothing short of what one has come to expect from the Four Seasons brand. For larger parties, call ahead so they can make it happen for you. Seasons is open for breakfast, lunch, and dinner.

Yoshi's (p. 169): This venue can easily accommodate really large groups for dinner. Management is good about organizing these meetings, and large, private rooms are also available should you need them. The menu is creative, and a lot of it is Japanese fusion, rather than straight-up Japanese; the sauces tend to be a bit sweet, which pleases most American palates. With the jazz club and concert hall available for live concerts, it's most appropriate to treat your clients to one of the shows at Yoshi's. The full menu and bar is available to order from the concert hall, but you can easily host dinner in the restaurant and move the party over to the hall for drinks. Yoshi's is only open for dinner, and is available for private parties.

Recipes

Creamy White Bean Bruschetta

This simple bruschetta appetizer is served at Internos Wine Bar in San Francisco. Created by owner Adnan Abudaken, the dish presents beautifully but also melds the deep flavors of beans with accents of yogurt, lemon, and tomatoes. Paired with wine or on its own, it's a terrific appetizer or snack for any time of day—and good for you, too.

Serves 2

2 cups dried giant white beans, rinsed and soaked overnight
¼ cup olive oil, plus extra for drizzling
¼ cup fresh lemon juice
½ cup plain yogurt
2 tablespoons sea salt
1 tablespoon ground cumin
½ cup tahini
4 slices ciabatta bread, sliced ¼ inch thick
A handful of cherry tomatoes
Basil

In a saucepan, boil the rinsed beans in about 2 cups water for 30 minutes.

In a food processor, mix the olive oil and lemon juice until combined.

Once the beans have boiled, drain and add to the olive oil and lemon juice in the food processor. Add the yogurt, salt, cumin, and tahini. Process until creamy.

Let the mixture sit for 30 minutes.

Toast the ciabatta bread slices.

Cut a handful of cherry tomatoes in half.

Once the bread is toasted, assemble bruschetta by spreading the creamy white beans over the toasted bread. To finish, add the cherry tomatoes and sprinkle with chopped fresh basil and drizzle with olive oil.

Courtesy of Internos Wine Bar (p. 262)

Hukilau's Classic Poke

Very few things say "Hawaii" like poke (in the Hawaiian language, "poke" means to cut or slice into small pieces). Poke is indeed considered to be a local food—it's not uncommon to walk into a local grocery store or even a convenience store in Hawaii and find tubs full of various kinds of poke for sale. Though the element of raw fish makes it similar to Japanese sashimi, poke uses chunks of fish that are doused and/or marinated in a soy-based sauce.

Simple and easy to make, the main ingredient is fresh, sashimi-grade fish. Prepare the dish as a starter or appetizer and you'll be sure to hear "That's ono!" ("delicious" in Hawaiian) all night long.

Single Serving

- 6 ounces #2+ grade ahi tuna loin
- 1 tablespoon sesame oil
- 2 tablespoons soy sauce, to taste
- ¼ cup finely chopped red onion
- ¼ cup finely chopped green onion
- ¼ cup coarsely chopped limu (Hawaiian seaweed), if available (regular seaweed is acceptable, too)
- Crushed red pepper to taste

Slice the ahi tuna into 1-inch cubes.

In mixing bowl, toss the cubed ahi with the sesame oil and soy sauce.

Toss the mixture until the ahi is well-coated and then add the red and green onions.

Add ¼ cup of the coarsely chopped limu seaweed and toss again.

Add crushed pepper to desired level of spiciness and add additional soy sauce, if needed.

Cover and store in refrigerator for 2 hours.

Toss once over and serve cold.

Courtesy of Hukilau Hawaiian Restaurant (p. 263)

Chantenay Carrot Soup with Turmeric Dates & Almonds

Anything that Chef Mark Sullivan touches turns to culinary gold. From simple burgers to creating an explosion of flavors with complex fish and protein and vegetables from completely different regions, he heads up the famous Spruce in San Francisco with a menu that highlights the freshest of local, sustainable ingredients. Perhaps it's the use of these ingredients that makes it possible for him to create the most savory soups in San Francisco as your first course. Below is an example of the magic he can work with fresh carrots—and it turns into a creamy yet refreshing bowl of soup with slight notes of almonds and distinct waves of cardamom. This is not your ordinary carrot soup! While Chef Sullivan utilizes Chantenay carrots at Spruce for the delicate and distinct sweetness in this particular carrot, regular carrots may be substituted in this recipe, if Chantenay carrots are not readily available.

Serves 8

Chantenay Carrot Soup

½ cup extra-virgin olive oil

4 cups sliced yellow onions

1 square foot of cheesecloth

1 ounce fresh ginger, peeled and thinly shaved on a mandoline

8 fresh cardamom pods, toasted lightly

12 sprigs fresh thyme, slightly bruised

4 cups sliced Chantenay carrots

1 teaspoon turmeric powder

4 cups Chantenay carrot juice

Salt and finely ground white pepper to taste

In a heavy-bottomed pot over medium heat, sweat the yellow onions in extra-virgin olive oil until tender, about 25 minutes.

Spread out the cheesecloth and add the shaved ginger, cardamom pods, and fresh thyme sprigs. Tie the cheesecloth off and add to the sweated onions.

Add the sliced carrots and turmeric powder, stir, and allow to cook until the carrots are tender, about 25 minutes.

Add the fresh carrot juice and bring to a simmer.

Blend in a high speed blender, and pass through a fine-mesh sieve.

Turmeric Date & Almond Emulsion

8 Medjool dates, seed removed	4 tablespoons cider vinegar
½ cup toasted Marcona almonds	Salt to taste
	2 cups cream
½ teaspoon aleppo chile pepper	1 small pinch saffron threads,
1 teaspoon turmeric powder	about ½ teaspoon

Place all of the ingredients, except for the saffron threads, in a sauce pot and simmer for 5 minutes.

Lightly toast the saffron threads in a dry pan and add to the date-cream mixture. Let steep for 5 minutes.

Place the mixture in a high-speed blender and puree until silky smooth. Pass through a fine-mesh sieve.

Add the mixture to a thermal whip canister, charge with NO_2, and reserve for garnishing soup.

Courtesy of Chef Mark Sullivan of Spruce (p. 200)

Spaghettini with Cured Tuna Heart & Egg Yolk

Chef Chris Cosentino, host of Food Network's Chefs vs. City, *is the Executive Head Chef at the famous Incanto in San Francisco, co-owned with Mark Pastore. Incanto specializes in rustic Italian, and this dish is one of the restaurant's top sellers. With one bite of this pasta, I was amazed at the flavors of the amazing blend of saltiness added by the cured tuna heart and the richness that the egg yolk adds to the dish.*

Serves 4

1 pound spaghettini
2 tablespoons slivered garlic (3 or 4 medium-size cloves)
Dried aleppo chile flakes (a pinch)
2 tablespoons olive oil
¼ cup roughly chopped flat-leaf parsley

2 tablespoons roughly chopped fresh oregano
1 lemon, zested using a microplane rasp
Salt and black pepper to taste
4 egg yolks
Cured tuna heart

Place large pot of water on stove to boil and season with salt. When water reaches a full boil, add pasta. Follow package directions for cooking time. Drain.

In the meantime, in a large sauté pan over high heat, combine the garlic, chile flakes, and olive oil, stirring frequently and being careful not to let the garlic burn.

Add the herbs and lemon zest and sizzle in the oil.

Add the freshly cooked, drained pasta to the pan and remove from the heat.

Season to taste with salt and pepper, being sure to go light on salt since the tuna heart is salted.

Place pasta on hot serving dish; make an indent in the pasta and place the egg yolks in the center. Using a coarse microplane, shave the tuna heart over top of the pasta. Serve immediately.

Courtesy of Incanto (p. 106)

Chicken & Andouille Gumbo

New on the San Francisco restaurant scene is Boxing Room, the hippest eatery in town, at the moment serving up alligator meat, head cheese, flounder, and all kinds of Creole cooking, created by Executive Chef Justin Simoneaux, who was born in Louisiana. Chef Simoneaux is currently one of San Francisco's youngest chefs and comes with years of experience from the Moss Room at the California Academy of Sciences, as well as other well-known San Francisco eateries. As authentic as it should be, he offers a flavorful bowl of gumbo at Boxing Room, and we're thrilled that he agreed to include the recipe in the book. Flavors abound in this dish, with the sausage enhancing rather than masking the chicken. Add some rice to this dish to enjoy the intense flavors of this broth at home.

Serves 4

- 2 tablespoons canola oil
- 1 medium onion, cut into 8 wedges
- 1 cup 1-inch pieces of celery
- 1 cup 1-inch pieces of carrots
- 1 3- to 4-pound chicken, cut up
- 5 cloves garlic, smashed
- 1 bay leaf
- 1 teaspoon black peppercorns
- 5 sprigs fresh thyme
- 1 gallon water
- 2 tablespoons salt

Preparing the Chicken Meat and Stock

In a 2-gallon stockpot, heat oil over medium-high heat. When oil is hot, add onion, celery, and carrot and cook, stirring regularly, until vegetables are caramelized.

Add remaining ingredients and bring to a boil. Let simmer for 45 minutes to an hour, or until chicken is cooked through.

Strain liquid from chicken and vegetables with a fine sieve, pick out the chicken, and reserve for making gumbo.

Preparing the Gumbo

1 cup canola oil
1½ cups flour
2 cups chopped onions
1 cup chopped celery
1 cup chopped green bell
    pepper
½ cup chopped red bell pepper
3–4 cloves garlic or to taste
1 pound andouille sausage, cut
    into ½-inch slices

3 quarts hot chicken stock,
    reserved from above recipe
1 bay leaf
Picked chicken meat, from
    above recipe
1 cup ½-inch pieces fresh okra
1 teaspoon chopped fresh
    thyme
Salt and pepper to taste
Cayenne pepper to taste

In a 2-gallon stockpot, heat oil, then whisk in flour and stir constantly until roux becomes a pecan-brown color.

Add onion, celery, and peppers. Cook until vegetables are wilted (about 3–5 minutes).

Add garlic and sausage and cook for another 3 minutes.

Add the stock and bay leaf. Stir regularly to ensure that the roux does not burn. Bring to a boil and let simmer for about 30 minutes.

Add chicken meat, okra, and thyme. Continue to simmer for another 15 minutes.

Season with salt, pepper, and cayenne to taste.

Courtesy of Boxing Room (p. 144)

Potato-Wrapped Cannelloni of Beef Brasato with Truffled Verdure

Provided by co-owner and Executive Chef Suzette Gresham of Acquerello, this modern adaptation of the classic cannelloni was created by Chef de Cuisine Mark Pensa as an unconventional way of serving up this timeless dish.

The flavorful and rich, moist meat filling, made in the style of a brasato, is placed into a paper thin potato cannelloni in lieu of pasta, resulting in a masterful presentation that resembles pasta but combines the classic tastes of meat and potatoes.

Despite its length, the recipe is really quite simple once you have completed the preparations.

At Acquerello, they utilize boneless short ribs taken from the flap closest to the chuck, but chuck roast can just as easily be used at home. Ideally, have fresh truffles available to shave onto the final dish.

Serves 8–10 (depending on serving portion)

Braising the Beef

2 tablespoons rendered beef fat (or olive oil)

Kosher salt to taste

Freshly ground black pepper to taste

8–10 pounds boneless beef short ribs

1 head garlic, cut in half

4 celery stalks, cut into large chunks

2 medium yellow onions, peeled and cut into large chunks

3 or 4 carrots, peeled and cut into large chunks

4 sprigs fresh thyme

1 sprig fresh oregano

2 bay leaves

1 7-ounce jar concentrato pomodoro (tomato paste)

1 quart Italian red wine (try Barolo)

2 quarts chicken stock

2 quarts water

Heat a heavy-bottomed pot, add rendered beef fat and quickly coat the pan. With salt and pepper, season the short ribs and add to the fat and sear the meat on all sides. Remove meat and add the halved head of garlic and chopped vegetables into the same pan and sauté; add herbs and sauté until slightly caramelized. Return meat to the pan.

Add the tomato concentrate. (If it's an American brand, diluting with water will be appropriate.) Work the paste over the sauté, and once mixed well, add the wine. Cook 8–10 minutes (until alcohol has evaporated), and add equal parts chicken stock and water, just enough to cover the mix.

Put over low heat, cover, and cook gently for 2–2.5 hours until the meat is tender, never allowing the mixture to boil. This part should preferably be done the day before in order to allow the meat to cool in the liquid and rest in the refrigerator overnight.

Red Wine Syrup

2 cups red wine
¾ cup granulated sugar

Place the wine in a heavy-bottomed small pot and reduce it by half. Remove from heat and add the sugar incrementally as you taste for viscosity. Return to heat and cook only until wine and sugar are incorporated. Remove from heat and let cool.

Place a small amount of liquid on a saucer into the refrigerator. In 5 minutes, check for tackiness: Put a "bead" of liquid between two fingers and make sure a thin line forms when you pull apart your fingers. If not, return to heat and reduce further until this happens. Set aside for use in the beef filling.

Making the Beef Filling

1 bunch fresh Italian flat-leaf parsley, chopped

If cooled overnight, lightly reheat the meat and vegetable concoction. Once heated, separate the meat from the vegetables and put aside; with a slotted spoon, remove the vegetable chunks from the liquid and put aside (this is the mirepoix you will use later), and pour remaining sauce through a strainer—this should yield approximately 2 quarts of liquid.

In a pot, reduce the liquid sauce by 75 percent; put aside.

While still warm, pulse the meat with half of the cooked vegetables until no large chunks are present and the meat is smooth in texture. Transfer to a large stainless steel bowl and drizzle with a small amount of the wine syrup and the reduced braising liquid you just made. Mix well, add the parsley, and season with salt and pepper to taste. Don't make it too sweet.

Sauce

2 tablespoons rendered beef fat (or olive oil)

3 pounds scrap or stewing beef

1 head garlic, skin-on, cut in half

5 ribs celery, roughly diced

2 yellow onions, peeled, roughly diced

3 carrots, peeled, roughly diced

1 spear fresh rosemary

½ bunch fresh thyme

1 7-ounce jar Italian concentrato pomodoro (tomato paste)

8 ounces red wine

3 quarts chicken stock

1 tablespoons black peppercorns

1 small Yukon Gold potato, peeled and cubed

In a heavy-bottomed pan, heat to medium and pour in the beef fat or olive oil.

Render and sear the beef to achieve slight caramelization. Pour out any excess fat and add the halved heads of garlic, allowing them to color. Add vegetables and sauté; add herbs and the concentrato pomodoro. Allow the mixture to "rust" for 15 minutes but do not scorch.

Deglaze with red wine, and cook down approximately 5 minutes.

Deglaze with chicken stock.

Add peppercorns and cook for 45 minutes to 1 hour at a slow simmer. If the liquid needs more body, add the cubed potato; this provides a silky finish.

When it begins to look like there isn't enough liquid left and the meat is poking up, remove from the heat and let steep overnight, or strain immediately.

Strain through a heavy metal china cap strainer and push through to get every last drop of liquid. Strain again through a finer strainer and return the sauce to a pot, reducing further for approximately 20 minutes, or until the sauce reaches a consistency where it will coat the back of the spoon. Cover and set aside.

The Assembly

3 or 4 Yukon Gold baking-size potatoes

Kosher salt to taste

1 egg, beaten and mixed with pinch of salt and a drop of water

Nonstick cooking spray (like Vegalene)

5 6-inch squares parchment or baking paper

Peel the potatoes. On a meat slicer or mandoline, slice the potatoes ¹⁄₁₆-inch thick, letting them drop into a pot of water. Allow approximately 5 slices per person.

Bring a pot of water to boil and season with salt. Drop the sliced potatoes one at a time into the boiling water for 13 seconds each, remove, and immediately plunge into ice water to stop the cooking process.

Load your beef filling into a disposable pastry bag and cut off the tip; the opening should be about the diameter of a pencil. Set aside.

Remove your first 5 slices of potato from the water and pat dry, line up lengthwise on a cutting board, and cut one straight edge. Squeeze out the filling along this edge, and roll inward from this point into small burrito-like shapes.

Repeat for all slices of potatoes.

Set your beef-filled potato rolls on the parchment paper on a baking tray coated with nonstick cooking spray, brush top of rolls with egg mixture. Place in a 375–400 degree oven (depending on your oven) for 5 minutes.

Serving: Heat your plates and warm up the sauce.

Remove the potato rolls from the oven and equally space on serving plate.

With a spoon, nape the sauce over the rolls and finish with a broader flourish around the plate. Drizzle mirepoix right through the middle in a straight line over all rolls and sprinkle herbs on it if you wish. Shave thin slices of truffle over the "cannelloni" and serve.

Courtesy of Acquerello (p. 56)

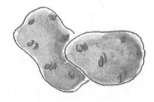

Hanuri Korean BBQ Kalbi

My go-to place for Korean food in San Francisco is Hanuri. Particularly excellent at the restaurant is the kalbi *(marinated short ribs) and the soybean paste–smothered pork belly. This dish is served up with a wide array of* banchan *(side dishes) and rice and can be grilled at the table during your visit. Or you can make this great recipe at home to cook on the grill or even under the broiler.*

Serves 4

- 1 cup soy sauce
- 3 cups water
- ¼ cup sesame oil
- ½ cup sugar
- ½ cup malt syrup
- 1 onion, peeled and sliced in chunks
- ¼ cup garlic, peeled and diced
- ½ jalapeño, to taste, seeded and sliced
- ¼ pineapple, enough to yield ¼ cup juice
- 1 teaspoon black pepper
- 2 tablespoons Liquid Smoke
- 5 pounds short ribs

In a large glass bowl combine the soy sauce, water, sesame oil, sugar, and malt syrup and stir to mix.

Add the sliced onions, garlic, and seeded jalapeño to the marinade.

Puree pineapple in the blender to yield approximately ¼ cup liquid; some of the pineapple chunks may be used. Stir in the pineapple liquid into the marinade.

Mix in the pepper and Liquid Smoke and stir thoroughly.

Wash the short ribs in cold water and let drain.

Place the short ribs into the marinade, cover with plastic wrap and leave overnight in the refrigerator to marinate. Either grill or broil to preferred doneness.

Courtesy of Hanuri Korean BBQ (p. 184)

Bonet (Chocolate Flan)

Albona Ristorante is the only Istrian restaurant in San Francisco; the cuisine is very similar to Italian but with more of an accent, if you will—and it's one of my favorites! While Executive Chef Samuel Hernandez makes some sensational starters and entrees, time and again I have skipped dessert after dinner elsewhere to run into Albona wanting the bonet. I have called ahead on my visits to the restaurant to make sure there is bonet; that's how serious I am about this dessert. Made by Chef Beatriz Hernandez, the pastry chef at Albona, this rich and decadent dessert is smooth in texture, full of chocolate flavor but not overpowering, and the ideal after-dinner treat. This recipe is for 12 servings, and if I were you, I'd calculate at least two servings for each person. It's that good.

Serves 12

12 4-ounce flan ramekins	Pinch of salt
5 cups white sugar, divided	8 whole eggs
3 cups whole milk	4 egg yolks
3 ounces bittersweet chocolate	4 ounces amaretto liqueur
3 ounces semisweet chocolate	4 ounces crème de cacao
1 cup amaretto crumbs	

Preheat oven to 375 degrees. Place 4 cups sugar in a saucepan on low heat, stir constantly with a wooden spoon until it turns a deep golden brown. Transfer the caramel to the ramekins in even proportions and let cool, about 20 minutes. In another saucepan boil the milk, the bittersweet and semisweet chocolates, amaretto crumbs, and the pinch of salt for 5 minutes.

At the same time mix the other cup of sugar, whole eggs, yolks, and both liqueurs in a big bowl and add the hot milk-chocolate mixture. Slowly whisk until well blended. Divide the warm custard among the caramelized ramekins and place all ramekins into a large baking pan at least 2" in height (or use two 9x13 pans to cook in two batches, if necessary). Pour enough hot tap water into the pan to come halfway up the side of the ramekins. Put the pan in the oven and bake for 55 minutes.

Take the ramekins out of the oven; remove from pan and cool to room temperature, cover, and refrigerate overnight. Unmold just before serving using a sharp, flexible knife around the mold and flip it onto a plate.

Courtesy of Albona Ristorante Istriano (p. 28)

La Quesada

Chef James Stolich heads up one of the hottest "underground supper clubs" in San Francisco—Cook with James. With his experiences throughout Europe and the well-known Quince in San Francisco, the dinners and classes he hosts at his home are among the hippest things to do in the city. It's eating out, but not quite; it's more like going over to a welcoming friend's house, cooking up a storm together, and then digging in.

La Quesada is a dessert he acquired from his beloved Spanish "mother," Lola, during his time in Santander, Spain. It utilizes milk and cheese—two plentiful ingredients in the Basque region, which is well-known for cows. With a slight sweetness, this creamy yet light dessert is reminiscent of a cheesecake courting flan—and it pairs wonderfully with coffee or tea.

Serves 8–12 (depending on serving portion)

6 ounces vanilla nonfat yogurt

3 triangles plain Laughing Cow Swiss cheese

12 ounces whole milk

10 ounces brown sugar

6 ounces unbleached all-purpose flour, plus 1 tablespoon for the baking dish

3 eggs

½ cup (1 stick) unsalted butter

Confectioners' sugar for garnishing

In a large mixing bowl, combine all ingredients except the butter and confectioners' sugar. (Chef Stolich adds, "I like to add the yogurt first and then use the yogurt container to add and measure the other ingredients. it's really 2 yogurt containers of milk, slightly less than 2 of sugar, and 1 yogurt container of flour. Just be sure the yogurt is the 6-ounce version.")

Use a hand blender to emulsify all of the ingredients, blending until smooth. Melt the stick of butter over medium heat in a saucepan. Pour the butter into an oven-safe baking dish coating it completely. Next pour the butter into the mixing bowl but do not clean the baking dish; you want a thin film of butter to remain. Blend the ingredients together once more. Sprinkle a tablespoon of flour into the baking dish coating the bottom of the dish lightly. This will help form a crust. Pour the entire mixture into the baking dish.

Place into a cold oven. Set the temperature to 350 degrees. Bake for exactly 1 hour. Remove and let rest for 2 hours at room temperature. Sprinkle the top with confectioners' sugar. Cover with plastic wrap and refrigerate for at least 2 hours before serving. The quesada will keep for 5–7 days refrigerated.

Courtesy of Chef James Stolich of Cook with James (p. 148)

The Starry Night

This cold beverage is the ideal balance of sweet and fruity while packing a great punch in each sip. Created just for the Food Lovers' Guide to San Francisco by the talented master mixologist Marc Goldfine from one of my favorite bars in the city, 83 Proof, this one is sure to please the masses as the scent of cinnamon and cherries takes over your senses and whisks you away.

Single Servings

1 cinnamon stick
1¾ ounce añejo tequila (preferably Partida or Siete Leguas)

⅓ ounce Heering cherry liqueur
⅓ ounce Licor Cuarente e Tres (Licor 43)
Whole star anise for garnish

Using a bar spoon, gently scrape the cinnamon stick 15 times.

Place all ingredients (except the star anise) in a mixing glass and fill the glass with ice. Stir for 25–30 seconds.

Strain into a Champagne coupe (saucer glass) or martini glass.

Garnish with one star anise floating on the cocktail.

Courtesy of Marc Goldfine of 83 Proof (p. 255)

Appendices

Appendix A: Eateries by Cuisine

Wooden Charcoal Korean Barbecue
    House, 205, 243
Yakini-Q, 169

Belgian
La Trappe Cafe, 41

Brazilian
Espetus Churrascaria Brazilian
    Steakhouse, 101

Brewery
Social Kitchen and Brewery, 198,
    257
21st Amendment Brewery and
    Restaurant, 129

Burmese
Burma Superstar, 178

Butcher Shop
Guerra's Quality Meats, 227
Mi Tierra, 132
Salama Halal Meat, 85
San Francisco Meats &
    Delicatessen, 228

Cajun
Boxing Room, 144, 269
Craw Station, 179

California
Coi Restaurant, 31
Namu, 23, 190

Cambodian
Angkor Borei Restaurant, 211

Caribbean
Cha Cha Cha, 145
Primo Patio Cafe, 118

Chinese
City View Restaurant, 30
D&A Cafe, 181
Good Luck Dim Sum, 182
Kingdom of Dumpling, 219
Mayflower Seafood Restaurant, 189
Pot's, The, 192
R & G Lounge, 44
San Tung, 196
Ton Kiang, 203
Yank Sing Restaurant, 130, 246
Yuet Lee, 241

Rhea's Deli & Market, 119
Toyose, 203
Wooden Charcoal Korean Barbecue
   House, 205, 243
Yakini-Q, 169

Latin American
Mr. Pollo, 114

Market/Farmers' Market
DeLessio Market and Bakery, 173
Ferry Plaza Farmers' Market, 52
Heart of the City Farmers'
   Market, 132
Ted's Market, 128
Tomales Bay Oyster Company, 237
Y&Y Vietnamese Deli, 208

Mediterranean
Foreign Cinema, 104, 248
Frascati, 65, 257
Goood Frikin Chicken, 218
Kokkari Estiatorio, 69
Paul K Restaurant, 161
Troya, 204

Mexican
El Burrito eXpress, 181
El Farolito, 98, 244
El Metate, 100
Gordo Taqueria, 183
La Corneta Tacqueria, 108
Nick's Crispy Tacos, 246
Taco Shop at Underdogs, 201
Taqueria Cancun, 127
Tia Margarita, 202

Middle Eastern
Old Jerusalem Restaurant, 115

Peruvian
La Mar Cebicheria Peruana, 40
Mi Lindo Peru Restaurant, 220
Piqueo's, 223

Pizza
Arinell Pizza Inc., 92
Giovanni's Pizza Bistro, 217
Goat Hill Pizza, 104
Little Star Pizza, 156
Mozzarella Di Bufala Pizzeria, 221
Patxi's Chicago Pizza, 160, 257

Appendix B: Dishes, Specialties & Specialty Food

Burgers

Burritos

Cake

Noe Valley Bakery, 133

Sophie's Crepes, 165

Index